נר ד' נשמת אדם

Yizkor menorah graphic

"The candle of God is the soul of a person" is the Hebrew inscription underne
menorah.

In all likelihood, this line drawing was inspired by the memory of the Krasnob
menorah. Page 162 [page 494 – Yiddish], [Page 209 – Hebrew]

Krasnobrod; A Memorial to the Jewish Community
(Krasnobród, Poland)

Translation of
Krasnobrod; sefer zikaron

Original Book Edited by: M. Kushnir

Originally published in Tel Aviv 1956

JewishGen
מרכז עולמי לגנאלוגיה יהודית
The Global Home for Jewish Genealogy

A Publication of JewishGen, INC
Edmond J. Safra Plaza, 36 Battery Place, New York, NY 10280
646.494.5972 | info@JewishGen.org | www.jewishgen.org

MUSEUM OF
JEWISH HERITAGE
A LIVING MEMORIAL
TO THE HOLOCAUST

Krasnobrod; A Memorial to the Jewish Community (Krasnobród, Poland)
Translation of *Krasnobrod; sefer zikaron*

Editor of Original Yizkor Book: M. Kushnir
Project Coordinator: Moses Milstein
Cover Design: Irv Osterer
Layout and Name Indexing: Jonathan Wind
Yiddish Translations: Moses Milstein
Photo Extraction: Sondra Ettlinger

Printed in the United States of America by Lightning Source, Inc.

Library of Congress Control Number (LCCN): 2022946272

ISBN: 978-1-954176-58-4 (hard cover: 238 pages, alk. paper)

About JewishGen.org

JewishGen, an affiliate of the Museum of Jewish Heritage - A Living Memorial to the Holocaust, serves as the global home for Jewish genealogy.

Featuring unparalleled access to 30+ million records, it offers unique search tools, along with opportunities for researchers to connect with others who share similar interests. Award winning resources such as the Family Finder, Discussion Groups, and ViewMate, are relied upon by thousands each day.

In addition, JewishGen's extensive informational, educational and historical offerings, such as the Jewish Communities Database, Yizkor Book translations, InfoFiles, Family Tree of the Jewish People, and KehilaLinks, provide critical insights, first-hand accounts, and context about Jewish communal and familial life throughout the world.

Offered as a free resource, JewishGen.org has facilitated thousands of family connections and success stories, and is currently engaged in an intensive expansion effort that will bring many more records, tools, and resources to its collections.

Please visit https://www.jewishgen.org/ to learn more.

Executive Director: Avraham Groll

About the JewishGen Yizkor Book Project

Yizkor Books (Memorial Books) were traditionally written to memorialize the names of departed family and martyrs during holiday services in the synagogue (a practice that still exists in many synagogues today).

Over the centuries, as a result of countless persecutions and horrific atrocities committed against the Jews, Yizkor Books (Sefer Zikaron in Hebrew) were expanded to include more historical information, such as biographical sketches of famous personalities and descriptions of daily town life.

Following the Holocaust, the idea of remembrance and learning took on an urgent and crucial importance. Survivors of the Holocaust sought out other surviving residents of their former towns to memorialize and document the names and way of life of those who were ruthlessly murdered by the Nazis. These remembrances were documented in Yizkor Books, hundreds of which were published in the first decades after the Holocaust.

Most of these books were published privately, or through landsmanshaftn (social organizations comprised of members originating from the same European town or region) that still existed, and were often distributed free of charge. Sadly, the languages used to document these crucial histories and links to our past, Yiddish and Hebrew, are no longer commonly understood by a significant percentage of Jews today. As a result, JewishGen has undertaken the sacred responsibility of translating these books into English so that the culture and way of life of these communities will be preserved and transmitted to future generations.

In 1986, a group of farsighted JewishGenners started a project to pool their efforts together in groups based upon their ancestors from each town and donate money to get the Yizkor books of their ancestral towns translated into English. As the translated material became available, it was made accessible for free at www.JewishGen.org/Yizkor. Hardcover copies can be purchased by visiting https://www.jewishgen.org/Yizkor/ybip.html (see below).

It is our hope that the translation of these books into English (and other languages) will assist the countless Jewish family researchers who are so desperately seeking to forge a connection with their heritage.

Director of JewishGen Yizkor Book Project: Lance Ackerfeld

About JewishGen Press

JewishGen Press (formerly the Yizkor Books-in-Print Project) is the publishing division of JewishGen.org, and provides a venue for the publication of non-fiction books pertaining to Jewish genealogy, history, culture, and heritage.

In addition to the Yizkor Book category, publications in the Other Non-Fiction category include Shoah memoirs and research, genealogical research, collections of genealogical and historical materials, biographies, diaries and letters, studies of Jewish experience and cultural life in the past, academic theses, and other books of interest to the Jewish community.

Please visit https://www.jewishgen.org/Yizkor/ybip.html to learn more.

Director of JewishGen Press: Joel Alpert
Managing Editor - Jessica Feinstein
Publications Manager - Susan Rosin

Notes to the Reader

The images in the original book were reproduced from photographs from the time of the first edition. These reproductions were already of poor quality, being pre-war and at least 30 or more years old. As a result the images in the book are not very good and the best achievable.

A reader can view the original scans of the book on the websites listed below.

The original book can be seen online at the Yiddish Book Center website:

https://www.yiddishbookcenter.org/search/collection/NYPL-Yiddish%20Book%20Center%20Yizkor%20Book%20Collection?query=krasnobrod&restrict=

or
at the New York Public Library Digital Collections website:

https://digitalcollections.nypl.org/items/38d303f0-7a76-0133-cb89-00505686a51c

To obtain a list of Shoah victims from Krasnobrod (Krasnobród, Poland), the reader should access the Yad Vashem web site listed below; one can also search for specific family names using family name option. These lists are continually updated by Yad Vashem, so it is worthwhile to periodically search these lists.

There is more valuable information (including the Pages of Testimony, etc.) available on this website: https://yvng.yadvashem.org/

A list of all books available from JewishGen Press along with prices is available at: https://www.jewishgen.org/Yizkor/ybip.html

Photo Credits

Front Cover:

Portrait of the Shul's Gabai, R' Aharon Lochfeld, of blessed memory.
Lochfeld managed to save the six-foot brass signature menorah from the Krasnobrod shul that was destroyed in 1915 during World War I. Lochfeld proudly returned the menorah to its proper place in the rededicated synagogue. Page 16 [Page 27 – Hebrew], [Page 241 Yiddish]

Back Cover:

Exterior View of the Original Beit HaKnesset in Krasnobród (circa 1910).
The photographs of the synagogue in Krasnobrod were originally published in research by Professor A. Shishko-Bohosh and were subsequently given to JewishGen with the permission of the author of the article, the engineer D. Davidovich. Pages 27 and 31 [Page 43 – Hebrew], [Page 260 – Yiddish]

Public domain map image sourced from Wojskowy Instytut Geograficzny, 1932

Back cover text
Pages 11-12 of the English translation
By Eliyahu Rind translated by Moses Milstein

Acknowledgements

My thanks to the dedicated folks at JewishGen for promoting the translation and publication of these memorial books. I believe we are conforming with the desires of the authors of these yizkor books by making their memories and testaments available to a wider audience, many of whom are no longer able to read the original Yiddish.

I would like to thank Lance Ackerfeld, Director of the JewishGen Yizkor Book Project for his invaluable help in all stages of the project; Max G. Heffler, and Jason Hallgarten, for their HTML expertise; Ala Gamulka for comparing the Hebrew and Yiddish sections for duplications; and Mira Eckhaus and Jerrold Landau for their Hebrew translations.
Thanks also to the publishing team led by Susan Rosin, Publications Manager; Jonathan Wind, layout and name indexing; Sondra Ettlinger, photo extraction; and Irv Osterer for cover design.

I dedicate this translation to my parents, Ephraim and Bela Milstein, from the nearby town of Shebreshin (Szczebrzeszyn), who doubtless knew some of the people in Krasnobrod, and shared in the joy and tragedy of the people of that part of Poland.

Moses Milstein
Pemberton, British Columbia
October 2022

Geopolitical Information

Krasnobród, Poland is located at 50°33' N 23°12' E and 151 miles SE of Warsaw

	Town	District	Province	Country
Before WWI (c. 1900):	Krasnobród	Zamość	Lublin	Russian Empire
Between the wars (c. 1930):	Krasnobród	Zamość	Lublin	Poland
After WWII (c. 1950):	Krasnobród			Poland
Today (c. 2000):	Krasnobród			Poland

Alternate Names for the Town:

Krasnobród [Pol], Krasnabrod [Yid]

Nearby Jewish Communities:

Józefów 9 miles SW
Zwierzyniec 11 miles WNW
Zamość 12 miles N
Tomaszów Lubelski 12 miles SE
Komarów 13 miles ENE
Szczebrzeszyn 15 miles NW
Narol 15 miles SSE
Lipsko 15 miles SSE
Bełżec 15 miles SE
Łukowa 17 miles SW
Jarczów 20 miles ESE
Lubycza Królewska 21 miles SE
Ułazów 21 miles SSW
Biłgoraj 22 miles W
Skierbieszów 22 miles NNE
Cieszanów 22 miles S
Mosty Małe 22 miles SE
Tyszowce 22 miles ENE
Izbica 23 miles N
Tarnogóra 23 miles N

Łaszczów 23 miles E
Tarnogród 24 miles WSW
Dzików Stary 24 miles SSW
Chłaniów 24 miles NW
Frampol 25 miles WNW
Grabowiec 25 miles NE
Cewków 25 miles SW
Goraj 26 miles WNW
Horyniec 26 miles SSE
Lubaczów 27 miles S
Potelych, Ukraine 27 miles SE
Uhniv, Ukraine 27 miles ESE
Kraśniczyn 27 miles NNE
Oleszyce 27 miles SSW
Rava-Ruska, Ukraine 28 miles SE
Turobin 28 miles NW
Gorzków 29 miles NNW
Żółkiewka 29 miles NW
Wojsławice 30 miles NNE
Krasnystaw 30 miles N
Chrzanów 30 miles WNW

Jewish Population: 1,378 (in 1900), 5,744

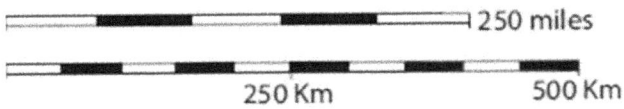

POLAND – CURRENT BORDERS

Map of Poland showing the location of **Krasnobród**

Table of Contents

Krasnobrod; a Memorial to the Jewish community (Krasnobród, Poland)

50°33' / 23°12'

Translation of
Krasnobrod; sefer zikaron

Editor: M. Kushnir

Tel Aviv 1956

Acknowledgments

Project Coordinator:

Moses Milstein

Our sincere appreciation to Yad Vashem
for the submission of the necrology for placement on the JewishGen web site.

We also would like to thank Ala Gamulka for her technical assistance in this project.

This is a translation of: *Krasnobrod; sefer zikaron* (Krasnobrod; a memorial to the Jewish community), Edited by M. Kushnir, Tel Aviv 1956 (H, Y 526 pages)

Note: The original book can be seen online at the NY Public Library site: Krasnobrod

קרסנוברוד
ספר זכרון

KRASNOBROD

A. MEMORIAL

To the Jewish Community

כל הזכויות שמורות
נדפס בישראל תשט"ז
Printed in Israel 1956

רשום זהרי, ת"א, פלטין 63462

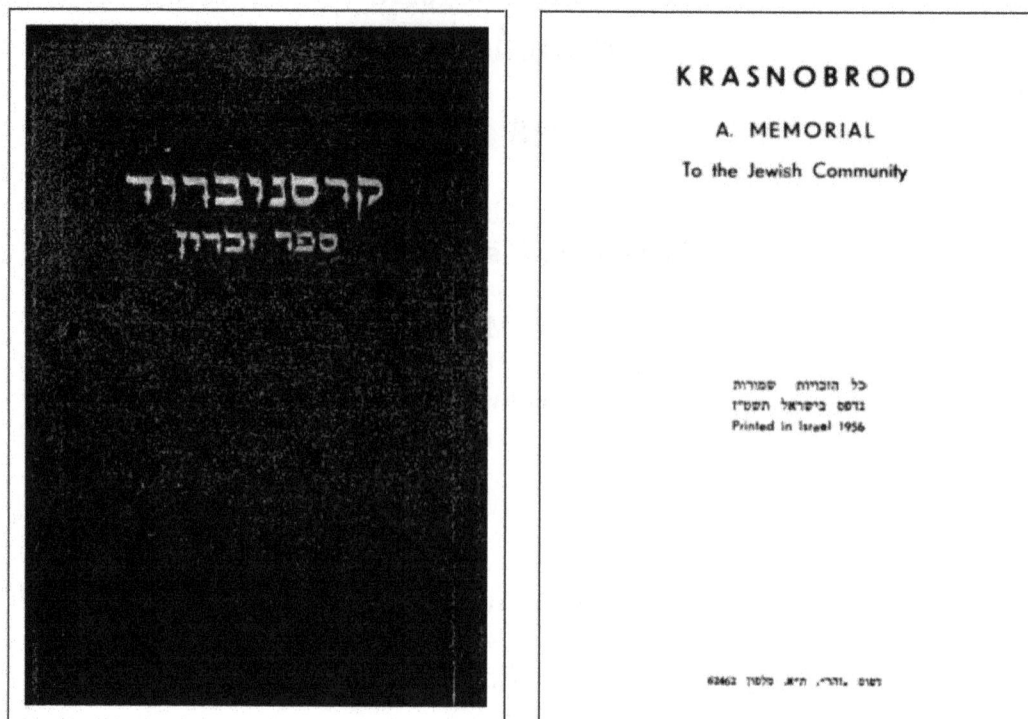

[Page 215 - Yiddish] [Page 7 - Hebrew]

A word from the editor

by M.K.

Translated by Moses Milstein

Quietly they lived, and quietly they died, the martyrs of the Jewish community of Krasnobrod, near Zamosc.

Quietly lived the shtetl and the Jewish community within, so quietly, like hundreds and thousands of other Jewish communities in Europe.

Quietly the martyrs perished in her, as quietly as hundreds and thousands of other Jewish communities in Europe.

Quietly they lived, the ordinary Jews, the kindhearted Jewish common people, storekeepers, businessmen, workers, musicians, teachers, grocers, and peddlers.

Quietly they perished while the whole world was in chaos, while mighty powers were engaged in a struggle to the death, and turned a blind eye to the disappearance of the Jewish people.

Quietly they lived, the kind and true Jewish mothers, and the still greater Jewish mothers who gave their lives to save their children.

Quietly they perished while the smell of their burning flesh issued from the ovens of the crematoria and spread over the whole world, and the mighty did not turn away and ask: who is it that is being burned alive?

Quietly they lived, the rabbis and scholars who subsisted on little, and devoted their days and nights to the Jewish Torah–moral foundation of the world.

Quietly they died, and the death throes of their bodies made the freshly dug earth heave.

Quietly they lived, the illiterate, the poor, butchers and their young helpers, the carriage drivers and horse handlers who loved to drink and break into a Hasidic dance.

Quietly they perished while the gas, which filled their lungs, crept into the palaces of the victors, and the "saviors of mankind" covered their nostrils with silk handkerchiefs and refused to ask whose lungs are being devoured.

Quietly they lived, the Jewish boys and girls who pined for revolutions, measured themselves against traditions thousands of years old, who yearned for a homeland, and left for lands far away.

Quietly they died while their brothers and sisters in other ghettoes raised the flag of revolt against the Nazi beasts.

Quietly there lived a Jewish congregation with simple longings; bread for wife and child, a book for the soul.

Quietly they perished, and quiet Europe became without Jews.

But in their quiet death they left us their will; to deliver their helpless cry to the world, and to deny rest to those who, with full knowledge, eliminated Jewish life in Europe.

We must not forget their lives and martyrdom. May it shine in our memories, and give strength to all those who lived through it without losing their humanity, and emerged alive from the fiery furnace.

Do not look for fine literature, or thrilling narratives in this book. Ordinary people wrote this, about ordinary lives that quietly passed away. Quiet lives, but very simple and beautiful.

These quiet lives, cut short before their time, demand: Remember them, pray for the exaltation of their souls.

—*Yitgadal v'yitkadash…*

[Page 217 - Yiddish] [Page 9 - Hebrew]

Sing![1]
(fragment)

by Itzchak Katznelson

Translated by Moses Milstein

"Sing, sing it one last time still here on the earth, throw back
your head, fix your eyes hard upon it
and sing it one last time, play it on the harp:
There are no more Jews! Murdered and gone for good!"

-- How can I sing? How can I raise the staring eyes
in my head? A frozen tear
has gathered in my eye…it struggles, struggles
to fall from my eye–but it cannot fall, God, my God!

"Sing, sing, raise your gaze to the blind heavens high above
As if there was a God there in the sky…wink at him, wink–
As if good fortune still shone its light upon us there!
Sit on the ruins of our murdered people and sing!

How can I sing–when the world is desolate for me?
How can I play with wringing hands?
Where are my dead? I search for my dead, God, in every pile of dirt
In every hill of ashes–O tell me where you are?

Shout out from every heap of sand, from under every rock,
From every bit of dust, from all the flames, from every wisp of smoke–
It is your blood and sap, it is the marrow from your bones,
It is your skin and bone! Shout it out, shout loud!

[Page 218]

Shout from entrails of the animals in the forest, from fish in the river–
They consumed you, shout from the crematoria, young and old shout,
I want a shriek, a cry of woe, a voice, I want your voice,
Shout, murdered Jewish people, shout, shout it out!

Don't cry to heaven–He hears you like the earth, like a heap of refuse,
Don't cry to the sun, nor speak to the light…ach, if I could
Extinguish it as one extinguishes a lamp in the miserable murderer's cave!
My people, you shone more, you shone brighter!

O appear to me my people, show yourselves, stretch out your hands
From the graves deep and miles long and densely packed
Layer upon layer, covered with lime and burned,
Up! Up! Arise from the deepest, bottom-most layer!

Come you all from Treblinka, from Sobibor, from Auschwitz
From Belzec come, come from Ponary and from yet more, from more, from more!
With eyes wide open, a frozen cry, a shriek without a voice,
Come from the earth, from deep sunken mud, from rotted moss–

Come the desiccated, the mutilated, the ground-up, array yourselves,
In a circle-dance, a large circle around me, a giant hoop–
Grandfathers, grandmothers, fathers, mothers with children on their laps–
Come Jewish bones from powders, from pieces of soap.

Show yourselves, all of you, to me, all come, come
I want to see you all, I want to look at you, I want
To look at my murdered people, in silence, silenced–
And I will sing…yes…bring me the harp–I am playing!

3"5.10.1943

Translator's note:

1.   Itzchak Katznelson was a well known and beloved poet in Yiddish and Hebrew. This fragment is from his poem, "Dos Lied Funem Oisgehargetn Yiddishen Folk," "The Song of the Murdered Jewish people." He was murdered by the Germans in Auschwitz in 1944.

[Page 219 - Yiddish] [Page 11 - Hebrew]

Introduction

Translated by Moses Milstein

With feelings of apprehension and reverence, we pass on this book–dedicated to the martyrs of our shtetl, Krasnobrod–to all those who were connected by an unbreakable bond to the Jewish community of Krasnobrod.

With some financial help, and the work of dedicated assistants, we succeeded in putting out this book. We tried our best to transmit and portray the life of our parents going back several generations, up to the last days of destruction.

With love and respect, and in plain language, we endeavored to pass on the stories from our parents about the generations that lived long ago. We have gathered together every memory about them, every legend, every occurrence, and memorialized them in this book.

The book fulfills another important task by gathering together the testimony and materials relating to the terrible Hitler years, the years of death and destruction. We are aware of how important it is to forever remember this era, to tell the terrible truth about the suffering our people endured in the Hitler years.

We believe that with this book, we have accomplished two things: to make sure that the greater, non–Jewish world will not forget what they have done to us; and that we will never forget what the *Amalek*–German did to us.

The book is published in the two languages near and dear to our people: In Hebrew, so that the younger generation who were raised in that language can look into the past, and derive inspiration from Jewish tradition, beliefs, and morality. And in Yiddish, to enable those brought up in the language to return to those wonderful years of their youth. To walk again around the little shtetl streets, to meet those near and dear people, to feel the atmosphere of love and devotion, and to better understand and feel the pain and tragedy that afflicted us all.

We believe that this book will be received with thanks and veneration, as a cherished reminder of everything that has now disappeared. Just as our parents and grandparents used to write the *yohrzeits* of the departed on the title pages of holy books, this book will remind us of the *yohrzeit* of the martyrs. With the *yohrzeit* light shining, anyone turning the pages of this book will remember, with holy trembling, the martyrs who died "*al kiddush–haShem v'ha'am.*"

[Page 223 - Yiddish] [Page 13 - Hebrew]

History of the Jewish Settlement

Chapters of Krasnobrod History

by Eliyahu Rind, Haifa

Translated by Moses Milstein

It is, unfortunately, difficult to establish exactly when the Jewish community in Krasnobrod, near Zamosc, was founded.

According to certain known facts, we can assume that a Jewish community already existed there 500 years ago. There was a cemetery hundreds of years old, on the road to the village of Hitek, left of the woods on the sand. The remnants of tombstones found there is evidence of this fact.

In 1914, when the Russian army was fortifying its position in the shtetl, and digging trenches, they uncovered a tombstone in good condition. They were able to make out the engraved title of a respected Jew who died in the year 5337, that is, 379 years ago. From this, we can conclude that a Jewish community had already existed there years earlier.

When Rabbi Nachum Feigenboim, *z"l*, (originally from the shtetl, Lamaz, in Lithuania) was informed of this, he, along with several community leaders, went out to the site and concluded that it had once been a cemetery. They also decided that a small wall should be constructed as a sign to future generations that this is a holy place.

The age of our community can also be demonstrated by the fact that half the cemetery was full and some of the gravestones are 300 years old. I believe that the community was founded by a given number of families who intermarried. This must be the reason why almost half of the families in our shtetl had the same surnames. Also the ancient wills and testaments provide evidence that Jewish assets were held by a few families only.

According to an old legend, the shtetl lay in another place entirely hundreds of years ago, somewhere around Greshtis mountain, and it was called Chelmnitz. But after the shtetl was completely destroyed, the Jews moved lower down, closer to the river Wieprz, and rebuilt the town under its new name.

It is hard to know where the legend originated from, and how true it was. I have childhood memories of the great fires that wiped the town off the map, and living among the peasants until the town was rebuilt.

The Jewish community before the First World War.

Our shtetl, exactly like all the Jewish shtetls in Poland, was home to Jews from a variety of circles and social classes. Business owners, merchants, grocers, tradesmen, laborers, and *dorfshendler*. They were not particularly worried about making a living. Their reward was living respectfully. They lived together in peace and unity. They were mindful of prayer and the injunction to "love thy neighbor as yourself."

Our community always strived to acquire the most renowned rabbinic personalities as our spiritual leaders.

Four generations ago, the spiritual leader of our congregation was Harav Mordechai Yosef Babad, a descendant of Tarnopol. His place was passed to his son, R' Israel Yakov Babad. After him came Harav Zvi Yechezkel Michelson, later to become *Rosh Bet Din* of Warsaw. (Died under the Nazis.)

After R' Michelson left Krasnobrod, the aforementioned R' Nachum Feigenboim, also of renowned rabbinic lineage, a brother–in–law of the Radziner rebbe, R' Gershon Chanuch, was engaged. In his later years, he published a book, "*Halachta Rabta L'shavta.*" He died in 1917.

The old folks used to tell us that the rebbe of Lublin, the "seer," came from Krasnobrod. They would even point out the house where his wedding took place, to substantiate the legend.

The rebbe of Lublin, the "seer," was betrothed to a tenant farmer's daughter from the village of Katchuka, 5 *verst*[1] from our shtetl. The wedding was to be celebrated in Krasnobrod. When the bride was brought under the *chupa* the "seer" said, " The sages of the Talmud say, "*Asur l'adam sh'yikdesh et ha'isha ad sh'yirenah*." Thus, I want to see her before I take her for my wife." When they lifted her veil and uncovered her face, he declared that he would not marry her because he saw a cross on her face. The wedding did not take place. Later, it was said that she left the *derech hayashar* and converted.

The rebbe from Lublin's real wedding also took place in Krasnobrod, and the house where it took place was known.

The following story about the time of Chmielnicki was told in our shtetl.

When Chmielnicki's forces got closer to our neighborhood, the Jews of Krasnobrod began to lobby the noblemen of Kranobrod, Bander and Jadamow to keep them safe. They promised to protect them for a large sum of money, and they fulfilled their promise.

At the time, Chmielnicki's general staff were quartered on Jadamow's estate. The army remained in the Bander forests and avoided the shtetl. As a result, the Jews escaped mass murder.

Some bandits still managed to get into town, and coming upon a wedding in the *shul's* courtyard, they shot the bride and groom. They were both buried there.

We all knew that, on the north side of the *shul*, between the *shul* and the *beit hamidrash*, there was a little mound indicating the grave. The *cohanim* avoided the area and took the path between the *beit hamidrash* and the public baths.

The really old people, that I can remember from my childhood, were always telling us about how well previous generations got along together in peace and unity, how they were true Chasidim, and followed the ways of their great rabbi, the *Besht*, and his disciples.

Until, that is, the well–known "*makhloykes haskholes*[2]", broke out among the Radziner Chasidim between those who wore "*tikheyles*[3]" threads in their *tzizes*, and all the other Chasidic dynasties who were against it.

The quarrels spread to all the Jewish residents of Polish Russia. It was especially acute in our region. The rabbis called them "*makhloykes kerakh*" meaning the towns of Krasnobrod, Rajowiec and Chelm. In these areas, they even came to blows, and a strong enmity grew between the Chasidim on both sides.

This resulted in marriages arranged between other towns, and thanks to that, the shtetl began to grow and increase in population. New Chasidic *shtieblach* were established. Everyone "did their own thing" and travelled to their rebbes.

In the end, it was a quarrel for the sake of heaven, and slowly, the fire of fanaticism extinguished itself. Nevertheless, the enmity was felt for years, and if I am not mistaken, it was the reason that *Harav* R' Zvi Yehezkel Michelson left the chair of the Krasnobrod rabbinate.

Krasnobrod was not even listed on any maps until the First World War, and carried the qualification of "*Osada*" (settlement). This gave her the privilege of benefitting from the few rights that were granted to the peasants in the 19th century when they were freed from serfdom.

By decree, a certain portion of aristocratic land was granted to the peasants as compensation for their years of servitude. Our community was also given a portion of forest, and everyone's portion was recorded by number and boundaries.

In order to avoid arguments where someone preferred a nicer piece, or someone got a less well–treed portion, it was decided to sell the land, and share the proceeds equally.

R'Meyerl–a scholar–who was a good writer, was chosen to carry out the transaction.

The city was divided into sections, and it was announced that the forest was being sold without the land beneath, only the right to harvest trees was sold.

The company, Federbush, from Lemberg, bought the right to the timber for a sum of close to 50 thousand rubles, and began to work immediately. Some Jews from our town were also employed there. I remember two of them, Tevel Schreiber, and Israel Leib Eilboim. They worked there as employees.

It is to be remembered that in the serfdom era, Jews were obligated to work for the nobility along with the *goyim*. They were allowed one exception, not to work on Shabbos or the holidays.

The forest was actually called the "Jewish Forest," and I can remember parts of it from when I was a child. Every *Tisha B'Av*, when we were freed from going to *cheder*, groups of us got together, and with sacs in our hands we would go to "our" forest to gather nuts. Even though it was our Jewish forest, we still ran away in fear if we encountered *shkotzim* because they often greeted us with blows, or snatched away our hats.

No one of my generation knows what was done with the large sum of money that flowed in from the forest. Nor were any documents found. It didn't take long, and the land left from the logged–out forest also went over to *goyishe* hands. In their land–hunger, they gladly bought it from the Jews. The few who did not immediately sell, gave it over to the peasants to sow. In return, the farmer would bring them a sac of potatoes or a measure of wheat for *Shmurah Matzah*. Slowly, the peasant became the *de facto* owner of the land.

One Jew nevertheless, stubbornly refused to sell his part of the land. That was Arche Schlegel–a pious Chasidic Jew–who worked the field with his children, planted along with the farmers, cut and gathered the wheat in sheaves. He was the only one among the shtetl Jews who still occupied himself with that kind of work, really the "Last of the Mohicans."

R' Arche Shlegel

But even he gave it up later, thus putting an end to the chapter, "land," that our community received as a great prize from the Polish aristocrats.

One portion alone remained in Jewish hands, and was never sold, and that was the portion of woods and field owned by Berl Knebel (Yokele's)

In the year of the "jackpot," Purim was happily celebrated with no poor people. Not one pauper was to be found in our shtetl, and no begging hand was outstretched.

The musical Purim troupe led by Moishele Sofer and his retinue of old men from the Belzer *shtiebel*, among whom I remember: Mendele Beker, Elhanan Shuster, Matieh Ber, and Azriel Beker.

They had two goals: First, to get everyone happily singing holiday songs; and second, to raise several hundred rubles to be donated to *Hachnoses Kalah*.[4]

One of the elders in shtetl told me that, years ago, he had lived for a while in Josefow where he had a little shop. He made a living with his business, but did not have a dowry for his daughter. It was almost impossible to marry a daughter without a dowry in those days. Nevertheless, he told no one about his poverty.

One day, Moishele Sofer, *A"H*, came to see him and asked him: "Why aren't you getting a husband for your daughter, ha?" And with that he took out 200 rubles, put the money on the table, and quickly left.

R' Shlomo Bergstein, an old man, once told me that this very same musical troupe of Belzer Chasidim from our shtetl recognized "Yoshe Kalb" in the Belzer court. He had lived in Krasnobrod for a time. They were the chief witnesses in the great *Din Torah*[5]. Years later, when I saw the play, "Yoshe Kalb", by I. J. Singer, in the Yiddish theater, I was reminded of the tales I had heard during my childhood.

Before World War I, there were about 400 Jewish families in our shtetl. To this we must add some tens of Jewish families living in the surrounding villages who were in every way like the Jews of the shtetl. Among them were scholars, Chasidim, and simple warm–hearted Jewish folk. They participated in shtetl society along with everyone else. Their children either studied in town, or they brought the best *melamdim* and teachers to them. All the folk tales and jokes about illiterate villagers did not apply to the Jews around our shtetl. They came to the shtetl as equals, and brought the finest presents and donations. They occupied important leadership roles along with the important men of the shtetl.

I remember that every *Rosh Hashana* they would leave their well–established homes and come to town in wagons fully loaded with packs. Everyone already had a place to stay for the holidays. You could feel the love that Jews had for one another, and the holiday peace that pervaded the shtetl.

It is certainly possible that today, when we evoke the memories of our shtetl, everything seems brighter, more beautiful. It's possible that today we see only good things, cherished stories, true brotherhood and love among Jews–and it's possible that we are not inclined now to see the negative sides–which there undoubtedly were–of our shtetl Jewish life. Nevertheless, we know that life was brighter, that beauty shone from Jewish life and filled us with faith and meaning that were the foundation of our lives.

We were 20 km from Zamosc, the district seat, to which we were closely tied. We would go there to see doctors, on business, and for all kinds of government things. Even though Zamosc was a center of *Haskalah*, it did not affect our shtetl, and the *Haskalah* spirit did not "infect" our youth.

Up until World War I, there was not a Jewish boy who had shaved his beard. There was hardly any difference in appearance or dress among the various social classes.

After a day of work and trade, everyone went to his *beit hamidrash*, and the melodies of those studying rang through the town. At dawn, the *shammes* woke the shtetl for *Avoydes Haboyre*, knocking three times on every Jewish door, and not missing anyone.

On Shabbos and the holidays, when the whole town's Jews dressed in their Shabbos clothes, the women in their Jewelry, and everyone going to *daven*, one could really feel the holy spirit entering every little Jewish corner. When a rebbe came to visit, the celebration was tremendous. *Goyim* passing by would listen with envy to the *zmiros* singing that came from every Jewish home.

On summer Saturdays, the women would sit outside their homes and loudly read together the *Tsenerene*.

On Shabbos, in those days, no one dared to cross the *tkhum* on the other side of the bridge, or the other side of the shtetl. The pious Shmuel Zeinvl, A"H, established an *eruv, al pi ha'din*. If the *shkotzim* tore down the wires, he would take Ber Tentser or another of his students, and quickly repair the *eruv*.

As soon as *Rosh Chodesh, Elul*, was observed, the city acquired a different appearance. The fear of the coming Days of Awe made everyone more religious, and reflections on atonement occupied everyone's mind.

In the evenings, after *mincha* and *ma'ariv*, most people remained in the *beit midrashim* or *shtiebls*. They began to study. Large naphtha lamps were lit to make it easier to study. Some held a candle in their hands, deeply engrossed in their reading, ignoring the wax that dripped, like tears, onto the old, yellowed pages of the holy books. On Thursday nights, some stayed up all night studying.

After a boy had his Bar Mitzvah, he would stop going to *cheder* and went on to the *beit hamidrash*, or went to another city to the *yeshiva*. They studied *chumash* with *Rashi*, *Gemara* with *Tosafot* and *Mefarshim*. But they insisted that *Nevi'im* and *Ktuvim* not be taught. The Chasidim did not think it was desirable to study them.

It was said that our *melamed*, R' Baruch Yokele's Glustman, was studying *Tanach* in secret with the *Malbim*[6], which according to Chasidic thought, was strictly prohibited. One could believe it of him. He was a learned scholar with greater understanding than any other *melamed* or scholar in town. His method of teaching was unique. He could also write in several languages: Yiddish, Hebrew, Polish, Russian, German, and a little French. It's hard to know how he learned these languages, because he never travelled away from home. He certainly didn't learn them from his father, a poor *melamed* from the little shtetl of Komorow.

During *Slichot*, Zalma Ber (he was a shoemaker) would begin waking people up at 3:00 o'clock in the morning.

One night, Zalman Ber awoke at midnight, and not having a watch, he got up, took his wooden hammer, and set off to wake people for *Slichot*. People, tired, sleepy, got up, woke the boys older than 12, hastily poured out *negelvasser*, lit the lanterns, and set off for *the batei midrashim*. The houses where no grown–up girls were left (girls who were not yet married did not go to *Slichot*) were shut with padlocks, and the rest went off to beg God for health and a livelihood. The bandits quickly sniffed out the situation, and when the people returned at dawn, they found heir houses emptied out. A pity on poor old *shammes* Zalman Ber who received his share from the outraged owners.

"*Min hametzar karati yah*"…with awe and fear and deep mysticism, the whole congregation stood at the blowing of the *shofar* with holy fervor in their prayers. Above, in the women's gallery, the women and girls sat in their finest dresses and jewelry, and looked down through the large windows on the men in *shul*. From time to time a man would glance upward, but remembering what sort of day it was, he would quickly return to his prayers.

Once finished *davening*, everyone went home to eat, and then quickly returned to the *beit hamidrash*. No one dared take a nap, becaue it was written in the holy books, that it was forbidden to sleep during the day of Rosh Hashana: you could, God forbid, sleep your good fortune away. After *mincha*, the crowd went singing to the river for *tashlich*. The men took over the whole bridge, the women standing along the banks, and all the sins and sorrows were shaken into the water. Returning, it seems, one walked easier, as though relieved of a heavy load. One felt the kind of spiritual enjoyment which nourishes the soul and the body together.

How fanatic our shtetl was can be illustrated by the following: Just before World War I, a respectable man from our shtetl gave his daughter in marriage to a young man from Warsaw. As soon as the young man arrived, the news spread that he was an *apikoros*, even though he was wearing a *kapote*, and a Chasidic hat. Because his beard was pointed and his *payes* weren't as long as those in our town, they viewed him as an *apikoros*. Chasidim did not trim their beards, and were scrupulous in not throwing away any hair that might fall from their beard.

It did not take long for them to divorce. There was no place in town for such an *apikoros* as this Chasidic, young man was.

A fire broke out in the shtetl, in the middle of the night, during the week of *Shavuot*, 1913. Two warehouses full of goods burned down. One warehouse, filled with glass, was owned by Pinyele Glatter. The second, full of flour, belonged to Myer Fuchs. The fire quickly grew and could not be extinguished. More than half the shtetl was consumed in flames. The other half, with the *shul*, and the *batei midrash* were spared. The shtetl rebuilt itself so completely that, at the time of the First World War, no traces of the fires remained.

But a new fire arrived, one that enveloped the world and set it ablaze with the flames of war. It did not spare our shtetl.

During World War I

During the first mobilization of the Tsarist army, about 20 Jews from our shtetl were mobilized. They were quickly sent to the front.

On a Friday, they assembled the mobilized group in the middle of the market, before being shipped out. The howls and cries from their families could have moved a stone. When the group began to move out, and the farewells began, the wailing reached the heavens. On this Shabbos, families were left orphaned by the departure of their husbands, fathers, and sons. This Shabbos was disrupted in the shtetl of Krasnobrod where for generations, Shabbos was a symbol of rest, joy, and holiness.

Dovid Ben Yechezkel (Yakov Ber's) andAvigdor Rind in the Tsarist army

If my memory does not trick me, those mobilized were: Shalom (Naviner) Fersht, Yitzchak–Hersh Weissfish, Nachman Shtokhammer, Avigdor Rind (my father, *A'H'*), Moshe Kupfer (the hat maker), the three Krelman brothers, Chaim Pipek's son (the old man was later dragged into the Austrian army as a spy) Matye Knebel, Yakov Leibreiner, Leibish Fuchs (Mendel Beker's son), Nathan Interboich (today in America), Velvel Hackman, Israel Tabak, and others. (The last two did not return).

When the front approached Komorow, the military authorities ordered the evacuation of the shtetl. There were trenches already dug surrounding the city. There was generalized panic. In haste, people dug graves, and buried their fortunes. They fled in search of a place to save themselves, taking only what they could carry. The deserted shtetl was later destroyed by the battles, and burnt down.

After a while, as the battles moved further away, the Jews began to return. They settled in the ruins, or stayed with *goyim* in the surrounding villages, and began to rebuild the shtetl anew. But the *shul* and the *beit hamidrash* remained in ruinous condition for years.

They *davened* in *minyans* in the private homes of Pinchas Rothheiser, Hersh Geist, Itche Lefler, Shlomo Bergstein, Shmuel Levenfuss, Shmuel Gurtler, and Itche Bleichman.

In 1917, Rav R' Nachum Feigenboim died, and the only one to carry on was the moyre–hoyre, R' Mair Zilberman.

Under Polish rule

When the first Polish government came to power, a town council was created, and the Jews elected the clever Moshe Eli Chaim Gerzon. Although he was a zealous Chasid, he mastered both speaking and writing in Polish. After his death, R' Shmuel Gurtler became the representative, a post he held until the Devastation.

The Polish authorities had scarcely had time to solidify their power, before the peasants began to rob and plunder Jewish possessions. Every Sunday and Tuesday, they would descend in large groups to rob Jewish stores. Whoever tried to resist them was met with blows. *Goyim*, who we personally knew well, came with iron bars and axes, and without shame or fear, they broke open the doors of stores, and took whatever they pleased. The three Polish policemen in town were not to be seen, nor did they try to stop the robberies.

The Jews in the villages also were included in the terror. Their homes were ruined. The windows broken, the possessions taken. The days, and especially the nights, were passed in dread. It was a miracle that they did not yet take to murdering people, and were occupied only with stealing Jewish wealth.

During market days, Sunday and Tuesday, the Jewish stores were locked. But the Jewish stores needed the two days of business, and as a result, there was an economic decline.

Delegations to the *starosta* in Zamosc were sent frequently to ask for help with the bandits. Other than fine words, no help was forthcoming. Despair crept into every home, and fear was reflected in people's eyes.

One fine Tuesday, groups of policemen arrived from the direction of Zamosc, armed with rifles and grenades. They took over the center of the city and all the surrounding streets. At the same time, from the Tomaszow side, organized bands of bandits appeared carrying weapons. They came in the hundreds, and immediately began to pillage, in view of the police.

But when the police began to beat them with rubber batons, and fired a few salvos into the air, they fled like rats to their dens. The city became quiet after that.

It must be said that if we had mounted a resistance and not allowed them to run wild, we would not have reached such a state of robbery, and we would have restored order with our own efforts. In order to prove this, I will present several facts:

On a certain Sunday, a bunch of bandits grabbed old Yokele Knebel, and began to cut off his beard with a knife. Hersh Sender's (Lefler) was a witness to this, and not being able to stand the humiliation, he grabbed a stick and threw himself on the shkotzim. His brother–in–law quickly came to his aid, and the bandits ran away in fear.

A group of Krasnobrod young men in the Polish army

It was quiet for a short time, and it was thought that life was back to normal. It turned out though that the cup of sorrow was not yet full. In 1920, Petliera's bandits came to town, and for 24 hours they ran rampant, raping women, plundering Jewish possessions, beating, stripping naked two Jews and murdering them: Chaim Schneider and Shloimele Melech.

* * *

After six hard years of pain and sorrow, the shtetl became quiet again, and life normalized and bloomed again. The rabbinate proclaimed a day of prayer and a *Tanes–Tsiber*[7]. All the stores were closed and business stopped, and the whole community gathered at the *shul*, and offered prayers. At the exit, the *gabais* collected donations from the assembled.

A few months later, the *Linat Hatzedek*[8] group celebrated a *Hachnasat Sefer Torah*[9] in the *shul* ruins. R' Yosef Rind, a former Krasnobrod resident who had returned from America, was present. Upon seeing the ruins of the *shul* he delivered a passionate *drasha* calling for the restoration of the *shul*. A committee was soon established to reach this goal with the participation of everyone according to their abilities.

The best master builders were brought in from everywhere, and the *shul* was quickly built. Moishele Sefer, *A"H*, painted it in beautiful colors. The big, six–foot, brass menorah was brought back, which the *gabai*, Aharon Luchfeld, had saved from the fires, and *Chanukat–habayit* was celebrated with great joy.

It was a real *yom tov* then in the shtetl. Old and young were dressed in their holiday best. Music (brought in from Lublin), was playing, people danced in the streets and visited family at tables laden with the best. It could really be said:

He who has not seen the *simcha* at the Krasnobrod *beit haknesset*, has never seen a *simcha* in his life!"

R' Aharon Lochfeld, z"l

Control of the *shul* went to the *Chevra Kedisha*. Its *gabai* became the *shul gabai*.

At the *Simchat Torah kiddush*, the battle to elect a new *gabai* for the coming year began. *Motzi Sukkot*, everyone would get together at the rev's house, and hear who was nominated. After that, a child would draw the ballots with the names out of the rebbe's yarmulke. That's how the *gabai* and two of his deputies were elected. Sometimes, a *gabai* was hired for an additional year. This happened only with someone who managed the financial side well, received fat burial donations from the heirs of the wealthy, and who, every Shabos, provided a *Kiddusha Rabba* for the congregation.

I can remember the following *gabais*: Aharon (Israel Kupiec's) Lochfeld, Eliyahu Zimmerman, Yosef Lederman, Shmuel Rind, Yosef Friedlender, Mordechai Gurtler, Itzhak Hersh Weissfish, Shmuel Levenfus, Shimon Untzig, Berl (Naftali's) Steinberg, Chaim Untzig, Aharon Shmuel Miltz, Itche Moishe Untzig, and the director of the shul, Leib Borg.

New winds in Krasnobrod

Our shtetl was small in size, but large in quality of life. In this, it was no different than in larger Jewish settlements in Poland.

Our youth, who passionately embraced life, and the challenge to bring a new agenda into Jewish life, encountered substantial difficulties. It required much courage and endurance to break down the wall of old ideas and customs behind which our parents took refuge, staying true to the conservative way of life of previous generations.

Quarrels and fights increased between parents and children. They spread from the home to the schools and synagogues. The battles between the older generation and the awakening youth became sharper and more determined.

When the Balfour Declaration was announced, we wondered around drunk on nationalist dreams and fantasies. We eagerly read every newspaper and journal that we could get our hands on. Nevertheless, we lacked the power to organize and accomplish something.

Finally, some of the youth joined the central committee of the *Keren Kayemet L'Israel* in Warsaw, and received from them instructions on how to organize the activities.

Their opponents, the youth of Agudat Israel, began a counter–action and brought in a *Rav*–a speaker. They distributed for free the orthodox organ, *Der Yud*. The older generation gave them all the help they needed. They were able to get the attention of the shtetl youth for a while, but not for long.

In 1920, the house of Berish Givertz became a Zionist center. The majority of the youth went there. We acquired a gramophone, and thus were able to listen to the speeches of a great variety of Zionist leaders, whose names were written on the records. They were sent from the central K.K.L. The establishment of the Zionist movement in Krasnobrod became a fact.

We took to the work with youthful passion. It was not easy to distribute the blue, white tins. Nevertheless, we managed to take an important position in the K.K.L. In 1923, commendations for their activity were received by: Yakov Zimmerman, Yehoshua Babad, Yehoshua Gurtler, Alezer Glickman, Sholom Aharon Rendler, and Eliyahu Rind–the author of these lines.

Because of the great storm caused by our activities, our parents became calmer, and slowly made peace with the idea of our abandoning the "*Derech Hayashar.*" We conducted meetings without disturbances, and we planned to establish a library at the Zionist organization, the first of its kind in the shtetl.

The library, and its books, was to be open to anyone. More than once, parents stormed in shouting and hitting their son or daughter and dragging them home. Nevertheless, we managed to enlarge the library and buy new books.

The work for the K.K.L was proving to be difficult. I am reminded of an episode from the first "*Chamisha esser b'Shabbat*" action that we carried out: We received, from K.K.L. central, various kinds of dried fruit, and small paper bags. All night we sat and filled the bags. In the morning, on a frosty day, we set off to sell the little bags. Buyers there were none of, but insults to our appeal there were plenty of.

The single unified Zionist organization in the shtetl did not long maintain its oneness. Gradually, each group began to organize itself separately. Speakers, and organizers from various Zionist parties visited, and increased the rift in the shtetl.

At the congress elections, the most votes went to *Poalei Zion* with its youth wing, "*Freiheit–Dror.*" *Mizrahi* came second, and third, the General Zionists and their two spin–offs, *Al Hamishmar*, and *Et L'banot*. The Revisionist party in our town was very small, but it had several active and dedicated members: Bintche Rosenfeld, Mechl Meyer, Yonah Lerer, and Yodl Untzig (today in America).

The *Bund* and the Communists had very interesting and knowledgeable members in their organisations. They also had a splendid youth wing.

In 1929, the Polish police carried out night arrests of the members of the Communist party, and sent them to various prisons for long terms.

The drama society, under the direction of Yehoshua Babad, produced a host of pieces which went off with great success, and contributed greatly to the cultural development of the youth.

Agudat Israel was left weakened organizationally when it lost the youth. Not willing to give up, they decided to "monopolize" education. They established a *cheder* under the name of *"Cheder Yesodei HaTorah."* Among the founders were: Chaim Untzig, Baruch Eli Broder, and Motl Halperin.

At the top of *Agudat Israel* were, apart from those already mentioned: Itche meir Kupiec, Aharon Greenboim, Moishe Helfman, Moishe Margolit, Zvi Steinberg, Zvi Broder, Itche Knebel, Israel Lochfed, and others. When the *cheder* closed after a short time, they began, with fanatical bitterness, to harass the Zionist youth who were still in the *batei midrashim*. Every Shabbos they created scenes and refused to *daven* with them.

In order to avoid the confrontations, they organized *minyans* for themselves. With time, the *minyan* grew, and became a place of true unity.

In their battle to "save" the youth, the Radziner Chasidim came to the conclusion that they needed to bring in a *"Manhig Ha'ir,"* and not continue with the scholarly R' Meir Zilberman. They succeeded in influencing several Gerer Chasids and together, without the consent of the majority of the residents, brought in a *Rav* for the shtetl.

The outrage over the action of a small group of Chasidim was great. A huge quarrel erupted. The other side also brought in a *Rav*, a local from the Babad family, *Harev* Menachem Manish Margoliot. The majority demanded of the minority that they retire their candidate. But they refused with the argument that the Chair of the Rabbinate belonged to them in as much as the late *Rav* R'Nachum Feigenboim was a Radziner Chasid.

After much quarreling and investigating, a *Din Torah* was handed down by several prominent rabbis–headed by the Tarner *rav*–and they ruled that the first rabbi must leave the city, and that Harav Menachem Manish Margoliot, the rabbi picked by the majority, should stay. He remained our spiritual leader from 1923 until the Destruction.

* * *

In the period from 1920–1930, the economic situation of the Jews was quite good. It was a prosperous time. About 30 of the residents were engaged in the lumber industry, one of the good businesses in Poland. This stirred feelings of envy among the Christian neighbors. They took to business themselves, built stores in the center of town, and tried to conquer the Jewish businesses.

When this failed, they proposed to the authorities that the market be moved outside of town, ostensibly for sanitary reasons, but as a result the Jews would lose business. They also picked out the suitable spot for the market, naturally in a completely Christian neighborhood. They immediately began to build stores and opened two bakeries.

In a short time, farmers were no longer seen in the shtetl market. Jewish economic life fell with one blow. In light of this situation, the prominent people of the shtetl went to see the priest to get him to influence the farmers. A delegation that travelled to the *starasto* got no answer. A delegation headed by Eliyahu Zimmerman went to Warsaw to see the Jewish deputies in the Sejm. They brought along lawyers, headed by Dr. Hartglass. And after long interventions the decree was voided. The shtetl breathed easier for a short time.

In 1932, the members of the Zionist *minyan* began action to take Jewish education away from the *cheders* and their old–fashioned *melamdim*.

A group of sixth grade schoolgirls in the folkshule

The issue was real also because the children attended the Polish state school and after half a day of studying in a modern, bright school building, they had to spend the second half of the day in cramped, dark, and often dirty *cheders*.

Understandably, our actions simply meant a revolution in the shtetl. First of all, it was compared to conversion, and secondly, it threatened the livelihood of a group of *melamdim* who were, moreover, not capable of any other kind of work.

A group of schoolgirl members of "Hashomer HaDati."
In the center is the counselor, Itah Margoliot
(All perished under the Nazis)

The *Mizrachi* party, according to a directive from *Yavneh* central in Warsaw, started to organize a *Yavneh* school. The Polish school authorities began to raise objections and refused to consider the school under any circumstances. They could not allow the freeing of Jewish children from the obligation to attend a government school. After long negotiations, they came to an agreement that the children would attend the Polish school, but were exempted from religious studies.

After getting the government's permission, we got a place at our *chaver* Bintche Rosenfeld. *Yavneh* central sent us the pedagogue, B. Kohanovitz, as teacher (from Jedwabne by Lomza). To teach religious subjects, we hired the best *melamed* in town, R' Chaim Untzig.

In a very short time, the children could speak Hebrew, knew well the *Tanach*, mastered the religious studies, and were happy with their school. The zealots did not however, stop their attacks, slandered ceaselessly, insulted the parents, and plotted endlessly.

R' Chaim Untzig, hy"d

Unfortunately, there also came to be conflict between the teacher, Kohanowitz, and the Chasidic *melamed*, Chaim Untzig. Untzig saw Kohanowitz as an *apikoros*, a transgressor of Chasidic laws. R' Chaim Untzig began to write complaints to *Yavneh* central, and even to the president of *Mizrahi*, Harav Brodt, Z"L. As a result, Kohanowitz left his job, and a short time later, the school closed.

The eve of the destruction

Already by 1936–1937 we could feel the growing Polish anti–Semitism and its goal of ruining the Jewish population, robbing them of their few rights, breaking them economically, and drowning them in bloody pogroms, according to Hitler's design.

The *goyim* began to increase pressure in the city, opened stores and competed with the Jewish small shtetl merchants. Insults to Jews became frequent. When hooligans harassed a Jewish business, the Police commander urged them on, saying that Hitler was what was needed for the Jews. On market days, the Polish storekeepers brought in pickets to sand in front of Jewish stores and let no one in. We felt the full meaning of premier Skladkowski's famous "*Owszem.*"

Under the conditions of the time, it wasn't even possible to dream about mounting a resistance. The Poles were hoping for it. At the time, Nachum (Sender's) Lefler, told me he was becoming ill from watching, with hands tied, the scenes of hooliganism. I heard the same from Moishe Shnor whose windows were shattered by hooligans.

The proposed law banning kosher slaughter by the Polish Sejm got the shtetl worked up. The religious assembled at the synagogues hoping that their prayers would avert the decree. Our rav was summoned by the Zamosc rabbinate and the *kehila* directors. They asked him to put together a delegation of community leaders from Krasnobrod and Zamosc in order to influence the *graf*, Podakowski, a member of the Polish senate and friend of the Polish president,

Maszcicki. The *rav* turned to R' Shmuel Gurtler, a visitor to the *graf's* house and factor of his mill. He arranged with the *graf* to meet the delegation.

Taking part in the delegation were the Zamosc *rav*, several local community members with Ben–Zion Lubliner– the *kehila* chairman–at the head. And the Krasnobrod *rav* and community leaders headed by R' Shmuel Gurtler. As expected, the delegation returned with a negative answer, and received nothing from the *graf*.

R' Shmuel Gurtler, hy"d, chatting with graf Podakowski

Blood libel

In the winter of 1937, a 10–year old Christian girl mysteriously disappeared. Her neighbors were Jews.

The anti–Semites began to spread malicious stories saying that the Jews murdered the child to use her blood for making matzos. Soon witnesses popped up who "swore" that they personally saw and heard the Jews murder the child. The *goyeh* who washed clothes at the rebbe's house testified that she had seen full bottles of blood in the rebbe's credenza. The frenzied Christian population, on a Sunday, went to the cemetery and began to dig up the fresh graves looking for the girl's body. After pleading with the *starosta* the police ordered a halt to the desecration of the Jewish graves.

In spring the mystery was solved, and it was found that the child had drowned in the river. In the winter, when the river was frozen, people would take a shortcut from one side of the shtetl to the other by walking across the ice. The

Christians who used the water from the river, and washed their clothes in it would chop a hole in the ice to do it. One evening, the parents of the child went to a wedding on the other side of the river leaving her at home. Late in the evening, the child decided to go to her parents, and in the dark, fell into one of those holes in the ice, and disappeared under the ice without a trace.

Erev Pesach, her little body was found at the mill's sluice. The medical commission concluded that the child had drowned and had been under the ice the entire time.

The beginning of the end

The Second World War broke out on September 1, 1939. Thus began the last chapter in the history of the Jewish community in Poland. In the bloody flood, the Jews of Europe, and with them, the Jews of Krasnobrod, were drowned.

In the very first day of the war, the anti–Semites and the police strutted around, and in victory, began to demonstrate their rule over Jews. Friday evening, during *Kabbalat Shabbat*, they invaded the synagogues, evicted everyone, and ordered them to go home, lock their doors and windows, and sit in the dark. No one dared to say a word, and the order was quickly followed. We sat in the dark and listened to the hysterical laughter of our Polish rulers who walked by our windows as "victors" and expressed their glee at the fear of the Jews.

Erev Rosh Hashanah, the Nazi troops marched into our shtetl and brought horror and terror with them. Some Jews left town and moved in with the Christians in the suburbs. The next day, after Rosh Hashana, the city was virtually empty. Because of fear of the front, people fled to the woods. Monday morning, shooting broke out from both sides, and victims of the shootings were Moishe Ben Itche Fuchs, Shmelke Ben Ephraim Shtemer, and a third young boy from Cracow. The three boys were searching for a hiding place and perished together. From our hiding places in the forest, we saw the shtetl enveloped in flames. The fires were lit by the Polish troops, and the shtetl went up in smoke. Thursday, when we got back to the shtetl, we could see the whole disaster…

Beneath the ruins and ashes, we found half–burned bodies whose identity we could not establish, because the shtetl was full of refugees from the Cracow region. Eighteen Jews were buried that day without the ceremonies and wailing customary to Jews in normal times. The Polish populace helped the Germans to discover the hiding places and cellars where people's valuables were buried, and shared in the loot. In Leibish Lerner's cellar, aside from merchandise, the books from the *rav's* library were buried there. Upon finding the books, they built a fire and threw them in, distributing the loot by the light of the pyre.

On Yom Kippur, several *minyans* were organized. *Kol Nidre* was observed in total fear. With broken hearts, they sang the holy prayers, and silently, each person begged God to save him from the evil–doers. After the prayers, rumors were spread that Russia had entered the war. On Yom Kippur day, at around 10:00 am, rifle gunshots were heard. When we went outside, we saw German soldiers lying near the pharmacy by the little bridge, and shooting in the direction of the sand hill. A few hours later, the Germans left and Polish army soldiers marched in, mostly cavalry and artillery units. They arrived from the Zamosc side, and left via the Tomaszow side. Suddenly, we saw a carriage and mounted horsemen of the the general staff, and a whole contingent of high ranking officers from the Polish army. We doffed our hats and greeted them, and Baruch Eli Broder approached them with the question of whether we should remain in town or flee. Without waiting to hear him out, they answered sarcastically, "Complain to Hitler, not us!" That answered deepened our distress, and more people crammed into the darkened rooms where the *minyanim* were held, and continued to pray.

When *musaf* was starting–R' Chaim Untzig was the *Baal Tefila*–we became aware that something was happening outside. A number of rider–less horses appeared in town. Soon we could hear shouting and saw small groups of Polish soldiers fighting with bayonets against German units. In fear we fled the praying. Soon after, we heard the noise of motorized divisions, and a German troop on motorcycles entered. One of the German came over to the window of our minyan and asked if there were any Jews there. Receiving no reply, he disappeared. A grenade exploded right by the window and deafened us, and forced us to go deeper into our hiding places.

Around 4:00 pm, when it had quieted down and not a sound was heard, people began to venture outside. We saw two armed German soldiers, wearing steel helmets, standing near Moishe Greenbaum's house, and patrolling the street. We went up to one of them and asked if we could stay here, or if we had to leave. He did not answer, so we went over to the other soldier. He advised us to leave immediately, and no later than 6:00 pm, because from that time on there was going to be mayhem.

We were seized by panic, and not stopping even to get dressed, we grabbed our children and ran for the forest. We had barely got away before a mighty cannonade of heavy artillery began. The explosions were truly deafening. It lasted for 24 hours without letup, and after 2 days, the fighting continued with breaks. When we ventured out, we saw dead bodies from both sides littering the roads. In the shtetl, the dead bodies were piled together with the corpses of horses and cows. The new bridge was destroyed and the devastation was complete.

The Germans began to force Jews to remove the corpses. The *goyim*, on the other hand, roamed around looking for something to steal, not scrupling even to remove the boots from the dead Polish soldiers.

When the Red army marched into the shtetl, we breathed a little easier. Some goyim were frightened enough and returned the Jewish possessions they had stolen, claiming that they had found them. We believed the war was over, and we could return and rebuild the shtetl.

Our joy was short–lived. We quickly discovered that the Russian army was retreating to new borders, and that our area was going to go back under the Germans. Some Jews held that we should leave with the Red Army, and others that we should stay. I was of the same opinion. On *Hoshana Raba* morning, my friends came to visit: Zvi Shoch, Moishe Haz, Yehoshua Babad, Fishl Schlegel. (They all perished). They decided they would stay put together. But if the Germans were to evict them, they would take their children and go to the Russian border. I could not promise them anything, because I was getting ready to go to travel to my grandfather in Tomaszow.

When I got to Tomaszow, I found the city was almost empty. Jews were fleeing en masse, and the Soviet army was driving from house to house, and trying to get the people to leave with them. I also decided to save my family and myself and we got on a Russian autobus that took us to Rawa Ruska. *Shmini Atzeret* morning, I tried to convince my uncles, Itche and Meyer Fuchs, to leave with us. They answered that although they feared the Germans, they didn't want to desecrate the holiday. At *motzi yom tov*, they would travel to the rabbi in Belz and ask him what to do. My mother agreed with them, and we said good–bye not knowing that we were saying farewell forever.

A few weeks after we got to Rawa Ruska, my friend Zvi Shoch came to see us. With tears in his eyes, he said to me, "Eli, I am petrified knowing that I am going back to the murderers. I know I'm going to my death. But I can't stay here when my wife and children are over there. Whatever is gong to happen to them, it will happen to me too." And that is how they left us, our nearest and most beloved, those who could not bear to be separated from their families and were martyred.

The road of pain

Weeks and months passed. We, on the Soviet side, learned to feel at home in the new society, under the new conditions of life, and we even lived reasonably well. From our old homes, we received disconcerting news, each time worse than the last. However, we did not forget our old home. We were filled with longing in our hearts waiting for something that would come, even though we had no clear idea of what that would be.

There was a proclamation that all the refugees were required to appear on a certain date to register themselves, and to receive Soviet passports.

The refugees were into into a panic not knowing whether to take out Soviet citizenship and give up their Polish citizenship, and possibly lose their right to return to Poland after the war. The majority declined to comply with the authorities demand. The Soviet government's instinct was to see this–and rightly so–as an act of unfriendliness towards the authorities. They prepared train transport, and in the summer of 1940, they arrested all the refugees without passports, and their families, and sent them to the farthest reaches of Russia, mostly to Siberia.

Up to 100 people were packed into the railroad cars. For many weeks, we traversed Russia, in filthy conditions, dying for a drink of water.

Finally, we were distributed to various camps and forest settlements (*fasialkes*) isolated in the Taiga hundreds of kilometers from a city. Our job was to cut trees in the Ural forests, and prepare them for use by the government.

There has been much already written about the Soviet camps and Gulags, so I'm not adding anything new when I talk about the hard penal work, about hunger and filth. About the awful cold that lacerated our bodies, about those who fell at their work like fallen trees and never rose again. I will, however, pass over the opportunity to relate this nightmare, and will instead remember the tragic fate of Abraham Ben Shimon Greenboim, 39 years old, who, in the middle of the day went out to gather some twigs, and disappeared without a trace in the deep Taiga.

We endured all the pain that fate had in store for the few remaining Jews, until we lived to see the day when, on the way home, we crossed the Polish border, and received the first "welcome" from the Poles in the form of stones, curses and shouts.

Our years–long dream of our old home, and meeting again with the rest of the family was shattered in a terrible awakening. The Jewish homes in Poland lay in ruins, and not even a trace remained of the old, so creative, Jewish way of life. Even the graves were desolate and destroyed. Our parents, brothers and sisters, wives and children, grandfathers and grandmothers lie slaughtered in mass graves and the earth screams to the heavens at the outrages inflicted on her.

Liberated Poland welcomed us with murdered Jews, with being dragged from trains, with interrogations–where are you coming from? With pogroms in Kielce and Cracow.

With cutting looks and hidden fists ready to shatter our lives.

Through the hardships of the *she'erit hapletah* in camps in Austria, Germany and Italy, through the danger–filled routes of the illegal immigration, we came to the shores of our homeland. Our brothers and sisters welcomed us, and we began to set down roots in our own Jewish land, drawing from it spiritual nourishment to replace the severed Jewish branch, and giving rise again to proud and free generations.

Pinchas Diamond as soldier in the Jewish Brigade

Let us, in the telling of our lives, in the reestablishment of the Jewish people, find some good from our lives, a consolation for our tortured souls and healing for our lacerated bodies.

Let us remember our holy families with reverence, and honour all those who were sacrificed in the name of the people of Israel.

May these pages serve as a monument on the graves of the holy community of Krasnobrod, near Zamosc.

Translator's notes:
1. A verst is a Tsarist Russian measure equal to 1.06 km
2. quarrels
3. sky–blue thread in biblical days woven into *tallit*
4. Communal help for young girls without resources to marry.
5. Lawsuit in rabbinical court
6. Rabbi Meir Leibush ben Yehiel Michel Wisser
7. Exceptional collective communal fast–day.
8. A charitable organization
9. Inauguration of a sefer Torah

[Hebrew page 43]

The Synagogue in Krasnobrod

by Engineer D. Davidovich, Tel Aviv

Translated by Mira Eckhaus

The synagogue of the Krasnobrod community in Lublin County belongs to the type of synagogues with four main supporting pillars, which was very common all over Poland from the end of the 16th century to the beginning of the 19th century. The synagogue was built in the Baroque style and excelled in its beautiful exterior, and in particular, in its wide windows with a semi-circular arch as well as its picturesque two-story mansard roof.

[Hebrew page 44]

[Hebrew page 45]

Note: The photographs of the synagogue in Krasnobrod were published in the aforementioned research by Professor A. Shishko-Bohosh and were given to us with the permission of the author of the article, the engineer D. Davidovich.

[Hebrew page 46]

In the spacious prayer hall (approximately 13x14 m), it is worth mentioning the four rather simple rounded wooden pillars that supported the flat ceiling and divided the area of the synagogue into nine equal areas. Similarly to the synagogue in Vyshgorod, there is no match here between the period in which the synagogue was built, (it is estimated that the synagogue was built at the end of the 17th century, as evidenced by the platform that was built in 1680) and the style of the interior. In fact, the four pillars of this synagogue testify only to a certain traditional connection with the period of the first synagogues with four pillars - and they should perhaps be seen as a sort of a hint of that period, since these pillars are not organically connected with the beautiful wooden platform, which was indeed built between them, but at some distance from them.

"A row of holes in the western wall serves as a connection between the interior (that is, the prayer hall) and the women's section, which is located above the "polish". A second part of the women's section, similar to the previous, is on the ground floor, on the side of the north wall, and completes the space of the synagogue. Apart from these, a wooden gallery for the children was preserved here[1]". The most beautiful examples of this kind of structure were found only in certain synagogues in Greater Poland (such as: Pinchow, Zamosc, Vyshgorod, Gabin, Grojec) and in the synagogue outside the city of Lviv. The function of the gallery inside the synagogue hall is not clear to this day. Gloger describes such a gallery that is in the Renaissance style synagogue of Zamosc, in his book "Construction with Wood and Wood Products in Old Poland"[2] and defines it as chorek, which means the small choir gallery which is intended for the children of the "cheders"[3].

[Hebrew page 47]

"The wooden furniture, such as the large table, which has upright style lines, the book stands (the "stenders"), etc., represent the artistic, folk character. Other furnishings, such as the wood-carved platform and the Holy Ark are works in the style of the Baroque period[4]."

We will also mention here Eliyahu's chair with the wooden tympanum, the shape of which is very similar to that of Eliyahu's chair in the synagogue in Shebreshin, the Hanukkah lamp with the seven candelabrums and its delicate shape, which was found next to the Holy Ark, as well as a row of beautiful brass chandeliers ("spiders"), which are typical of most ancient synagogues in Poland.

The synagogue was destroyed by the Nazi invaders and no remnant was left of it.

Engineer D. Davidovich

***

We were lucky that we managed to get photographs of the old synagogue, which went up in flames in 1915, during the First World War.

On the western wall of the synagogue was engraved the date 5422-1661, probably the year its construction was completed. Its antiquity was also evidenced by the thick walls, the windows that were placed at a great height, right under the ceiling, as well as the double tiled roof.

There were two women's sections in the synagogue. One on the west side, above the men's section, and the second women's section was on the ground floor, near the north wall to the front. On the eastern side, there were two large boxes, built as two altars. Throughout the year, the boxes were covered and on the right-hand box stood the large copper Menorah. On the eve of the Day of Atonement (Yom Kippur), the covers would be taken off. Those who came to the synagogue would stick large memorial candles in the sand that filled the boxes, which would be lit until the end of the holiday.

[Hebrew page 48]

The interior of the building was lit by the many copper lamps that were hanging from the ceiling on long chains near the four pillars that supported the roof, and in the middle of the synagogue above the "bimah ." On the bimah was a table and "Eliyahu's chair." On the southwestern corner rose a fenced balcony reached by stairs. This place was sacred to the schoolchildren, so they would also be able to see what was happening, without the elders hiding it.

And here is the place to mention Rabbi Shlomo, the cantor, who was at the time the most famous in town. For many years his name was mentioned with respect and appreciation. It was said about him that when he started in the Days of Awe with "Hamelach", the whole building trembled. If my memory serves me correctly, Rabbi Shlomo died in 1910. He was succeeded by cantor Rabbi Haim Bergshtein.

In the western wall of the synagogue there was a deep hollow, with two glazed doors, and in which an "eternal flame" (Ner HaTamid) burned. An incident from my childhood is related to this corner. I was about 7 or 8 years old at the time, and since my father was then in the army, I went alone on the eve of the Day of Atonement (Yom Kippur) to pray the Mincha prayer. When I came out of the synagogue, I was amazed. Next to the eternal flame stood a thick-bearded Jew, in his hand a whip with two long straps, and in front of him Jews prostrated themselves, rolled up their capote, and the old man whipped them. A great fear fell upon me. For some reason I remembered at that moment the stories of fear that were told by my friends. The dead who come to the synagogue to pray, about Lilin and the ghosts that dwell in the attic and whoever goes up there never returns. I ran home as fast as I could. Since then, I have been careful not to glance at this corner.

I remember that for a long time this did not let us rest. One day we decided to do something about it. One day, when we were free from the burden of cheder, a group of us children got together, and we decided to go up to the attic. We held each other's hands after checking our tassels seven times, and with trembling hearts we went up. We found piles of Machzor and Techina books that had turned yellow from age and the tears shed on them by mothers and grandmothers from generations before us.

A. Riner

Translator's notes:
1. A. Szyszko-Bohusz, materialy do Architektury boznic w Polsce, Krakow 1926, p. 20
2. Z, Glogier, Budownictwo drzewne I wyroby z drzewa w dawnej Polsce, Warsaw 1907 p. 18
3. In his above-mentioned research, Shishko Bohosh also mentions such choirs in the other synagogues described by him. The synagogue outside the city of Lviv, which was publicized, among other things, due to the boycott that was announced in it for the first time against the Hasidim, according to the decision of the 4 countries committee and the rabbis of the country from the year 5482 (1722) - such a gallery was found and it is indeed mentioned in this boycott that was announced by Rabbi Ya'akov Yehoshua, the author of "Pnei Yehoshua": "On those who sinned in blowing the shofar and blowing out the candles and all the people stood and listened tremblingly to the words of the curse and school children who were placed in rows on the **western gallery**(my emphasis - D.D.) answered after them Amen with a loud voice". By M. Balaban: "To the History of the Frankish Movement", first part, Tel Aviv, p. 65)
4. Shishko Bohosh, in his aforementioned research, p. 24.

[Page 260 - Yiddish] [Page 47 - Hebrew]

The Old Synagogue

by Eliyahu Rind

Translated by Moses Milstein

We were fortunate to have acquired these photos of the old Krasnobrod shul which had burned down in 1915 during the First World War.

Outside view of the old shul

The western wall bore the date 1661. Its antiquity was seen in the thick brick walls, the windows, the tall transom windows, as well as the double shingle roof. The shul had two women's shuls:

[Page 261]

[Page 262]

All the photos of the old shul were published in the work of Professor A. Shishka Bohush, and were passed to us by Eng. Davidovitch of Tel-Aviv

[Page 263]

One on the western wall, high above the anteroom, the second below at the northern wall. A strong impression was made by its interior appearance. Up on the eastern wall, there were two brick boxes that gave the impression of two altars. To their right stood a brass menorah. They were covered up during the year. But on Yom Kippur, they were uncovered and the big yizkor candles were placed in the sand they contained. The shul was lit by the many brass chandeliers that hung from iron chains beside the four lecterns, right in the middle of the shul, at the *balemer*. The Torah reading table was on the balemer, and Eliyahu's chair. In the corner of the west wall, there was a little wooden balcony with small stairs for the cheder children.

We should also mention the cantor, R' Shloime, who was renowned in the shtetl, and was spoken of for years with reverence. It was said that when he sang the "*Hamelach*" during the Days of Awe, the whole building trembled. As far as I remember, he died in the year 1910. After him, R' Chaim Bergstein was taken on as cantor.

There was a deep niche in the corner of the west wall that was covered by a set of small glass doors where the Ner Tamid burned. I am brought back to this corner by an episode that occurred in my youth. I was 7 or 8 years old when my father, A"H, was in the army. Erev Yom Kippur, I went to daven Minchah alone. As I was going home, I stood struck with fear seeing an old man at the Ner Tamid holding a whip with two long leather straps. Men lay down at his feet, whispered a prayer, and received lashes. Fear ran through me at this scene. As children, we had heard many frightening stories and legends about the shul. It was said that at midnight, the dead come to pray there, that there are spirits in the attic, and whoever goes up there, does not return.

[Page 264]

I also remember that when we got older, free of cheder, a group of us boys got together, and holding on to one another, we climbed up to the shul attic. We found mountains of torn religious books, and women's prayer books that were soaked in the tears of generations of our grandparents.

Haifa

[Page 267 - Yiddish] [Page 51 - Hebrew]

The Town

[Page 267 - Yiddish] [Page 51 - Hebrew]

My Little Town Krasnobrod

by Efraim Lochfeld, Haifa

Translated by Moses Milstein

It is hard to find any consolation in the terrible tragedy that was inflicted on our people, and especially the Jews of Poland. A large Jewish community, rich in spiritual and material worth, was cut away. Desolate and lonely now are the Jewish cities and shtetlach where for hundreds of years the Jewish people lived and grew.

I accept the decision to publish this book, which will perpetuate the memory of the Jews of Krasnobrod, with thanks. I return to my childhood years, and I gather them into my memories as I remembered them, and I see myself again on the streets of our shtetl.

* * *

On an ordinary weekday, the shtetl was humming with workers and the pursuit of a living.

At dawn, the *shammes* went around waking everyone up for "*avoydes haboireh*", interrupting the sleep of those who were slow to get up. Soon after, shutters and doors began to swing open. The streets filled with young kids and old folks who were hurrying to the *beit hamidrash* for *Shachrit*. The uniquely religious melody of the prayers in the grey dawn would escape the houses and fill you with *Yiddishkeit* for the whole day.

After *davening*, came a day of business and labor. The storekeepers at the entrance to their stores, the tradesmen in their workshops, the *dorfsgeyer*[1] in the villages looking for businesss in *goyishe* farms, and the timber merchants in the forests where they would–from morning to night–measure and select wood.

In the evening, people would get together again in the *batei midrashim*, and collectively *daven Ma'ariv*. After prayers, there was no rush to go home, some stayed to study a portion of Mishnah, others to catch up on "politics." A newspaper used to arrive in town two to three days after its publication, and those who read it were the "experts" on the latest political goings–on. From politics, they would pass on to gossip and take to task the wealthy of the shtetl.

The shtetl took on a completely different appearance with the coming of Shabbat.

The preparation to welcome the Sabbath as an important guest began as early as Friday after lunch. Representatives of institutions would go around to the houses to collect the donations from the "*pushkes*[2]." Organizations such as *Linat Hatzedek, Hachnasat Orchim, Tikkun Soferim*, and others. The god–fearing Henieh, wife of Leib Cohen, collected *chalahs* and other food that she distributed to the poor. Work was still being done when the bath bell began to ring announcing that the bath was heated.

The *schwitz*–bath where buckets of water were poured onto red glowing stones were crammed with Jews. They would spread out on the steps and groan with pleasure as they beat each other with soft brooms. They left the *schwitz* sweaty and red as beets but with a feeling of lightness as if they had cast off the burden carried on the shoulders of the Jewish people.

Soon, the *shammes*'s call to "Light candles!" is heard, and the women hurry to end their preparations for Shabbat. Suddenly, one remembers that she had forgot to buy something. Swift as an arrow she flies to the store and begs the storekeeper to sell it to her, and he, the crook, even though he is afraid to desecrate the Sabbath, he accommodates her, not wanting to lose the money.

Finally, the shtetl became quiet and calm. The workweek had ended, Shabbat is coming.

Shabbat candlelight sparkled from the houses, and winked to each other. The people in shul are welcoming the Sabbath, and the voice of the cantor singing "*Lecha dodi*" is heard through the windows. And the voices of the congregation respond.

The crowds go slowly home, loudly wishing each other "*Gut Shabbos.*" Everyone goes home to a clean house, sits down at the Shabbos table, and enjoys with pleasure the dishes prepared by his wife, the good housekeeper. The *zmires* sung by the sated, *Shabbesdikeh* singers carry on late into the night.

Shabbos at dawn, the swifter ones would go to the *mikvah* and from there to the first *minyan*. There were some "experts" and music lovers" for whom one *ba'al tefila* wasn't enough, they had to go to several *batei midrashim* to hear others. Others would get up early in order to study a little Mishna before going to shul.

After eating the fatty *cholent* and kugel, the older people used to retire for a nap and the young people would go outdoors to enjoy Shabbos their own way. In the winter they used to see each other at various youth lectures, and in summer they would go out for walks in the surrounding forests.

There was a Jew in town called R' Shmuel Zainvel Melamed, *z"l*, who undertook the *mitzvah* of maintaining the *eruv*. It was his custom to walk around and check the *eruv* every *erev* Shabbat to make sure there were no, god forbid, breaks. Early Saturday morning, he would go out to see if anything had happened to it overnight. He did not deviate from his task even on Yom Kippur.

At the boarding house of R' Itche Rath

In the center, seated is the Razdititsher rabbi, and next to him is Moishe Diamant, A. Rind, B. Sushchak, Sh. Broder, Z. Broder, and a group of children

And if something did happen to it, R' Shmuel Zainvel went into action and informed all the *batei midrashim*, and *minyanim*, that the *eruv* was torn and that it was forbidden to carry anything. On such a Shabbos, the *daveners* returned wrapped in their *talissim*. More than anyone, the youth rejoiced at this, walking around in their best, with snuff boxes in their pockets, and large, colorful, kerchiefs around their necks.

During my childhood in Krasnobrod, there was no modern shul. The children studied in the *cheders* under R' Shmuel Zainvel, and R' Bonimel Melamed.

In those small, dirty rooms we spent entire days, until late in the night. We were constantly in fear of the rebbe's little whip. How we yearned to be out in the fresh air! If someone arrived late, he had the honor of meeting the rebbe's little whip. We must however, acknowledge that from these little dirty rooms emerged some scholars and *goanim* of Torah and wisdom.

There was also R' Yoel Lehrer's *cheder* where Yiddish reading and writing were taught. This school differed from the others in terms of progress, but was exactly the same in terms of sanitation. R'Baruch Yokel's (Glistman) opened a modern *cheder* where they also taught grammar and Hebrew.

When I got older, I transferred to the *beit hamidrash*. I was immediately given the social activities job and became a bit of a "leader." I joined the *Tikkun Seforim* group, and every Friday I would go around soliciting donations for the group and for *Linat Hatzedek*. And *Gemilut Chasidim* as well. Through my visits to the houses, I got to know our Jews more closely. I saw them as they were "opening their wallets." There were those who gave little even though they had a lot, and there were those who would give you their last piece of bread. And how could one not give? This noble streak also finds itself among our brothers in Israel. At the first assembly in Haifa on 6.11.49 a *gemilut chasedim* fund was established named after "The martyrs of Krasnobrod" which aids over 80 people from our shtetl.

Who among us remembers the welcoming home of R' Moshe Greenboim–"Kutche, as he was called–whose house was always full of visitors from elsewhere, who stayed and ate there. *beit hamidrash* boys would also go there for a bit to eat.

New times

After World War I, new winds began to blow through our shtetl as well, and plans were made for a people's library. Thanks to the enthusiasm of the youth, the library was established, and books of modern Yiddish literature began to push aside the Gemara. A reading room was established which was full every evening with young people thirstily drinking at this freshly opened well. Later, a drama circle was established under the leadership of Asher Handelsman and Yehoshua Babad.

One of the performances of the drama club
Seated, center, Yehoshua Babad, hy"d

At the head of the cultural work was a committee of 11 people. At the first meeting the following were elected: 1. Gitl (Tentser) Barg–chairman) now in Israel); 2. Yehoshua Babad–vice–chairman; 3. Yakov Zimmerman–secretary; 4. Yehoshua Gurtler–vice–secretary; 5. Yehoshua Shnur–treasurer; 6. Reuben Kramer–vice treasurer; 7. Abraham Borg (now in Israel); 9. Moshe Kam–relief librarian; 10. Chaim Leib Germanhoz (now in Argentina); 11. Yakov Papir.

The spirit of the times dominated our town. Cultural movements taking place in larger cities came to us. The youth began to organize in parties and youth movements, joined the central bodies, and began activities of their own.

Agudat Israel founded a branch headed by R' Chaim Untzig, and Baruch Eli Broder.

The *Mizrachi* party also had a fine chapter headed by R' Israel Babad, Leizke Gurtler and R' Shraga Feivel Frumerman (now in Israel). The *Mizrachi* branch also had a youth wing called *Hashomer Hadati*.

A wide–ranging, active program was brought by the *Poalei Zion* party and its youth organization *Freiheit*. At the head of party work were the active doers: Yehoshua Gurtler, Zvi Arieh Briks, Shalom Aharon Rendler and Yehoshua Babad. At the head of *Freiheit* were the young members: Zob Gurtler, Malke Schlegl, Shlomo Babad, Shimon Kupiec (now in America) and Shikeh Gree.

The General Zionists had a small branch with Yakov Zimmerman, Mendl Farber, Eliyahu Dimand, and Eliezer Gurtler at the head.

A group of General Zionist youth with their counselors

There was also a branch of *Hechalutz Haklali* which sent a few members on *hashkara*, and some of them went on to make *Aliyah* to Israel. Of those who did not live to make *Aliyah*, I want to mention the young people: Eliyezer Liebl, Blume Tentser, Yosl Kupiec, Simcha Broder, Shmuel Yosef Entner, Devorah Langer, Zob Gurtler, Ita Margalit, and others killed by the Nazis.

The anti–Zionist workers parties, the Bund and the communists, also had their branches in our shtetl. The executives of the Bund were the comrades: Yehoshua Shnur, Reuben Kramer, Yakov Geistat. The communists were led by the comrades: Yakov Kramer, Aharon Rofer, and Yakov Shnur (Today in Poland).

It was not easy to break the opposition of our parents. There were some who alerted the authorities to our activities and received a welcome reception such that the library was to be closed.

But help came to us unexpectedly. There was no *rav* in our town, and in the meantime, questions were referred to a *dayan*. As soon as it was decided to get a *rav*, two opposing camps formed. One camp, headed by R' Eliyahu Zimmerman, and a second camp by the Ger and Radziner Chasidim. A quarrel developed which drew in everyone in the shtetl. Oaths and curses were exchanged. One side banned the kosher slaughter of the other and so on. In the fire of the war we forgot about our Zionist activities. We had shown that we had been able to strengthen our organization and to spread our ideas more widely among the youth. And more than once the central committee expressed its recognition of our work.

After other rabbis from other shtetls mixed in, the whole quarrel about the rabbis was brought to a *Din Torah* before the Tarnow *rav*, R' Meir Arik, of the giants of the older generation. He ruled that the rabbi picked by the majority should stay in town, and the other rabbi should be made whole with a sum of money. In this way, the town acquired a *rav*, peace at home, and also a Zionist youth club and a library.

We, the Zionist youth suffered for years from our fanatically religious parents. Nevertheless, we did not forsake our Jewish traditions and customs. When we were finally on *hachshara* and working in the sawmill we would still often get to the *beit hamidrash* and get a page of Gamara in, until the zealots chased us out.

In 1927, the Zionist youth decided to carry out a Purim evening with a benefit bazaar for *Keren Kayemet L'Israel*.

Some of the fanatic parents, headed by R' Moshe Leib Borg, R' Moishele Sofer, and R' Shmuel Gurtler, determined to wreck our event. They forced their way into our hall, and began to dance Chasidic dances. We did not surrender, but with a courageous effort, we managed to drive them out of the hall. The evening went off with great success and brought in a lot of money for *Keren Kayemet*.

As the years passed, some of the youth left on *Aliyah*. Their inspiring letters home opened the hearts of their parents. And following that, Jewish homes opened to the blue boxes of K.K.L., which found its place beside the *pushke* of R' Mair Bal Haness, *Matan B'Seter*, and other Jewish *tzedakah* boxes.

"Yasha Kalb"

R' Moshe Sofer once told me a story that probably also served as a motif for the play "Yasha Kalb," by Y.Y. Singer.[3]

There was once a young man in Krasnobrod, an orphan by the name of Yosef. He was an odd person, a fool, and they called him "Yasha Kalb" because for every question he answered only yes, or no. The local Jews used him for various jobs and paid him with a token[4]. Most of the time, he could be found in the cemetery where he sometimes helped the gravedigger dig graves. In return, he received bread and tea and a place to sleep.

With time, he was taught by R' Moshe Sofer to write psalms in *mezuzot*. He did not, however, devote much time to it, and as before, did all kinds of jobs hanging around cemeteries. When the gravedigger drove him away, he slept in the *beit hamidrash*.

And this was the way Yasha Kalb lived, lost and in tatters, and crowned as the town fool. And then a plague broke out in town. The town began seeking atonement, and monitoring the actions of its own people. Then they remembered Yasha Kalb. In order to stop the evil causing the plague, they honored Yasha and married him to the orphan daughter of the gravedigger. They erected a *chupa* in the cemetery and conducted the marriage according to the custom. The rich gave dowry furniture, and the shtetl celebrated happily and enthusiastically, because in the meantime, the plague had passed.

A short time after, Yasha disappeared, and no one knew where he was. Some said he left with the missionaries; others claimed that the peasants had murdered him. After a while, Yasha Kalb was completely forgotten.

One day, news arrived that the Zhinever rebbe's son–in–law, R' Moshe Chaim Kaminer had disappeared a short time after his wedding. For a while, the news was the talk of the town, until it too was forgotten.

About a year later, R' Moshe Chaim Kaminer returned home. His father–in–law welcomed him with great joy and arranged a big banquet to which the rebbe's friends and Chasidim were also invited. The feast took place in the home of the Belzer rebbe who was a brother–in–law of the Zhinever rebbe. Present at the Belzer rebbe's at the time were his Krasnobrod Chasidim, R' Moishele Sofer, R' Mendel Fuchs, Elhanan and Eli Shuster, and Berish Grinboim. That's how they ended up being invited to the feast.

After some generous wine drinking, when the crowd was festive and happy, the son–in–law was brought in. The Krasnobrod Chasidim were stunned to see that R' Moshe Chaim Kaminer, the rebbe's son–in–law was really Yasha Kalb from their shtetl! R' Eli Shuster immediately arose and let loose with a fiery slap. A terrible scandal broke out. The Krasnobrod Chasidim shouted that he was Yasha Kalb, the son–in–law of the Krasnobrod gravedigger. On the other side, the Zhinever Chasidim were ready to tear them to pieces, "You hear? What a libel! And on the son–in–law of their rebbe?" Only Yasha Kalb was silent as a fish in water, and did not utter a word. The riot increased and the scandal even more. Finally, it was decided to bring the whole matter to a *Din Torah* of the greatest rabbis and Torah scholars.

R' Moishele Sofer, and the gravedigger and his daughter, the *agunah*, came before the Bet Din and laid out their claim–that they see Yasha Kalb who grew up in their shtetl and was married to the daughter of the gravedigger. The Zhinever rebbe and his followers showed that he had given certain signs that were known only "between a man and his wife," and further that he was able to remember the page of Gemara he was studying with the rebbe the night before his disappearance. Both sides presented logical arguments. The *Din Torah* went on for months.

The ruling, attended by thousands of Jews from the whole region, decreed that Yasha Kalb/Moshe Chaim Kaminer, must divorce both women following which he had the right to marry whichever of the two he desired.

That was the end of a story that disturbed the Jewish community of the time, and that found its expression in Jewish literature and the Jewish stage.

Translator's notes:
1. Ones who buy and sell with the villagers.
2. *Pushkes* are little tin boxes for depositing coins from a benevolent society, present in most homes.
3. Also a novel in Yiddish with the same title by Y.Y. Singer
4. a "token" can be exchanged for a bit of food

[Page 279 - Yiddish] [Page 71 - Hebrew]

My Home

by Yocheved Gurtler-Nuss

Translated by Moses Milstein

From my earliest years, I can recall that our home was the first in the shtetl to host gatherings where people would get together to discuss various social and political issues.

Shtetl youth felt stifled in the confines of the fanatically Jewish religious homes. The besmedresh ceased to be the source of meaning in the lives of the young. They were beginning to be drawn to a new life, to other sources. But all doors were closed to them. Their parents did not permit them to think differently than them, and they certainly did not permit us to gather together and, God forbid, deviate from the "right path."

They found the appropriate place for get-togethers was our house. Maybe it was because my father was no longer alive, and my mother, in her loneliness, agreed to it. Years later I learned that my father, soon after WWI, had given my brother a sum of money to found a library. So it was no wonder that our house became the place for social gatherings. In this way my whole family got drawn into social and political life. I also remember the shelf of books in our house that we used to lend out to people.

I remember the first plays the drama society put on and prepared in our house. Among others there were: "*Der Batlen*," "*Der Vilder Mentch*," "*Der Man Untern Tish*," etc. Troupes from out of town that used to come to Krasnobrod, also stayed in our house.

I saw everything, I went everywhere, and not coincidentally, I was drawn into the current of social life before I even finished school.

[Page 280]

I was especially active while my brother, Velvl, went on hachshara with the intention of making aliyah to Israel. Unfortunately, it was not to be. He got sick on hachshara and died.

After finishing school, I joined the "scouts" organization along with my girlfriends Tzipeh Gurtler, Baltche Krelman, Libeh Alboim, and other boys and girls.

We were kids from poorer homes, and we wanted to be part of a movement that fought for a better tomorrow in a socialist Eretz Israel.

Other girls in my group like, for example, Raizel Reif, Blume Glickman, Rivke Holzberg, Roise Dichterman, Rivke Freiman, Leah Fuchs, etc. joined the General Zionist youth movement, *Hanoar Hatzair*. Nevertheless, we remained good friends, going on walks together, taking pictures together, and carrying on our lives together.

A group of Krasnobrod girls

[Page 281]

The beautiful days of our youth are unforgettable. Every moment, every event is memorable. I remember so well, the May First celebrations in the forest, together with Sroltche Goldgrober, the regional get-togethers, the summer colonies in our forest. I can't forget the interesting discussions with chaver Shike Gree. How much energy our educators like Esther Kamm, Ruchel Kupiec, Laizer Libel, devoted, and taught us to be proud and free workers.

How beautiful the days of our youth were. Our feet never tired of dancing the horas, and our songs flowed like a river. Everything we did was done with heart, faith, and spirituality. Every activity of the movement filled us with pride, every May First celebration led us to believe that we were partners in the great Socialist movement, every shekel contributed gave the certainty that you were building your own homeland with it.

I remember still today, the departure of Esther Kam for Eretz Israel. I remember the singing of Iteh-Chaye Rechls that captivated us and woke up the shtetl:

"We are young,
and that is beautiful…!"

The years went by quickly, and we followed along. From "Freiheit" in the scouts, and later in the Poalei Zion party. We were active everywhere, and everywhere we found a spiritual freedom.

Krasnobrod my dear little shtetl how strongly we loved you! How dear you were to us with your blooming trees, your forest, your kind, simple, Jews who all knew each other, celebrated together at simches, and helped each other out in difficult times.

[Page 282]

The "Freiheit" organization in 1930

I can see before me Getzl Erlich and his wife Matl Elke's. I learned tailoring from her, and I knew what kind of people they were, with warm Jewish hearts, always ready to help out with an act of charity, a kind word, and material help in cases of need. They never bragged to anyone about it, weren't arrogant, but quietly and honestly they shared their love with people.

And Itche (Mendele's) Fuchs. How much goodness he possessed. Never refused to lend money to the needy, even borrowing from someone else when he did not have enough, and never demanding repayment of the debt in order not to, God forbid, humiliate a fellow Jew.

And Tcherneleh who tried to support my mother when she left in fear of the oppressor.

[Page 283]

She never lost her faith in God, and was sure that he would not forsake his people, that He would listen to her constant prayers, and that he would protect her. Why Tcherneleh, for what sins did your faith fail you?

* * *

1939–the horrible year of destruction and misfortune–drove us from our homes, forced us to become refugees, wandering in strange cities and countries.

Thanks to Shikeh Glatter who convinced us to flee, we survived the plague of Hitler.

But none of us imagined that we were leaving our homes forever, that we would never again see those who remained behind, that we would become alone and orphaned.

My sister Perl and her family perished, as well as my brother Moishe and his family, my dear Reiske Holzberg and her family, and Shikeh and his family. They are all gone, those who were a part of my life, who granted me love in those beautiful youthful days, heartfelt friendship, and belief in mankind.

After years of homelessness and wandering aimlessly, we arrived in the free homeland that we had dreamed about and sung about for so long.

* * *

Twelve hundred souls whose blood sated the earth of Krasnobrod, that is the tragic end result of our shtetl. Our best years lie trodden underfoot beneath this cipher, the most precious hopes and longings, the most intimate feelings that nested in our hearts. who like doves, stretched out their necks under the knife, before they even had the chance to have even a taste of life. Tzipeh, Baltche, Libeh and all the others, precious and innocent, who were brutally crushed under the boots of the Nazis, and their accomplices, the Polish degenerates.

Within this number is a web of death containing my dearest girlfriends

[Page 284]

Krasnobrod my Jewish shtetl, who can forget you!

Haifa

The "Freiheit" organization–1936

[Page 285 - Yiddish] [Page 67 - Hebrew]

The "Freiheit" Movement in Krasnobrod

by Esther Kamm

Translated by Moses Milstein

The large majority of the youth of Krasnobrod belonged to the "Freiheit" movement in spite of the opposition from their parents who were against any youth movement that distanced its members from piety, traditional ways of life, and which provided alternate goals in life.

The youth, hungry to start living, thirsting for freedom, and new ways of living, overcame the resistance of their parents, broke down the walls of old ideas, and found their way to the youth movement.

"Freiheit" instructor's course in Krasnobrod forest

The Freiheit organization grew. Its ranks were bigger and fuller, its work more diverse, broader and deeper. Every evening, the Freiheit locale echoed with singing, and the enthusiastic footsteps of the *hora* dance. Sometimes, the walls of the hall could not contain the numbers, and they poured out onto the street. The respectable people were angered by this, and the pious were beside themselves at such "wantonness."

If we tired of dancing, we would sit in a circle around Hersh Leibl, and he would narrate "From Zion, her land and her holy soil." We would listen to him with mouths and ears open, with longing in our hearts, absorbing his inspired descriptions of a new way of life being built by the new Jew, in the land of our fathers. His call to personal development, to readiness for any sacrifice for the people and the land, became so clear and understandable then. He awakened in us love and friendship to all people, belief in a new world, in a just, socialist order.

We spent our evenings like that, and also Saturdays, and holidays—the most beautiful and unforgettable years of our youth.

Later, we founded a drama circle under the management and direction of Yehoshua Babad. He was one our best and truest comrades as well as being a talented youth worker. Neither he, nor Hersh Leibl Briks, lived to reach Eretz Israel, and perished under the Nazis. Their memory will be forever etched into our hearts, along with the memory of all the dear comrades who gave their utmost for our freedom movement.

We used to take kids from the street, teach them to read and write, tell them about the role of our movement, and they would listen to us, be inspired and pay attention, and understand. We led them to a new way, planted hope in their young hearts, and gave them something to strive for.

Who can describe the strong friendship and unity that reigned among the youth in the ranks of Freiheit, and also in the ranks of other youth movements? We used to light a torch in the night, take each other by the hands with true affection, throw ourselves into dance, and sing whole-heartedly:

> *"Arum dem fayer*
> *mir zingen lieder…"*

There once was a shtetl, and in her, young people, full of life, brimming with energy, a youth that had its hopes and dreams, its aspirations and fantasies. A youth that filled us with pride and confidence gave courage and endurance, assured a certain continuation for the Jewish people, and provided reserves for the *chalutz* camp in the rebuilding of Eretz Israel.

Where is this youth that was exterminated by dark powers, the murderers of our future!

Only a few came from the ruins. They came to the dreamt-of land, saved from death and annihilation by a miracle, and brought us the terrible news of destruction and death.

From this precious youth, this wonderful youth movement, only a small bundle of memories remain, like an open wound that burns with any motion, and deepens the pain.

[Page 288 - Yiddish] [Page 67 - Hebrew]

The Hachshara [pioneer training]

by Gitl Knebel-Belman, Haifa

Translated by Moses Milstein

Whenever I think of Krasnobrod, the memories come pouring out.

From the mountain of memories, I want to single out and describe *hachshara* in kibbutz Dror in which a big group of young people from Krasnobrod participated.

The first steps in the *hachshara* kibbutz were difficult. Hard, unaccustomed work, hunger and deprivation, greeted us, and tested our zeal and faith.

Members of HeChalutz on hachshara
First on the right, A. Lochfeld

At first we worked in a greenhouse in Zolkow. After that, we went to Kamianka-Stromilowa where we also discovered the bitter taste of unemployment and hunger.

But we were young: our faith—a torch; our love, a flame; and our will, unbending. From this we drew strength and endurance for the new life that awaited us.

After a year of *hachshara*, we returned home to prepare ourselves for aliyah.

Those were wonderful, joyous days. Hope grew in our breasts. The hora dance stirred our blood, and our joyful singing pierced the heavens, awakened the youth from their apathy, and the shtetl from its sleep.

Joyful too was the evening celebration of our leaving on aliyah to Eretz Israel. We were truly drunk with our good fortune. Those who remained behind envied us, the ones who were worthy enough.

The heart weeps for all those who did not make it, for all those who were cut down in the bloom of their youth in a foreign, savage land.

Holy and precious is their memory.

[Page 290 - Yiddish] [Page 78 - Hebrew]

Nothing Has Changed

by Yakov Lochfeld, Haifa

Translated by Moses Milstein

The river snakes placidly and quietly between the fields, and flows to the far–away marshes. Only here, at the concrete bridge, do the waves become more turbulent, frothing between the stones of the Tarnobrod bridge, sounding as if they had something to tell of the nearby shtetl's past…

And much, much does the river have to tell. Just yesterday, the day before yesterday, it happened. Jewish daughters would come here to wash dishes, to rub and polish pots and pans, to scrub the plates and bowls.

Especially after a Shabbos or *yom tov*, they would come here, the young Jewish girls. A little brother would also come along to help carry the things home. While the sisters were busy with the washing, the boys would hike up their pants, play and splash in the water, run around and wrestle. The work done, the girls would carefully gather up the sparkling clean dishes, place them in a big bowl, and return home with careful steps.

The river gave the town much, very much. Summer, *erev* Shabbos, young and old would go down to the river some distance away from town. They would dump their clothes on the green lawn, and go for a swim in the calm water. Older Jews who could not swim, used to stand near the shore and dunk themselves, and wash *lekoved* Shabbos. They would get home in time for *kabbalat Shabbat*. But the young people were loath to leave the beach. By the time they got home, the sun would already be behind the mountain, the shtetl already enveloped in dusk. The sound of the hammering on Jewish doors would be heard, telling the women that it was time to light the candles.

Throwing off the workweek, ridding themselves of their daily cares, Jews would eagerly go to *shul* to greet the Sabbath queen whether in the *beit hamidrash*, the *shul*, or in the Chasidic *shtieblach*. It didn't take long before the Friday night prayers carried through all the quiet streets of the shtetl…Later in the evening, *kiddush*, and *zmiros*, could be heard coming from the houses.

Saturday morning, the old, long–time *shammes* would stand in the middle of town and shout at the top of his voice, "*Yidn, in shul arein!*" And again they would go to *shul*…After the Saturday meal, they would go to the forest for a little fresh, pine–scented, air.

Vacationers in Moishe-Leib Barg's rooming house

Shabbos evening, the women would sit outside on their stoops and discuss female politics…Until, the first star appeared in the sky, and the night lights were lit. A new week had begun.\

On Tuesdays, the town got ready for the market. They began to set up the stalls early in the morning. They laid out their merchandise, each in his own way. Jews from nearby shtetls came to do business, to make money. Men went to the first *minyan* in order not to start late.

In the evening, after the market, debtors would hurry to pay off a loan, fulfill a debt. Others–to borrow money. Then they would prepare for the next market…In this way, with small worries, the days, the weeks, the years, passed.

For the coming generation, the older *cheder* boys, there was no future here. So they were sent away. Some went to a larger city to learn a trade, others to Lithuania, to the far–off yeshivas. They would come home once a year for a *yom–tov*. Childhood friends could barely recognize each other…

The shtetl itself also slowly changed its appearance. Electricity was brought to homes. The interior rooms were lit up. The deep mud in the middle of the market was drained, and bricks were laid. But with this, there came a new problem–antisemitism. A great wave of antisemitism flooded the Polish towns and cities, and our Krasnobrod among them. Until greater sorrows arrived, the invasion of Poland by the Nazis.

The first days of war

It happened, as we know, in 1939.

The first messengers of death and annihilation arrived in their blue uniforms, in their Panzers, and threw fear into the Jews of the shtetl. People ran into their homes, locked and bolted their houses; mothers clutched their children to their breasts in fear and waited for mercy to come from heaven. After a short time went by with no harm, they began to slowly emerge from their houses onto the street. Small groups got together. They wanted to find out what was happening, to hear some of what others thought. There was a theory that these had been scouts. And they did indeed quickly disappear.

The Jews didn't know what to do, what the situation was. They tried to find out by telephoning to nearby shtetls to find out what the situation was. In the meantime, the retreating Polish army, badly broken, marched into town and readied positions for battle. The steel German birds began to spit fire and devastation. The first Jewish victims fell. It was chaos. The shtetl became the front. People began to flee their homes. Either with packs or just as they were. They fled to the nearby forest to hide in the valleys.

The battle began, and the cannons of both sides echoed terribly in the darkness of night. At every blast, mothers cuddled their children to their breasts, as if to shield them with their bodies.

This went on day and night. Drenched from the rains, frozen by the cold nights, with empty stomachs, they hoped for a change, an end to the troubles…In order to protect themselves from the rain and the bullets, they dug bunkers. At great risk, they stole onto a farmer's field in order to still their hunger with a potato or a turnip. Several days went by, but the situation did not change. On one dark night, a red glow was seen in the region of the shtetl. Someone cried out, "The shtetl is burning!" The next day, we got the news that the whole market square was burned down, the area where mostly Jews lived. Just a few houses on the Tomaszow road remained.

Under the Nazi boot

With the occupation of the shtetl by the Germans, the robbing of Jewish property began. German soldiers, along with the Polish antisemites, broke into cellars and took whatever was there. They were living it up. Staying in the forest made no sense anymore. We went back to the shtetl. At the edge of the forest, dead Polish soldiers lay. The air was full of the reek of dead horses. The shtetl was unrecognizable. The Jewish houses with the grey roof shingles were all burned down, turned to coal and ashes. Burned corpses lay here and there. The Germans detained people and ordered them to remove the dead bodies. The Germans amused themselves, lording it over the Jews, cutting off beards and *payes*, and dragging them about by their *tzitzit* and *tallit–katan*.

Homeless, without a roof over their heads, the Jews fell into despair and depression. They crammed themselves into the few remaining Jewish houses. A few days later, we got the news that the Russians had entered the nearby town of Tomaszow. Not much later, the Russians marched into our shtetl. Jews began to breathe a little easier. They went out on the street a little more freely. It was thought that salvation had arrived. But our relief was short–lived. The Russians soon announced that they were retreating. According to the Russian–German agreement, our region was to fall under German rule.

Varying opinions were heard. Some held that it was urgent to leave with the Russians, but others could not bear to leave the place where they were born. No one knew which option was the right one. Some argued that that, in any case, there was nothing to lose by leaving here, with no roof over one's head. The tragic farewells began between children and old mothers and fathers. Families were split up, and went off to wander in far away, foreign places…

For the Jews who stayed behind, a horrible life was beginning. With each passing day, more Jews died. Each morning was greeted with terrible dread. Great was the grief of the mothers who did not know what the fate of their wandering children was. And great, and endless was the pain and terror of the children and relatives of those left behind under the bloody rod of the Germans.

The days were gloomy and grey, and the nights dark with suffering. An eternal darkness enveloped the shtetl of Krasnobrod. The sun with its warm rays darkened the brightness of a clear day. Fear descended on everyone with the coming of night, when a dark fate always picked someone to tear from their home. Sleepless nights began. We were afraid of the slightest sound. A leaf falling from a tree, the wind blowing against the shutters, made our hearts tremble…

The Jews of the city were broken spiritually and physically, their courage and self–worth crushed. Living corpses with yellow patches and *Magan–Davids* on their arms. And perhaps the *Magan–David*, the symbol of Jewish bravery, gave them some hope and courage to want to live and fight with all their strength to get through the day, to push through the terrible night. But the terrible nights kept on coming, stretching out to infinity. Long nights of fear, of Jewish tears, of pain wracked groans, of tears from mothers of murdered children, of lamenting from widows over their strangled husbands, of sisters wailing over the death by fire, while still alive, of their brothers, of the heartrending cries of Jewish daughters for their slaughtered mothers. This was how the painful life of the few remaining, still breathing Krasnobroders, dragged on.

The German command created a *judenrat* in order to suck money out of Jews, and to obtain slaves for all kinds of labor. It was also more convenient for them this way. With the help of the Judenrat, they could keep an eye on every Jew. Things went on like this until 1941 when the Nazis invaded Russia. The sufferings of the Jews became even more acute and more tragic. The year 1942 brought the total annihilation of the Jews under the boot of the Nazis. The German murderers drove the remaining Jews out to Izbica where they murdered them along with Jews from the surrounding areas. Many were savagely killed in the shtetl itself and buried in mass graves. Many of them were burned alive. The last few remnants of the Jews disappeared with the smoke.

Only a few managed to escape to the surrounding peasant villages and hide. Some were murdered shortly before Germany's defeat, shortly before liberation, at the bloody hands of the Polish partisans and the peasants with whom they had sought shelter.

The shtetl of Krasnobrod became one entire cemetery. The earth is soaked with Jewish blood and mixed with the ashes of their burned bodies.

Nothing has changed

The year is 1950. Eight years after the tragic annihilation I stand and stare at the empty places once filled with Jewish homes, once resounding with Jewish life. The row of wooden houses, all built in the same style, looked like one long house with one long porch.

How long ago was it when, on such a warm summer day, the *cheder* boys would come out and play. Pushing and laughing, some of the mischievous ones would climb onto a roof and lie down and warm themselves in the warmth of the sun, or run to the river to bathe and practice their swimming.

When winter came, and the mud which had been formed by the harvest rains began to freeze, the river too began to ice over. The young boys went sliding on the still thin ice…

When the snows came, the young kids would take their sleds and go sliding down the slopes of the Krasnobrod mountains. They would try to overtake each other by climbing higher and higher. The sleds flew lightening–fast, from the mountaintops down to the shtetl, across the Zamosc road, and down to, the frozen river. They took care not to slide into the unfamiliar swamps.

The shtetl lay sparkling white as if covered by a sheet. And when the sun appeared from behind the clouds, the roofs shimmered and sparkled as if studded with diamonds…

But no! These are only paper dreams! There are no more Jewish children, no shtetl, no Jewish remnant. Krasnobrod has been transformed into a cemetery, but one without gravestones. A stranger passing through would never think that there had once been Jewish houses here, that this was a place that had pulsated with Jewish life.

The sun began to descend in the west, to the mountains, its last rays shining on the empty places and disappearing…The mountain's shadow spread and covered the site of the vanished shtetl of Krasnobrod in black sorrow.

The autobus from Zamosc arrived. Instead of Jews, only farmers and their wives are to be seen, pushing to get on the bus…

I cast a last look at my erstwhile home, at the forest, at the river. The natural features had not changed. Everything stood as before, as if nothing had happened…Nature hadn't changed. It was just Jewish life that had been extinguished, erased, and expunged.

———

[Page 299 - Yiddish] [Page 85 - Hebrew]

Episodes in the Life of the Town

by Mordechai Rapoport

Translated by Moses Milstein

I knew the shtetl Krasnobrod from my earliest days. I used to go there on business matters, soon acquired friends there, and in time, I became a resident. With permission, I will relate a few episodes from my time in Krasnobrod.

In 1928 I came to the market which was then near the church, outside town. One evening, while collecting money from the Christian merchants, I noticed 2 young Christians following me with the intent of robbing me. I didn't finish the collection, but jumped into a carriage, and quickly rode into the shtetl. The next day, some Christian merchants I was familiar with told me that my fears were not unwarranted, because they had been looking for me for a while.

* * *

A second encounter with Polish antisemitism occurred at the post office. Once I went to the post office, which was then in the courtyard, to send off a largish amount of money. The bank officer refused to take my money and scattered the coins across the floor. Thanks to my complaint to the head directors, he was dismissed from the post office.

After my marriage in 1931, together with my friends Eli Rind, Bunem Holzberg, Moishe Hoz, Fishl Shlegel, and Israel Babad, we founded a branch of Mizrachi and a minyan in Bintche Rosenfeld's house. We also undertook the establishment of a modern Yavne school. We brought the pedagogue, Kahanovitz, from Jedwabne, and opened the school. Unfortunately, it only existed for a short time. But in its time, it succeeded in planting the religious-nationalist Zionist spirit.

[Page 300]

I shudder when I remember how the shtetl looked after the fire caused by the Hitler murderers. We came from our hiding places in the forest, and did not recognize the shtetl. Ruins everywhere. Burned bodies, and around us the happy mugs of the Polish robbers and looters. Their mocking laughter drove me from the shtetl forever.

Tel Aviv

———

[Page 301 - Yiddish] [Page 77 - Hebrew]

by Reisha Lehrer

Translated by Moses Milstein

My birthplace, Krasnobrod, was a small, poor, and little known shtetl. It was not distinguished by famous customs, rabbinical personages, or the highly-educated. But whoever got to know it well knew that our Jewish community was blessed with the quality of generosity and readiness to help others. Even though there were few wealthy people, no one who was poor was left helpless when in need.

Engraved into my memory is a specific incident that illustrates clearly the character of our community. In 1936, a Bilgoraj train crashed into a wagon with Jewish passengers and two Jews died.

As soon as this became known in the shtetl, people began to think about the widows and orphans that were created. In the course of 3 days, over 500 Zlotys was collected–a significant sum in those days–and it was used to help out the future of the orphaned families.

This is how it happened everywhere. As soon as a need was detected, it was quickly addressed.

May those who occupied themselves with this work, and lived by the rule, "Love your neighbor as yourself," be remembered.

[Page 302 - Yiddish] [Page 63 - Hebrew]

Social Awakening

by Shmuel Gurtler

Translated by Moses Milstein

With the end of the First World War, and the end of Polish-Bolshevik conflict, a social awakening in Jewish life arrived like the morning star after a dark night. A fresh wind blew in and awakened the hidden, dreaming cultural forces of the shtetl.

The youth quickly began to escape from the strictures of dated ideas and customs. With their abundant unused energy, they took upon themselves the burden of becoming the bearers of a new Jewish culture in the narrow dark alleys of the shtetl.

The call from friends Leibke Kupiec, Yossef Lam, Chaim Babad, and Israel Babad to cultural work was received happily, and during the first meeting, it was decided to found a library, and name it after Dr. Ettinger.

The news about the library quickly reached the older generation. The thought that "Satan" had snuck into the Chasidic stronghold of Krasnobrod caused them to mount a war against the apikorsim and kofrim[1]. There were some Jews who knew how to approach the powers that be, and soon the local and regional authorities were "keeping an eye on" those who were not "kosher" enough for the older generation. The notion of founding a library was postponed.

Some time passed and a new cohort of young people arrived. They again raised the idea of cultural activities, the first of which was founding a library. The battle with the older generation renewed itself, and became even more impassioned and stubborn.

Youthful fire, the enthusiasm for new ideas, gave courage to this particular battle and promised success for the young.

[Page 303]

Soon after, a committee was formed that brought a request to the authorities to allow the founding of a library at the Tarbut[2]. They supplied the names of 10 responsible people. In those days, a quarrel had developed regarding rabbis, and 2 opposing sides had formed. When a request came from the authorities for information on the 10, the head of the community, in confusion, did not appreciate the reason, and unwittingly gave a glowing recommendation for the 10. When he did come to realize that it was in reference to the founding of a library, and that he himself, with his own hands, had added fuel to the fire, he pulled out all the stops, and began to make big problems for us. We had been working in secret, but the authorities finally figured things out, and began to carry out investigative searches. Some of the books were with the writer of these lines, and some with Yehoshua Babad. We would have come to a bad end if they had found them on us. Luckily, our friend, Feivel Frimerman was the soltis[3], and he led the police to other Jews with similar names. The police of course found nothing and left without having achieved their purpose.

We decided to transfer the library to Hersh Mazes's warehouse–the brother-in-law of Abraham Barg. We carried on our work there for a long time, until we received official permission from the authorities.

Our joy at the legalization of the library was great. We saw ourselves as victors in the fight against the spiritual ghetto we had been confined to for years. But we soon came up against new difficulties, the first of which was where to house it. No one was willing to rent us a room, recoiling from us as if we were apostates. In the end, we were able to resolve the problem. There was an old commode in Yosef Lam's house, certainly from king Sobieski's time. We used one of the drawers, and the library, with luck, was opened. Comical though it may seem, that drawer performed a serious cultural job. People came there to exchange books, read newspapers that we acquired, and every Saturday, there was a reading by Hersh Leibl Briks.

[Page 304]

A group of youths

Standing, first row above from R to L: Velvl Gurtler, Itke Alboim, Sholem Shlegel, Grune Gurtler, Shloime Babad, Malke Shlegel
Second row: Seated, Blume Tentzer, Freise Eisen, Freidl Knabel, Neshe Leon

Later, we acquired a room, and we were able to show what we were capable of. A drama club was formed that put on several one-act plays like *Shimshon Hagibor, Der Meshugener in Shpitul*, etc. The pious folks could not reconcile themselves to our activities, and they created great problems for us whenever they were able. Once the Rosh HaKahal, in the presence of our members, referred to us in insulting words. We therefore took him to court. Seeing that his position was precarious, he called as witnesses, the parents of our members. Thus a series of trials and quarrels in the home began. In the end, we won the trial, and silenced our opponents as a result. Interestingly, the Rosh HaKahal later became our friend, and the literary trial of Uriel Acosta took place in the big hall of his tavern.

[Page 305]

The trial drew many people from the surrounding cities and shtetls who were vacationing among us in the countryside. We conducted the trial at a high level, and took advantage of the intellectual abilities of the vacationers. During vacation season, we used to carry out a strong cultural and educational program. Naturally, there were people of many different political parties among the intellectuals taking part who affected us politically. Political parties of every direction, with no exceptions, were founded.

Nevertheless, our interactions were the friendliest. The most painful discussions never disturbed our relationships nor caused animosity. Truly Meshiach's time.

Part of the youth of that group made aliyah to Eretz Israel. Some immigrated to various countries overseas. Others abandoned the "foolishness" and were drawn into the hard battle to earn a living. A younger generation grew up and took their place, and injected fresh blood into our collective life.

This is how it continued until the arrival of the storm that tore out the deeply rooted Jewish community and destroyed it forever, and destroyed as well the fruitful, creative people who were the youth of Krasnobrod.

Haifa

Translator's notes:
1. Free thinkers and heretics
2. A network of Hebrew secular schools
3. Village magistrate

[Page 306]

Letters in my Drawer

by Gitl Barg, Tel Aviv

Translated by Moses Milstein

I stand by the open drawer of letters, as if by a grave. Letters–the accumulation of years–lie here. Every letter someone's soul, someone's life, an open wound. My sister, Bluma, writes me, "Dear Gitl, 26 months of *Hachshara* are not enough to make aliyah to Eretz Israel. I am waiting for your help." Pain, tear out my heart! Woe is me, I did not help her at all, I could not help! The letters lie here, and speak to me, demand, punish, and caress. They speak of what once was, and will never be again.

As if he were before me now, I can see my dear father, I can hear his voice saying, "Children, you must be good, love others as you love yourself, give *tzedakah*, and accumulate *massim tovim*." And he himself behaved the way he taught us to.

And here is my dear, good–hearted mother. She is happy that I finally achieved my goal, and am making aliyah to Israel. But she is very worried about my trip, and can't stop crying and sighing. Every sigh of hers, tears out a piece of my heart, steals from me a little bit of the joy of aliyah.

My sisters and brothers, and their children, do not leave me for a second. Every one brings me something; everyone gives me a gift as a memento. I still have many of the things given to me, a memento of my loved ones, though they themselves are no longer here. How terribly hard it is to comprehend that, from all of them, no one remains, that I will never see them again, never hear their voices again, never feel again the closeness and love.

I see you now, my dear friends, girls and boys, relatives and friends, as you all come to see me off. Our house is overflowing with people. My sister, Etl's, house is also crowded, and my dear friends fill the street. I hear Hersh Leibel Briks, and Yehoshua Shnur worriedly wondering, "Let's hope the sea is calm in such terrible weather."

My heart breaks when I am reminded of all this, the moment when I left them all. I remember how my beloved mother pressed me to her heart, "My child, you must go. Your beloved husband is there, your home is there." But I can't tear myself away from her. Every step takes me further from her, and I don't have the strength to go on. "God knows if I will ever see her again" is screaming in me. I can feel her last kiss. I never saw her again.

* * *

Krasnobrod, where I spent my childhood, the most beautiful years of my youth.

How beloved and dear is the name of my shtetl to me.

Krasnobrod. How horrible your name is to me, the shtetl of our doom, the place of our eternal, unrelieved sorrow…

* * *

I want to add here what I have learned about the death of my sister, Tzetl, and her family.

My sister, Tzetl, lived outside of the shtetl. That was why her little house did not get burned. That was the sad reason that she did not, like many others, leave the shtetl. My brother–in–law, Velvl, and two children went to Majdan where his parents had lived for years. Brocheh, their older daughter, and her husband and small child, were wandering around in the forest, in tatters and barefoot until they could take it no longer. Dying of hunger, they left to seek a piece of bread. The farmers killed her husband first, and then her.

Chanaleh, the second daughter, a very pretty girl, was found murdered in the forest. Tzetl escaped from the Izbic ghetto, then escaped from Beljec to Krasnobrod. She searched for a sign of any of her children. A few days before liberation, she was murdered by the *goyim*. Velvl learned that the children who had been with him had been murdered. One of his boys, it was reported, was thrown into a deep well. Overcome by grief and despair, Velvl committed suicide.

That is the horrible and cruel end of my sister's family. May the holy, innocent, blood that was shed, never be forgotten, and may it demand revenge from the German murderers and their Polish helpers.

[Page 309 - Yiddish] [Page 100 - Hebrew]

The Lord's Candle—A human soul

by Rav R'Chaim Shaul Ya'ave"tz

Translated by Moses Milstein

Even though I was not born in Krasnobrod, I happened to have spent a certain part of my life there, and I would like to describe some of the people I knew there.

I arrived in Krasnobrod in 1902, and there I found my friend and life companion, the estimable Jewish woman, Taube bat R'Yakov Ozer Kupiec z"l. I also became good friends with harav hagaon R'Nachum Feignboim, zts"l, whose door was open to everyone.

I developed an intimate friendship with R'Shmuel Leib (Zeltzer), shochet, z"l. He was one of the first chasidim, a scholar, and a big specialist in his work. Often when he encountered a difficult sugye[1] in the Talmud or tosafot,[2] I used to—as much as I was able—help him out with a peyresh[3]. And like someone who rejoices in a great victory, so he rejoiced over each new peyresh that I brought him.

So also was his son-in-law, R' Abraham Meir Shostchak, z"l, who observed all the laws faithfully.

I would also like to mention R' Shmuel Ozer and his son Mechl. R' Shmuel Ozer was a good-hearted Jew. Even though he lived in great poverty, he was always happy and received with joy both the good and the bad. A week before I left Krasnobrod, he asked me for a loan. I took out 25 Zlotys and gave them to him. He declined to take such an amount and only took 5 Zlotys.

And they, all the warm hearted, true Jews, students and scholars, were tortured with the most horrid suffering, to the death, by the enemy, may his name be erased, who had undertaken to annihilate the entire Jewish people.

I, who loved them with every fiber of my being, reawaken my memories of them in my mind, and may these few lines, written by one who sees himself as a brother in the family of Krasnobrod survivors, serve as a light to the memory of their holy souls.

New York

Translator's notes:
1. Talmudic question under study
2. Annotations to the Talmud
3. Commentary

[Hebrew page 101]

Memorial prayer

by Shlomo Zonshtein (New York)

Translated by Mira Eckhaus

For the ascension of the pure souls of the Krasnobrod martyrs.

May this memorial page, which I am writing here, be a spark in the eternal flame (Ner HaTamid), which will be in our hearts forever in the memory of the great mass grave of this holy community, which was cut down from the land of life, by an impure, vile and accursed nation until the end of all generations.

And may these letters in the memorial book be illuminated by the glow of the sky and shed bright light on the holy community that sacrificed their lives for the sanctification of the name of Israel among the Gentiles.

And when our children and our children's children see what is written in it, they will also know and will tell those who come after them about the heavy price paid by the exile generation. Let them see and know that they must protect their people's freedom and independence in this good land. And it will fill their hearts with strength and power, valor and courage of spirit, to fight for their freedom and to sacrifice their lives for it. And let this be a consolation for a life that was cut off, for a community that passed away, like a herd of sheep surrounded by coyotes. For a community that was mercilessly destroyed while no one did or said anything.

Krasnobrod was the first city that was burned down, and its people were the first victims who sacrificed their lives in the great conflagration that enveloped cities and countries, peoples and countries. These were also the first steps of the Nazis murderers on Polish soil.

As fate would have it, I was a witness to how the Krasnobrod community was burned and went up in flames. My eyes saw its first victims, whose bodies were found charred in the burning remains of the ruined houses.

Among these first victims I will mention a father and son, Shmuel Ozer Kupiec and his son Michael. Their faces were so mutilated that it was impossible to recognize them. We recognized the father by the small tallit that the flames, miraculously, did not corrupt, and this was a kind of symbol from Divine Providence, that only the body can be burned, but the spirit will remain forever. And no flame will be able to destroy the holy flame burning in the hearts of the people of Israel.

Among the ruins more charred bodies were found, but it was impossible to recognize them because they were the bodies of refugees whom no one in the town knew.

[Hebrew page 102]

On the same day of the fire, the Nazis also shot: Leibish Kramer, Shmuel (Shmilke) Shatmer, and the mentally ill Reuven. This was only the beginning - the beginning of the bitter end that befell our town, and then continued to a third of the Jewish people in the Diaspora. This was the beginning of the storm that dried up the spring of a living and deeply rooted Judaism, that was blessed with prosperity, and strength and wealthy in material and spiritual assets.

And just as the Jews of Krasnobrod were the first to be sacrificed, they were also among the last of the oppressor's victims. The latter did not die among the ruins of their homes, but in the land of Ukraine to which they fled, and where they hoped to be saved.

The murderers used to murder their victims in an orderly and cold manner. First, people without a profession were murdered. Then professionals would be murdered after exploiting their work and their professional skills. The survivors between one slaughter and the next, tried again to escape from the German-occupied land to the Romanian border, to "Transnistria". There, too, Jews were already living in ghettos and camps surrounded by barbed wire, but no one had yet heard of mass slaughters, as the Germans had perpetrated here. And so, the refugees risked their lives and stole away to the city of Zhmerynka and the city of Braila.

Until one day, Romanian soldiers surrounded the ghetto in Braila, and its surprised Jews, and led them all together to the slaughter place on the main road between Zhmerynka and Braila.

In this crowd that was led to slaughter were also a mother with her two daughters from Krasnobrod. The mother was Mira Kupiec and her daughters Hana and Bina. Their brother Avraham also walked with them. Hana kept her dignity until the last moment and did not agree to take off her clothes, as instructed by the murderers. She "won" and was murdered with her clothes on, and no one saw her nakedness while she was alive.

The disgrace they wanted to put on this holy Kosher daughter of Israel will stick to the murderers and their descendants until the last of them dies, and they will be an example to others forever.

And the glory of the names of the martyrs of Krasnobrod will live forever among the martyrs and the pure.

[Hebrew page 103]

A report about the first memorial assembly held for the martyrs of Krasnobrod that took place at Netzach Israel synagogue in Haifa on 15 Cheshvan 5710, 6.11.49

The memorial assembly was opened by the member Ephraim Lochfeld. He began by requesting we honor the memory of the martyrs with two minutes of silence. Afterwards, the member Lochfeld was elected as the chairman of the assembly, and the member Mordechai Rapaport was elected as secretary.

Permission to speak was given to the first of the eulogists, the member Moshe Fishl. He described the hardships that the Krasnobrod community endured under the hard rule of the Nazis. He described the *action* (the roundup of the Jews before sending them to the camps) as an eye witness to them. The first was during Shavuot in 5702, 1942. During the aktion, "judenrat" people and others were killed for not wanting to cooperate and betray their friends. Many were transferred to Belzec. The second aktion was in the month of Av 5702 (1942), when the Nazis set fire to houses with their occupants and about fifty people were burned to death.

The actions of the Nazis not only affected the living, but also the dead. The tombstones in the cemetery were removed and used to pave a road. The graves were plowed and sown. No sign remained of Krasnobrod and its dead.

After him, the member Aharon Untzig came up and taught the audience a chapter of Mishnoyat. He explained the value of studying for the ascent of the souls of the martyrs, in particular those who were not buried in a Jewish ceremony. He ended the "class" by saying Kaddish.

After that, Rabbi Yitzhak Meir Gurtler eulogized the martyrs. He based his eulogy on the verse from parashat Vayeshalach (Genesis 37), in which the sons of Yaakov said to their father: "They will not treat our sister as a prostitute", and the meaning is that the sons of Yaakov did not want to forsake their sister and demanded revenge for insulting her honor. And if we want to revenge the insult to the honor of our martyrs, we can only do so in our own free country. And again, he brought proof from the verse in Genesis 35, in which God said to Yaakov, "Get up, go to Bet El, and do not dwell in Nablus." Nablus was not considered an Israeli city at that time. The proof is from this, is that all the people of Israel, the sons of our father, Yaakov, must immigrate to Israel and live in the land and build it. And if we all live in the land and engage in its building, then we can avenge the insult to our nation and its martyrs.

The member Yoel Handelsman read scriptures in rhymes in the memory of the martyrs.

[Hebrew page 104]

Finally, the member Ephraim Lochfeld gave details and memories from the town. He talked about the martyrs and pure ones who sacrificed their lives to help the people from their nation. Those were: Yosef Goldstein and Fishl Shlegl, who were killed by the Nazis in the first aktion. He proposed that memorial assemblies be held every year on the day of the last aktion, which was the 15th day of the month of Cheshvan. His proposal was accepted unanimously.

We ended the mourning assembly with the prayer "God full of mercy" by the member Eliezer Lerner.

After the end of the mourning assembly, the assembled approached the practical part of the meeting. In this part, Mr. Lochfeld proposed the establishment of a committee. The following candidates were proposed:

1. Ephraim Lochfeld Haifa	9. Avraham Borg Tel Aviv
2. Shalom Zeltzer Haifa	10. Yehoshua Shlegl Tel Aviv
3. Eliyahu Rind Haifa	11. Avraham Glickman Tel Aviv
4. Pinchas Kupiec Haifa	12. Shmuel Untzig Tel Aviv
5. Shmuelke Gurtler Haifa	13. Avraham Elboim Jerusalem
6. Shlomo Babad Haifa	14. Mordechai Rapaport Ramla
7. Moshe Fishl Haifa	15. Moshe Fuchs Hadera
8. Avraham Giter Haifa	

After the candidates were approved, Mr. Lochfeld proposed establishing a charity fund, which would be a continuation of the charity fund that existed in the city of Krasnobrod. The purpose of the fund was to extend help to every needy member of the town of Krasnobrod who lived in Israel. He suggested that those gathered in the assembly make donations immediately, and with such donations the charity fund would be practically established. The proposal was accepted by unanimous consent, and everyone immediately contributed as much as they could.

With warm words and a call for unity, and maintaining a close relationship between the remnants of the people of Krasnobrod, Mr. Lochfeld closed the assembly.

[Page 311]

In the light of memory

by Esther Kam-Glickman, Holon

Translated by Moses Milstein

When we look back at the far away days of our youth, memories and impressions are awakened, and we feel an urge to tell, and tell, as much as we are capable of describing in words.

Of course the thousands of people who survived the Second World War, with all its hardships and terrors under Hitler's government, have much to tell and write about. But even for those who were far from their homes in that time, the shtetl, where they took their first steps on God's earth, is burned into their hearts…

I was a child like all the children in Krasnobrod. My parents—pious people—sent their children to *cheder*, determined that they would grow up with respect for all.

In those days, the Zionist movement was beginning, and Krasnobrod was hungry for every word about Zionism that reached it. Zionism mostly enthralled the young. Older people were against it. There were often quarrels between parents and their children. The parents tried to prevent their children from being swept along with the new ways. Great tragedies were played out in homes when a youngster went off to *hachshara* or aliyah to Eretz Israel.

I was also one of those who rebelled against my parents. My parents cried and argued, "Your Zionism has caused us shame and mockery, how can you do this? God will inflict sorrow on the whole house." Not a few of us old *chalutzim* remember this.

I remember that fateful day when I left the place of my birth, my home, left my father and mother, sisters, brothers, and friends, forever, and went to Eretz Israel. It was a sad moment, but I was determined and confident. I was full of hope that one wonderful day, I would be reunited with my loved ones. The letters I later got from my parents gave me courage and faith, roused me to be true to my people in my new land.

* * *

The year 1939 arrived. The war broke out. Letters from home no longer come. The only source of information is the press or radio.

We could feel a great tragedy developing. After work, our free time is spent by the radio. The Nazi army advances deeper and deeper into Poland. They take city after city. Story after story strikes us like thunder, and worries our hearts.

Day and night I would wonder: Where are my parents? Who knows what painful roads they now have to wander along? Do they have a place to rest their weary feet, something warm to keep them going? They were always in my thoughts, and at night, I would dream of them. Here—I see my father. He is begging me to send food to them, to Poland…They have nothing to eat…And I imagine I am speaking to my sister. She is mad at me for not bringing her over to me to Eretz Israel in time…In the morning I would wake from the nightmares tired and broken, unable to carry out my job. My eyes were never dry, always full of tears that it seemed would never end.

Yes, we who were far from the Nazi hell, also suffered during those sad times.

* * *

What I feared came to pass: "Now, you are alone in the world. There will be no more letters, no comforting words from your mother, or your sister. All your hopes are gone, and the little bit of *naches* that parents used to have from their children, and their children allotted to their parents has gone." And now it has all happened!…A heart feels, a heart cannot be fooled, it seems.

The Nazis plundered, murdered, burned. They tore children away from their parents, husbands from wives, and exterminated them all, and left eternal grief in our broken hearts.

How can you describe what you feel in words, and how can you forget the beloved shtetl, Krasnobrod, with her beautiful landscapes around her, the large, beautiful forests, where I spent part of my youth. We grew up together with our friends surrounded by the beauty of nature. We would spend entire days there in the summer, running around, singing, dancing…We would return home tired in the evening. What a warm home we had…

I will forever remember you, my Krasnobrod, with your small houses, and narrow lanes! I will forever carry in memory my beloved parents, my sisters and brothers, who were martyred. I will never forget you.

[Page 314 - Yiddish] [Page 86 - Hebrew]

The Town

by A. Diamant

Translated by Moses Milstein

It is not easy for me to write about memories of Krasnobrod. How can one "describe" a shtetl that had over 500 years of Jewish tradition? Harder still is to decide what and about whom to write. Is it possible to choose to write about one thing and not about another? Can one write about a shtetl of 400 Jewish families each of whom has its own history and traditions? Where every person had his own joys and sorrows, his own pleasures and worries. Where every tree could tell of generations of a pulsating Jewish life. And how much could the mountains and forests that surrounded the forest tell? How much could the river, Wieprz, tell abut the conversations between the mothers and grandmothers when they would come to wash clothes in its waters.

Unfortunately, we have only our memories to do so. Not possessing any other documents or materials, we are forced to search our memories in order to bring out the facts and events that will describe the life, and the destruction of the Jewish community in our shtetl.

There are various versions regarding the founding of Krasnobrod. One of them, which has some indication of authenticity, explains: In the fourteenth century, the Jews of Ukraine and Podolia suffered terribly as a result of the conflict between the Poles and the Ukrainians. A group of Jewish families came from Galicia and settled in Krasnobrod. The name Krasnobrod comes from 2 different words- *krasni brod* which means red dirt or dirty from redness, and red well. The name was given after big battles that took place in that area, and the ground was simply red from blood.

[Page 315]

Incidentally, I was in Brod, Galicia, which also has the name Krasni, during the war. There is a place there where hundreds of years ago great battles took place.

In the shtetl there were also tombstones over 400 years old. But the founding of the community actually took place much earlier.

WWI did not pass Krasnobrod by. It was burned down during the battles, plundered by the armies, Petlura's bands, and sometimes also by the Polish neighbors in the surrounding villages. They had to rebuild anew. Much effort and work was required until it was rebuilt and new life began to pulsate. Some of it was done with help from outside. Signs of an economic recovery based on business, trades, pedlaring–dorfsgeyer[1], among the Jewish population, began to be seen

Jewish Commerce

Ninety percent of business activity consisted of merchants who brought various kinds of merchandise from the big cities, and sold them to the Jewish and Polish population. The lumber business was a significant branch. Jews would buy up lumber from the nearby forests and send it off to Danzig and other places. With time, the lumber business developed greatly and a wood products industry also came into being–sawmills, furniture factories, etc. A lot of Jewish families earned their living by it, and some of them became very rich. The grain business also played a prominent role in the shtetl economy. They used to buy grains–wheat, corn, oats, barley–grind them into flour and sell it to other parts of the country.

[Page 316]

Trade in animals, cattle for slaughter, and horses was carried out by 2 or 3 families who passed it down from generation to generation. The cattle business was found in the hands of the "Zeinvelach", so called because one of the grandfathers was called Zeinvl. Almost all the sons, sons-in-law and their children took part in this business. Another person who was involved with the animal trade was Nachman Stockhammer who lived near the shul.

The Stockhammer family, Hy"D

He was a modest, and God-fearing person. He was never heard to speak harshly, and he lived peacefully with everyone. His house was always open to the boys from the besmedresh who came there to warm up. His wife, Beile-Bashe, also distinguished herself by her hospitality to guests. She never let a guest leave her house without having something to eat. It is my honor to memorialize, at least with these words, the memory of this woman, Beile-Bashe, who helped my mother in raising me, and whose house was a second home for me.

[Page 317]

The horse business was in the hands of several families originating from the Lefler family.

In contrast to other shtetls in our neighborhood, where the animal handlers were mainly from the lower classes, the "Zeinvelach", and the "Leflers" were faithful, pious Jews and well regarded business people. They willingly gave charity, gave their children a Jewish upbringing, and were well-liked in the shtetl. One of the Leflers, R' Itche Lefler, a man with a handsome beard, knew entire psalms off by heart. Every Shabbes, he would recite psalms before the davening began. He did not miss one day of davening. When I used to get up at dawn, and go to the besmedresh to study, he would always already be there, reciting psalms. He was usually accompanied by his brother-in-law, Abraham

Abis, also a horse dealer. He had another quality as well. Whenever a rabbi came to visit the town, he would have to stay at his house.

There were of course a few other families in the animal business, but the above mentioned families were the pioneers, and dominated the trade. It was the same thing with the butchers where 2 families, almost in a patriarchal way, were occupied with the meat business. One of them, the Tentser family, was a large family of observant Jews who guarded kashrut, and gave large donations. The second family were the Greenboim brothers, also a large family where almost all of them took part in the same business.

As much as I am able to remember, I will list the merchants of Krasnobrod by their line of business.

Lumber: Shmuel Gurtler, Pesach Helfman, Abraham Yakov Freund, Shloime Glomb, Lam-Levenfus families, Shulem Zeltser, Yosel Holz, and others. The first four were partners, and carried on a big businesses. But in the end, they were not successful and went on to other businesses; Gurtler to wheat, Helfman to a restaurant, Freund to textiles, and Glomb to leather.

[Page 318]

Textiles: Practically the first family in this branch was the family of Shloime Bergstein, or as he was called, Shloime-Gitl's. The family grew to be large, and all were concerned with this business. There were other textile stores like Shloime Kupiec–Shloime Menashe's–Binem Holcberg, Gerzon, etc. On the eve of the war, my father, may he live long, also took part in this business.

Leather: Moishe Yosl Goldberg

Iron: Pinchas Glater, who later immigrated to Eretz Israel, and gave his shop to his son Yehoshua, Leibish Gitl's, and Dovid Alboim.

Food and grocery: Nathan Lifsh, Berl Steinberg, Ozer Gortenkroit, Mordechai Gurtler, my father, and many others.

Handwork: In order to describe the Krasnobrod handworkers, one needs to be a very talented writer. It occupied a substantial and colorful stratum of the ordinary folk, hard working and filled with wisdom and folksy humor. Simple, pious people who, three times a day, tore themselves away from their workbenches and ran to the besmedresh so that, God forbid, they shouldn't miss Shacheris, Minche, and Maariv. They always remembered to recite a bit of psalms, and give their last penny for charity. They vied for synagogue service and sent their kids to the best teachers, turned them into "mentchen," who then left the shtetl, and went overseas to a better fate.

Shoemaker: Here too the trade was concentrated in the hands of a few families like: the Shtemers (the "Leifelakes"). These were all brothers, in-laws, and cousins. Almost all were slightly built with big beards; they each took after the other. Naturally, in time, the trade expanded and very many families drew their living from shoemaking and cobblering. Some of them later immigrated to South America, became rich and naturally forgot their shtetl and their acquaintances. I must mention certain shoemaker families like Yoine Alboim, Abraham Shnur, and Shiye Fuchs.

[Page 319]

Tailors: The preeminent family in this field was the Weissfish family, or as they were called, "Sralkelech," because their father and grandfather were called Israel Shneider. The family was composed of several of his sons and grandsons who were all occupied with tailoring. The grandchildren traveled away to big cities like Warsaw and Lodz, where they learned the latest styles and brought them back and made careers of it. Their parents had it easy previously sewing pants and the long kapotes. When the young people stopped wearing the long kapotes and began to demand modern clothing, the tailors had to acquire more knowledge and they went off to the big cities to learn the new styles.

Bakers: Several well-known families were engaged in this trade. They made good money, ran wealthy homes, and built nice bakeries and very nice houses. They gave their daughters nice dowries and made good matches. Families in the baking trade were: Fuchs or the "Mendelech," Rind, Rendler, Alboim, the "Chemtchicheh," Ben Zion Kam, and others.

There were other trades engaged in by Krasnobrod Jews like, for example, tinsmiths, carpenters, house painters, hat makers, watchmakers, barbers, locksmiths, but these were all just a few individuals.

[Page 320]

Carriage drivers: Since the shtetl had no railroad connections, or a highway, the only connection to the outside world was with horse and wagon. Several families drew their living from it: Shimon Balagoleh, Itchele Yosl's, Baruch Yakov Ulman, Nachman Gree, and others. They made the most money during the summer months, when hundreds of people came from the surrounding region for rest and recuperation in the Krasnobrod pine forests and sandy soil.

Peddler–dorfsgayer

Some tens of families were employed as peddlers to the villages. Like the other occupations, it was transmitted through the generations. There were 3 kinds of village peddlers: a) rich dealers who loaded up horse and wagon with merchandise they bought in the villages, stored it, and later sold it in large quantities b) poor dealers who in the space of a few days bought things from the peasants and sold them immediately in the city. The third kind of peddlers were the poor who had no means of making a living in the city. They would go out to the villages, and in various ways, earned some money.

Summary: These were the main types of business on which the economy of the Jewish population in the shtetl was based. The economic crisis of the thirties affected the Jews of Krasnobrod severely. Some became impoverished, and others had to work really hard to make a living. This led to the emigration of many families overseas. The youth dispersed to the big Polish cities to look for work.

In 1933-34, there were signs of improvement in the economy.

[Page 321]

But along with this, waves of antisemitism and boycotting of Jewish businesses arose. Polish businesses opened in competition, which with the help of wild unruly, pickets, began to break up and ruin the Jewish economy, and set the Jewish population along the road to hunger and need.

Fanaticism

At the same time, with the geographical separation from the outside world, the shtetl was also isolated from the social and political life of Polish Jewry.

The cultural life of Jewish men consisted of praying three times a day, and reciting a few psalms. Whoever was capable, studied Gemara with Tosafot and Mishanyot. Naturally, as the scholars had hegemony over Jewish life, the gabaim use to use all their wiles–not always honest ones–to maintain their dominance in the shtetl. There were individuals who would read a newspaper or a book from time to time, but that was done behind closed doors so that no one, God forbid, should find out.

The cultural life of women consisted of giving men the opportunity to study by helping them in earning a living, giving birth to and raising children. The Tsene Renne[2] was the main source from which our mothers and grandmothers drew their wisdom and culture. In the years following WWI, novels began to appear with tales of miracles performed by sages and pious Jews. But this too was only for certain individuals. The majority of women did not know how to read.

The Chasidim had a big influence in the shtetl. They used to travel to their rebbe several times a year, and sometimes the rebbe would visit the shtetl. Those days were like holidays for his followers.

[Page 322]

There were Chasidim from 4 rabbinical dynasties in town: Belzer, Trisker, Radziner, and Gerer. The relationships between the Chasidim were far from ideal. Quarrels and schisms were frequent occurrences. Separate prayer houses, separate shochets. When it came time to appoint a rabbi or a shochet, the debates and quarrels took up most of the public's time and resulted in creating enmity between people.

Awakening

The First World War shook up the shtetl and awakened it from its dreams, threw down the walls of fanaticism, and the breath of a growing Jewish cultural life blew in.

The thirst for knowledge about what was happening on the battlefields led to people beginning to read newspapers. Many refugees, who had returned to the shtetl after the war, brought news about Jewish life in other cities. Slowly, the desire for another way of life, began to be felt, and with it the desire to learn to read and write Polish, Yiddish and Hebrew. Some teachers adapted to the new requests and began to teach secular subjects. Some of the young, especially the girls, left to attend at the government elementary school.

The first library of Jewish books was created thereby laying the foundation for a new communal life that, in time, included all the Jewish youth.

The older generation did not stay indifferent. They dug in and began to fight with all the means at their disposal against the "plague" that had stolen into the shtetl. Quiet but serious fights went on between children and parents who would burn the books their kids brought into the house.

[Page 323]

The results of the battles were quite sad for the older generation. The youth became more motivated and did not give up, and responded with increased cultural activities. The times were full of dramatic tension. The struggle between generations is not an easy one and it demanded its sacrifices. The library became a symbol of their struggle. It developed the required strength needed for the interruption and the reconstruction of Jewish social life.

The social and cultural awakening led consequently to the development of a political consciousness among the masses. Political parties and their youth movements appeared.

The Parties

Unfortunately, we do not know the dates when the parties formed in our shtetl.

Mizrachi: The first to begin party organization activities were the Mizrachi members. They were youngsters who represented the religious way of life, and at the same time, Zionist work. They did work for Keren Kayemet L'Israel, and Keren Hayesod. They organized various Zionist events, and brought in speakers from larger cities. On the other hand, they did not interest themselves in culture-work, and did not organize any cultural events. They also tried to found a Yavneh school which lasted barely one year. The reason was, in my opinion, due to the failures of dedicated and capable members.

Poale Zion: The second party to get organized was Poale Zion. Thanks to the dedication and capabilities of its strongly idealistic members, in a short time, it expanded in quality and quantity. In time, they

[Page 324]

became the trend-setters of cultural life in the shtetl. They carried out successful theater presentations, and cultural events. Their youth organization, Freiheit, and the "Skoit," also developed an extensive educational program.

A convention of Hanoar Hazioni in Krasnobrod

General Zionists: The third party organized were the General Zionists of both directions (Al Hamishmar and Et Livnot). In actuality, they had begun organizing a general Zionist organization before any of the other parties, but it was interrupted by the death of Yakov Zimmerman. As one of the founders and organizers of the party, I remember well the colossal difficulties and interferences that we encountered in our activities. The interferences came from both the parents and the opposing parties. Thanks to the fact that the organization attracted a group of dedicated and aware ideologues, we were able to establish it on a solid foundation. We later had a big influence on the Zionist life of the shtetl. We also had a youth organization, Hashomer Haleumi, which later was called Hanoar Hazioni. It was in large measure due to the work of Mendl Farber who devoted much work and time to the General Zionist movement.

[Page 325]

A group of girl members of Hanoar Hazioni

[Page 326]

Bund: When the Bund was founded it had very few members. But it soon grew into a large and strong organization. Firstly, it was due to the fact that they had talented and politically conscious members like Yehoshua Shnur, and others. Secondly, the Communists, who had no legal organization, sent some of their members to the Bund in order to have a legal avenue for contributing to the debate. In the last years before the war, the Bund had shrunk considerably, and was barely heard of.

Communists: Right after the war, many young people, under the influence of the Russian revolution, joined the ranks of the Communist movement. Many were arrested, and one of them, Shmuel Weissfish, was murdered in jail. Others received heavy sentences. Some fled to Soviet Russia. And so, they fell apart. They never succeeded in accomplishing any organizational activities. Some of those who fled to Russia came back to Poland with the stream of repatriations after the Second World war.

Revisionists: The Revisionists had very few members and were not strong enough to mount their own party organization. They lacked the necessary organizers.

In the deepest sorrow and pain, I remember all these dear people, the simple, faithful Jews of the older generation, and the dear idealistic youth, their activists and educators.

Sorrow consumes the heart and there is no consolation.

Chaval al de'avdin velo mishtakchin![3]

Translator's notes:
1. Someone who carried on business visiting villages
2. Women's bible and other writings in Yiddish
3. Woe unto us, for he cannot be replaced.

[Hebrew page 97]

The destruction of the Krasnobrod Congregation

by Nathaniel Brenner (Jaffa)

Translated by Mira Eckhaus

There is no doubt that the impression of an adult from the sights he sees is deep. But no less deep is the impression of a little child from a sight that shocks him to the core of his childish soul, such as the sight of destruction, killing and devastation. The sight of the destruction of Krasnobrod was engraved on my heart and will never fade.

On the day the Second World War broke out, I was about 8 years old. I was with my parents, and my two brothers, and my sister in a village near Tarnogrod, where we stayed during the summer vacation period, and also because my father had some business in that area.

With the end of the summer vacation, we were about to return to Krasnobrod. My father preceded us and went to Bilgoraj. All of us, my mother and the children, got on the farmer's wagon and set off. We drove the whole night on a road that curved between meadows and stubble fields, in a quiet and calm landscape. Nothing disturbed the peaceful night, except for the barking of a dog, or the mooing of a cow. We were rocked by the wagon and dozed off. No one imagined the storm that would break out here in a little while. We arrived in Jozefow and continued towards Krasnobrod, and in the morning we arrived at its outskirts. We passed by the old cemetery and the pension of the late Moshe Borg. We entered the heart of the city, and there we noticed groups of Jews standing and arguing with great enthusiasm and interest, and a very worried look on their faces.

Such a sight in a quiet town like ours, and at this early hour, did not bode well. And indeed, when we arrived at the house of grandfather Rabbi Aharon in Babad, my good and dearest grandfather, he welcomed us with tears in his eyes. In a voice choked with tears, he informed us that war had broken out in the world. And he told us other bad news, news more bitter than death, that our father had been drafted into the army as soon as he arrived in Bilgoraj. The Polish government sent its best battalions, and as quickly as possible, to the front. I didn't get to see my father until a year later after he was captured and moved to Lviv.

The town was in turmoil. Chaos and confusion everywhere. The grocers immediately closed their stores and refused to sell food items. Cooking salt disappeared from the market. The residents began to hide everything that was valuable, some in the cellars and some in holes in the ground. The alarms became an everyday thing, airplanes appeared in the sky, and "experts" debated their identity for many days. Rumors spread about spies who had been parachuted in. The flour mill was closed to minimize noise, and telephone centers and vital points were guarded. The Polish army began to pass through town as they were retreating. We had never seen people and vehicles in such large numbers. The retreat was followed by acts of robbery, because the retreating soldiers were hungry and tired. As soon as the Polish army stopped coming through the town, rumors came of an approaching German army. And indeed, on Rosh Hashanah Eve, the first German tanks appeared from the direction of the Tomaszow road.

[Hebrew page 98]

After several days, the Germans disappeared and the Polish army returned and was seen in town. The knowledgeable people began to tell of a decisive battle that was about to take place between the armies. There was also someone who said that the Poles were going to blow up the safety bridge on the road leading to Zamosc. The neighbors who lived close to the bridge began to move to their relatives' houses, which were as far away from the bridge as possible. Since we were also among those who lived close to the bridge, we moved to Hashil Morer's house, where we found most of the people from our community, except for grandfather who was already ill, and preferred to move to Rabbi Shmuel Gurtler's house where he had prayed for years.

A short time later the battle began. Shelling, bursts from machine guns, noise, commotion, really like the upheaval of Sodom and Gomorrah. Several bullets hit the roof tiles and shattered them. The fragments fell in with a great noise to the dismay of the people who were prostrated on the floor, and who wept, wailed in fear, prayed or whispered a chapter of Psalms by heart.

Suddenly the shooting stopped, and after a while there was a huge explosion followed by an oppressive silence. Someone peeked out and said that a thick cloud of smoke was rising from the houses around. Soon we heard a shout: *Verfluchte Juden, Raus*! (Damned Jews, get out!) The door opened forcefully. Only then did we realize that the whole street, and also the house we were in, were on fire. There was an indescribable commotion, everyone began to run away. A stream of people pulled me out. My mother was lost and so was my 6-year-old brother. I ran through burning streets shrouded in thick smoke near houses that were burned to the ground. In the streets where the houses still stood, Germans passed with flamethrowers and set them on fire. Others accompanied the fleeing crowd with gunfire and bursts from machine guns. I was swept away with the stream of people heading towards the stream - to Mount Grabnik. We crossed the shallow stream and jumped intotrenches that had been dug at the time by the army and were abandoned. In the evening, we came out of the trenches. I found myself alone among strangers. Only later someone recognized me, and joined me to his family. He also told me that he had seen my mother coming out of the burning house with the new 8-month-old twins in her arms. My brother was also seen, but he probably went with a different group of people, while grandfather fled to another place.

[Hebrew page 98]

Days passed until we found each other. My grandfather moved to Zamosc, to his daughter Raizel Drong, may God avenge her. My mother, who was left without a house, with her four children, found refuge for a while in the house of Hadassah Blichman, the mother-in-law of the late Israel Babad (my uncle). Her house was near the school, an environment that was almost undamaged. After that it was decided that I would move to my uncle, Hashil Babad's, house, in a village near Jacnia. On my way there, I passed again through the ruined town. The streets were full of the stink of the corpses of horses and soldiers. Here and there, there was a charred or smoking wall that was like a tombstone to the great destruction. Even though I was a native of this city and knew it well, it was difficult for me to find my way in this ruin as there was no sign of a street or a neighborhood left. The hand of the destroyer, and the fire were in everything.

In the village I was a shepherd with other boys from the village until I was taken to Zamosc. There they informed me that my father, who had been captured by the Russians, had been released and was in Lviv.

And one day my aunt Pesia, my father's sister (now Pesia Roche, lives in Tira, near Haifa) came and took us to Lviv to my father. We had to leave grandfather in Zamosc. We could not take him with us because of his illness. He urged us to leave and go to my father. As for him, he believed that God would not leave him in times of trouble.

We never saw him again.

After 7 years we returned to the place where Krasnobrod once was. We could not find a trace of the town and its Jewish community. We found only hatred and sarcastic amazement that "there are still so many Jews left, despite everything that had happened."

Let this memorial book for the people of Krasnobrod serve as a monument to their lives and their holy deaths. Let the things written in it be a sign for future generations, and will instill in them courage and bravery to fight for the freedom of the people of Israel in the State of Israel.

[Page 327]

The First Memorial Assembly of Krasnobroders in Israel

Translated by Moses Milstein

The first memorial gathering of Krasnobroders in Israel took place on November 6, 1949 at the Netzach Israel synagogue in Haifa.

Ephraim Lochfeld, who opened the assembly, asked everyone to stand to honor the memory of the Krasnobrod martyrs. For two minutes the assembled stood in holy stillness communing with the near and dear ones who were so tragically cut away before their time. In those two minutes their hearts were gripped by deep sorrow for the orphaned family that had come together to say Kaddish for the holy Krasnobrod community, near Zamosc, that was destroyed.

E. Lochfeld was elected as chairman, and Mordechai Rapaport as secretary.

Moishe Fishl, one of the few survivors, recounted the terrible story of pain and torments during the annihilation of Krasnobrod.

With simple words, he described the terrible tragedy. In chapter after chapter he recounted the bestiality of the German murderers and their accomplices–the Poles.

After this, Aharon Untzig read a passage of mishnayes for the elevation of the holy souls of the martyrs, and ended with Kaddish.

R' Itzchak Mayer Gurtler delivered a eulogy for the martyrs calling on the assembled not to forget what the German Amalek had done to us, and the consolation of the building of Eretz Israel.

Yoel Handelsman read his writings dedicated to Krasnobrod.

[Page 328]

Ephraim Lochfeld related various facts about Krasnobrod life. His proposal that the day, tet'vav[1] Cheshvan, the day of the last aktion, become the memorial day for the Krasnobrod martyrs, was accepted.

After Eliezer Lerner recited El Maaleh Rachamim, the official part of the memorial assembly came to an end.

At the second session, a committee of the Krasnobrod she'erit hapletah was elected with the following composition:

1. Epharim Lochfeld, Haifa; 2. Sholom Zeltser, Haifa; 3. Eliyahu Rind, Haifa; 4. Pinchas Kupiec, Haifa; 5. Shmulke Gurtler, Haifa; 6. Shloime Babad, Haifa; 7. Moishe Fishl, Haifa; 8. Abraham Giter, Haifa; 9.Abraham Borg, Tel Aviv; 10. Yehoshua Shlegl, Tel Aviv; 11. Abraham Glikman, Tel Aviv; 12. Shmuel Untzig, Tel Aviv; 13. Abraham Elboim, Jerusalem; 14. Mordechai Rapaport, Ramle; 15. Moishe Fuchs, Hadera.

Lochfeld proposed founding a gemilut chasidim–a continuation of the gemilut chasidim in Krasnobrod–that would provide loans to help out the landsleit in need. The proposal was accepted, and those attending immediately donated their dues.

Lochfeld closed the session with moving words, calling for unity and strengthening among the she'erit hapletah[2] in Israel.

Translator's notes:
1.   15th of Cheshvan
2.   The 'remnant of survivors' (post WWII)

[Page 330 - Yiddish] [Page 106 - Hebrew]

Destruction and Holocaust

***Introduction

by M.K.

Translated by Moses Milstein

With the publication of these pages we are fulfilling one of the most important tasks we had set ourselves in bringing out this yizkor book.

These testimonies, experiences and memories make their way into the book without "historical" improvements. These events and facts are transmitted in different variations, sometimes by changing names and dates.

Today, 12-14 years after the tragic events, it is difficult to demand of those who miraculously survived the hell, an exact, chronological precision by recording the megillah of their anguish and torment. How can you demand of people who were in constant fear of death, persecuted and oppressed, hidden from the light of day, sundered from the world and humanity, hungry and thirsty, that they remember and transmit with meticulous precision everything they endured? Those who violated and murdered them, robbed and persecuted, witnessed and were silent, they have, of course, also written their bloody stories. From them, history will demand an exact reckoning.

We believe that the variability in the telling, the changing of names and dates, the separate issue of assessing the behavior of the Polish neighbor with respect to the persecution of Jews, make the experiences of the Holocaust era clearer and fuller, and permits us to understand and conceive how a Jewish community was slaughtered for their religion.

[Pages 331-361 - Yiddish] [Page 107-130 - Hebrew]

Pages from the Flames

by Moshe Fishel (Haifa)

Translated by Moses Milstein

(The days of devastation and death 1939–1944)

Moshe Fishel

The attack on Poland by the German killers took place the first of September 1939, two weeks before Rosh Hashanah.

On Erev Rosh Hashanah, some of the German mechanized divisions passed through our shtetl, Krasnobrod, near Zamosc. On the first day of the holiday, we could see them camped nearby. The holiday went by quietly. We saw no military in the shtetl itself.

After *Motzi Yom Tov* massive numbers of Polish military began to flow into town. Tuesday at dawn, a big battle occurred between the retreating Polish army and the Germans.

At the time, we were in Rav Margaliat's room. He was living with us in those days. The Germans entered our house and accused us of shooting at them. They threatened to shoot us. After much pleading and wailing we managed to dissuade them. Then they ordered everyone to leave town because they were going to burn it down.

The first Jewish sacrifices were: Shmuel–Ozer Kupiec, and his son, Michal. They were burned alive. They were found by Abraham Blechman, and Leibke Kupiec, Shmuel Ozer's brother. Others who fell that day were: Leibish Weinreich, the barber; Eliahu Liebel; the boy Moshe Fuchs, Itzhak Fuchs's son; a boy called Shmelke Shtemer, and a foreign boy whose name is not familiar to me.

On the second day, Wednesday, the Germans gave the Christian population permission to loot the remaining Jewish possessions. They raided the cellars where the Jews had hidden their few personal belongings and household goods.

On Yom Kippur, another battle took place between the Poles and the Germans.

In the first few days, the Germans detained R' Moshe–Yosef Goldberg, and Shmuel Ben–Yakov Gurtler along with other Jews and ordered them to bury the horses that had fallen. That night, after the work had been done, they ordered the exhausted Jews to remove their clothes and bury them along with the horses...They beat them mercilessly and then ordered them to dig up their clothes and go home.

During the months of October 1939 – January 1940, Germans would round up Jews for labor and torture them. The work consisted of demolishing the remaining houses and gathering the bricks and stones and transporting them to Lipsko forest. There they were building roads and installations for the German mechanized divisions. Jews also worked on the construction of an airfield at the village of Mirka, near Zamosc.

In February 1940, the Germans sent an order to the town regarding establishing a judenrat. The mayor of the town, Katowski, nominated the following for the judenrat: Moshe Hoz, Yosef Goldstein, Fishl Shlegel, Yosef Lam, David Levenfuss, Yehoshua Babad, Moshe Greenboim, Berl Shak, Yehoshua Wexler, Leibish Lerner, Hershl Shoch, and Leibish Eilboim. Twelve members altogether. Their first task was to register all the Jewish residents, and to open a file containing the details on everybody, especially their trade.

In the same month of February 1940, one fine day, the Gestapo arrived and began to confiscate valuable goods and merchandise from people's homes. They entered my father's home and took his merchandise. An aunt, Ettl Silbergeld, from Grobowiec, was staying with us at the time. The Germans beat her, and took her last 200 Zlotys. They brutally beat my brother, Yechezkel, with an iron bar. I was at the judenrat getting the files ready. They shoved me away from what I was doing and beat me.

The judenrat was required to carry out the commands of the Gestapo: Provide people for labor, and distribute the food they got from the *landrat*. Those capable of work received "certificates." The sick received certificates signed by a doctor stating that they were sick. We believed, and we convinced ourselves, that these "certificates" were important for our survival...

In May, or June 1940, two Gestapo details arrived in town and detained people, both the workers and the sick, and sent them to work in Belzec. Their "certificates" meant nothing at all. Of the 32 Jews sent to Belzec, I can recall: Leibish Lerner, Itzhak Greenboim, Moshe Greenboim, Ephraim–Ziml Goldberg, Aaron Gershon, Meir Krelman, Moshe Blumstein, Aaron–Laizer Shpeicher, Yosef Shpeicher, and Wolwish Tentser.

We prepared parcels of food to bring to them. It is 31 km from Krasnobrod to Belzec. We traveled on Shabos, because it was the only day they allowed food to be brought. The picture we saw was shocking. The Germans brutally abused the Jewish laborers. They forced them to sing Jewish songs while working, starved them, and beat them mercilessly.

The work was hard. They had to dig defensive trenches near the Soviet border that were 3 meters deep, with 3–meter high embankments around them, and 6 meters wide. The "work leaders" were Meir Zilf, and Brateczka, may their names be cursed. Later some were sent to work in "Czeszenow" and "Zulkow".

I was one of those who brought food to the workers. It was shocking to see the misery of my brothers.

We began to pay money to ransom the Jews. Little by little we managed to get everyone home. After the holidays, the last ones came home: Meir Krelman and Aaron–Gershon Kleiner.

The Gestapo announced that whoever worked in a post would not be bothered. People thanked God for this, thinking their security was assured.

One group of forty men worked on the road from the village of Jacnia to Zamosc. They were paid two Zlotys a day. This was the only place where anyone was paid. Everywhere else, labor was for free. They also worked in the Krasnobrod surroundings, in the nobleman Fodakowski's fields. The steward, in particular, sadistically harassed the Jewish girls.

In February 1941, the judenrat received a communication from Zamosc informing us that we must absorb one thousand, homeless, Jews. We sent a delegation to complain that there were only a few undestroyed houses left in town, and that the people themselves were impoverished. They had nothing left. There was not one place to receive the homeless.

On Friday, a group of Gestapo arrived, Brosch, and Fast, may his name be erased. They gathered the judenrat together and beat and tortured them so hard their cries could be heard in the seventh heaven. When one of the victims passed out, they revived him by pouring cold water on him, and resumed beating him.

The members of the judenrat who were the most horribly beaten were: Moshe Hoz, Yosef Goldstein, Leibish Lerner, and Berl Shak. The torturers taunted them: 'Now do you have place for them?'

My brother–in–law, Moshe Hoz, was laid–up sick a whole week after this. He was seen by many doctors. We feared he would not survive. His body was beaten and broken, covered with blue–black stripes.

It was the same with the other victims. After this, the murderers went from house to house, beating anyone they encountered.

A few days later, the refugees arrived. The killers brought the Zamosc judenrat along, and in a matter of a few hours, everything was organized. We all helped to hurry the newcomers into houses, because we wanted to see the thugs gone as quickly as possible.

Naturally, new calamities to add to the old were not in short supply. The newcomers were worn out, exhausted Jews, with no resources. They came from Lodz, Kutno, Wloclawek, all cities that were occupied by the German Reich.

We quickly formed an aid committee. Everyone who was able contributed from 5 to 20 Zlotys a month. For flour, which the community received from the *landrat*, we instituted a tax. Instead of charging 70 *groschen* a kilogram, we charged one Zloty. With this money we helped the homeless as well as those of our own who had no means of subsisting.

In spite of the fact that you could buy produce from the farmers in the villages, very few Jews ventured down those roads. It was a death penalty for a Jew to be found in the Christian villages. There were not a few times when the farmers would give potatoes or a bit of bread to the Jews. The situation with regard to food was the following: there was not enough to live, and not enough to die…

The aforementioned engineer Kotowski, worked hard to help Jews. He provided potatoes at government prices. Trees in the cemetery were cut down for heating fuel.

It was all of little help. The situation got worse from day to day, and every day, people died of hunger, cold and wretched conditions, so that we even got used to that…

Then an epidemic of abdominal typhus broke out. People ran to get a doctor's certificate so that they could be admitted to hospital. Without permission from the Gestapo, they were not allowed in.

The sick were sent to hospitals in Zamosc, Zwierzyniec, and Shebreshin[1]. Some of them were returned. The rest remained there…Many envied the dead, they had stopped suffering.

And suddenly–new troubles. The German army, which had been sent to the Russian front, marched through town. They pillaged and looted. They wreaked havoc in people's houses and in people's souls.

In October 1941, a group of soldiers broke into R' Nachman Stockhammer's house. They grabbed his daughter, Esther, and dragged her to the fields belonging to Stefan Kostrubiec. What they did to her there is not known. But the following morning, her brother, Shimon, came and told us that she was found dead in the fields. She had been tortured and shot. From what was seen, she must have lived and suffered for a time after she was shot. They saw how she had buried her face in the earth and had ended her life.

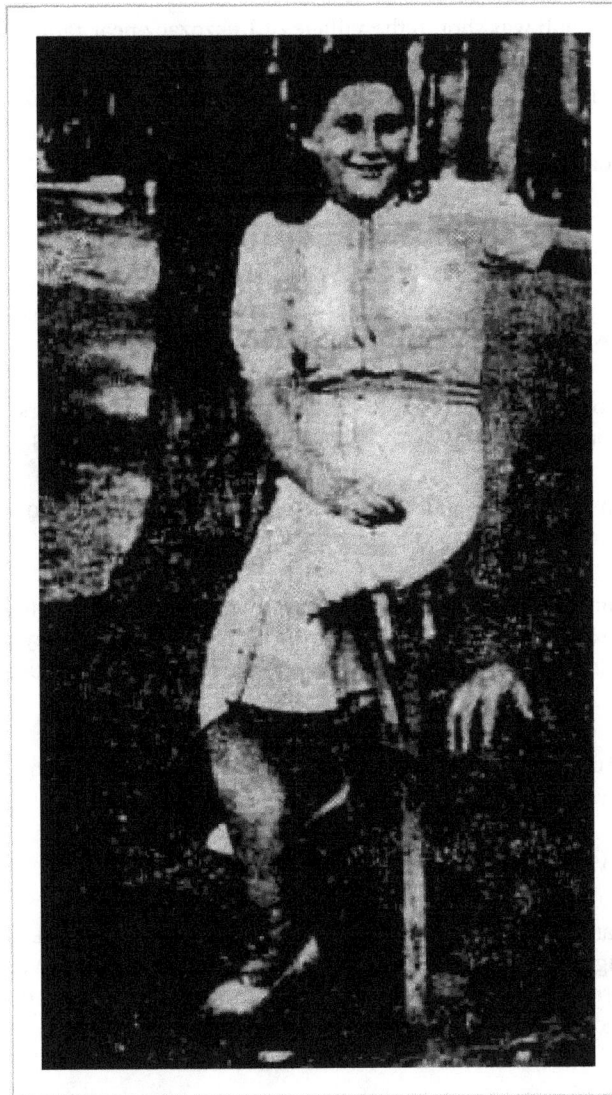

Esther Stockhammer, hy"d

On the evening of December 1941, a large company of soldiers that had been camped nearby, stormed into town. They broke down doors and windows, raped women, robbed, poured water on beds, and beat young and old. Our house was invaded by several soldiers. They poured a slop pail into mother's bed, and they beat my brother, Yechezkel, savagely.

When these left, others came.

I pushed against the door, but knowing I couldn't continue longer, my brother, Yechezkel, and I jumped out the window, naked in the cold, and ran away. They came into the house, did not bother the parents, and quickly left. When this had gone on for several days, the chairman of the judenrat, Moshe Hoz, went to see the administrator of the court, Telezinski, to ask him to request from the authorities an end to the searches. Since Germans were formally not allowed to interact with Jews, the argument succeeded. We did not see the soldiers again.

In March 1942, Laizer Weintraub was shot in the village of Luszczacz near farmer Kawka, by the little woods.

In April 1942, Pesach–Moshe Heisman and his son, Laizer, were shot. Motel Unzig was shot in Szur forest.

The sorrow and pain grew day by day, until the tragic end.

The Megillah of Sorrows

On Erev Shavuot 1942, Hershel Shuch, and David Glustman, travelled to Zamosc to get the flour ration. On the way, they were both detained by police in the village of Potoczek and imprisoned.

The city was devastated, worried about what to do. The "certificates" didn't work anymore. So, reasoning that a gift would help matters, they bought some big carps, whiskey, and other good things.

Naturally, nobody was keen to travel with all the goods to the killers…Moshe Hoz took on the task. He asked the Jews to pray, and he left for Potoczek. This was the first day of Shavuot.

A few hours later, a detachment of Gestapo arrived, and drove everyone out of town. Whoever could not flee in time was taken. Near Felix Kazenjowski's house, not far from Chaim Bronstein, they assembled them in rows. They went to the judenrat and commanded them to gather together all the jews for deportation. Those who tried to flee were shot on the spot.

Those shot were: Chaim–Rubin Strickler, Chaim Unzig's elderly mother, Aaron Unzig's mother, Chaya Kupiec and her daughter, and many others.

The herded– together Jews were taken to barracks behind the cloister.

The last ones caught, as I can best recall, were: R' Shmuel Gurtler, Esther Freind, Abraham–Yakov's wife. As the policeman was driving her along, she ran to the window of the judenrat and handed over a gold ring. After the Gestapo had brought everyone to the barracks, near the cloister, they went to the judenrat and demanded that they be treated to whiskey and cigarettes. This should be brought to them at the cloister.

We followed their orders…

They were seated around tables in Navojen's house, and they set themselves to stuffing themselves and swilling. Suddenly, Moshe Greenboim went by. He was on his way to the judenrat. The killers played a game: "Who can hit the Jew–dog?" They immediately began shooting. He fell. He moaned terribly and begged for help…

There was of course no help. Myself and Yosef Goldstein and another Jew whose name I can't remember, carried the unfortunate into Shimon Liebel's house and lay him on the bed. He suffered badly and begged us to kill him. The murderer approached and fired two more bullets into him and he was quiet...

In the meantime, Moshe Hoz returned from Potoczek. He had failed to meet Hershl Shoch, and Glustman because they had been moved to Zamosc. So I went with him to see Telezinski and to ask if maybe he could get us some whiskey. We were so foolish we thought that this would help... We did manage to get four liters of whiskey from him. Fishel Schlegel and Yosef Goldstein also found some whiskey. We were planning to deliver them to our persecutors. There were five of us: Me, Moshe Hoz, Leibish Lerner, Fishel Schlegel and Yosef Goldstein. We asked a Jewish policeman where the assembled Jews were being taken. He told us, to work in a camp near Chelm.

Fishl Shlegel—member of the Judenrat. Refused to hand Jews over to the Nazis.

As we got closer to the cloister, the mayor, Katowski passed by and winked at Moshe Hoz. "Why have you come? Take him into the *gemineh*," he said to us. "And tell him to run away through the back door. Because it looks bad..." He had heard the Germans discussing what they would do to us. But it was already too late. A Gestapo man came out and led us into the *gemineh*. They confiscated the whiskey and cigarettes. Then they lined us up.

The first one to be taken was Fishel Schlegel. He was shot behind the jail cell. The same murderer returned for Yosef Goldstein and took him to the Christian cemetery and shot him there.

It was my turn. Two SS men drove me, with blows from their rifles, to a car. I was certain that they were driving me to my death. Instead, they put me to work gathering together all the belongings of the captured Jews and transporting them to the barracks at the cloister. There were also Christian Poles doing the work.

Leibish Lerner was still alive. They brought me back from work and threw me into the cell where I found him. Later, a German from the *sonderdienst* came and ordered us to get on a wagon and bring bread for the "*verfluchte juden*". I asked him, "Where are we going to get bread?" "*Halt die schnauze, Jude!*" was his answer. On the way we met the commandant of the Polish police. I asked him, "Maybe you know where we can get bread?" But he did not know either...

We came to Chaim Bronstein's house, where we found several loaves of bread. When we got to Yehoshua Gurtler's house, the German tried to break down the door but couldn't. So he said to me, "*Jude, machst du auf!*" I answered that I couldn't and didn't say another word. I was afraid that there were Jews hidden inside. The *sonderdienst* grabbed an ax and tried to open the door and failed again. So we went on to Yehoshua Bronstein's house, found another couple of loaves and turned back.

As we approached the barracks we heard frightening wailing. R'Shmuel Gurtler was standing by the window and begging for water for the children. All the interned were thirsty. We went over to the organist's well. He gave us two buckets and we carried water to the unfortunates.

The whole way, the *sonderdienst* beat us, and then took us back to jail. The pain was so great during the day that we thanked God that we were back in jail. We sat there like that a whole night.

At around 5:00 o'clock, dawn, we looked out the window. We saw many farm wagons. Four people were seated in each wagon and all the Jews were taken for labor at Belzec

Belzec death camp

Then others were brought to the jail. Mashe Shpitseisen and her little daughter, and R' Moshe–Yosef Goldberg and his wife, Taubele. We were convinced we were all going to be shot. A little later, the mayor, Kotowski, came and released Mashe Shpizeisen and her daughter. About two hours later, the mayor returned and let me and Leibish Lerner out.

The *scharfuhrer* ordered us to find all the hidden Jews and begin to work again…So me and Leibish Lerner went to the forest to find the run–away Jews.

I argued with the *scharfuhrer* on behalf of Moshe–Yosef and his wife, asking him to free them because I needed them to help me. "Such old people are going to work?" he asked. I told him I would take responsibility for them. I had to sign for them and they were released.

Life began to "normalize." People began to return from the forests and other places where they had hidden.

They began to look for places to work. They wanted to work in the forests so as not to have to work in the city. No one slept at night, watching the Zamosc road with fear to see if the murderers were returning. But if you're alive, you have to eat. So they began to try to find ways to get flour. I went to Zamosc and they gave me flour for a month. When I asked for more, one of the the Zamosc judenrat said, "If you had had more people deported to Belzec, you wouldn't need more flour." I said, "If that's such a good thing, try it yourself."

One day a new blood–hound, a Gestapo from the village of Potoczek, arrived in town demanding that one of the judenrat should immediately come because he wanted a pair of boots.

I went down to Hersh–Leib's yard. I think Ephraim Zitser was there too. They gave me money which I used to buy boot leather. I was told to bring the leather to the Gestapo officer. I was afraid, but I had no choice. I went, and God helped me. I was successful. I settled everything with him, and he didn't bother us again.

At about this time, Hershel Shuch, David Glustman, and Mordechai Greenboim from Nemirowka,, escaped from the Zamosc barracks where they were held to be transferred to Belzec. They came back to the forest.

In July 1942, some Germans raided Chaim Bronstein's bakery. Itche Fuchs lived there. They took his daughter, Leah, and shot her on the spot. No one knew the reason.

Several days later, an SS group arrived wearing steel helmets, and carrying golden rifles. They surrounded the houses of Nathan Lifsh, Chaim Bronstein, and Yankel Laizer and set them on fire with incendiary bombs. The houses began to burn. Anyone coming out was fired upon. Everything, including the people inside, was burned.

I give here a list of the sacrifices that I can recall: Nathan Lifsh and his family; Berl Shak and his family and his mother–in–law, Leike Liebel; Shimon Liebel and his family; Yehoshua Wexler and his family; Yosef Aaron Shochet and his family and his father–in–law, Baruch Eli Broder, and his family; Yechezkel Unzig and his family; R' Yakov (Laizer's) Gurtler, and his daughter–in–law (Yehoshe's wife), and the children; Shmuel Rendler and his family; Moshe Aaron Freiman, Itche Fuchs and his wife; and Chaim Bronstein and his wife.

The fires burned until morning, and the bodies of the martyrs smoldered for days.

Later, the Germans raided the cellars and took everything they could find there.

Several weeks later they found Yosef Dichterman in the village of Kaczuka and shot him.

One day the Germans visited Leibish Lerner. He lived in Pinye Rotheiser's house. They took Shmuel Dichterman and beat him severely. Then they ordered him to dig a grave because they were going to shoot him. His family members began to lament so strongly–his son Isrulke was living there at the time–that they released him.

In August 1942, Hindeh Greenboim left Shoshke's house. A *sonderdienst* who was always in town saw her, and, simply, stoned her to death. This took place near Micholowski on the sand. He then called on the farmers to have them bury her. You could hear her cries as they buried her alive.

That same month, the Germans appointed Yakov Hersh Kreiden as chairman of the judenrat. He was a tailor and made clothes for them. So they appointed him to power. (Yakov Hersh remained chairman until the end).

One day he came to see us and reported that the *sonderdienst* had shot two Jews at the bridge. I was at Shmuel–Yankel Laizer's house. He lived at Todzik Shpiro's. Yakov Hersh Kreiden ordered us to bury the two Jews. Shmuel Gurtler and I went. We also took Yakov Hersh along. There we found a boy of about 17, and a man of about 40. They had both escaped from the Zamosc ghetto. They had Aryan passes and were trying to get to Czechoslovakia or Hungary. The *sonderdienst* recognized them. He shot the older man on the spot by the bridge. When he tried to shoot the other one, his gun jammed. He chased him until Franek Marusha's fields, and there he beat him with a club. The *sonderdienst* was still standing there when we came to bury the boy. We heard his strangulated breathing...In Franek Marushak's field, we dug a grave, broke some branches and laid them in the bottom so that it would become a coffin. We wanted to wait until his soul left his body. But the murderer returned and ordered us to bury him alive. We lowered the martyr into the grave and our hearts bled...The farmers stood around and looked at us with sadistic satisfaction at how low we had fallen...

A few days before the big *aktion* in October, Yehoshua–David Goldstein was travelling from Krasnobrod to Hutow. People were afraid to spend the night in town. A Gestapo member accosted him near the *sazhelkes*, and killed him. He was buried where he lay. Exactly where, I don't know.

On the eve of the big *aktion*, Sunday, October 10 1942, Aaron Greenboim, Shimon's son, came to Krasnobrod from Zamosc. He worked and lived in Zamosc. His father and both of his sisters, Leah and Chaya, were in Krasnobrod. He went to Ettl Schleger's home. She was then living outside town by Gresztis hill, at the peasant woman Dzadowska's. From there, it was easy to escape. I was also there. I was standing and *davening*. A young boy came running in, Shmuel Tentser's son, Bereleh, and told us that in Shebreshin, Jewish men and their families had been rounded–up. They were put in cattle cars and taken to Belzec. Along the way, he was pushed out of the window by his mother. Then she jumped out after him. They were shot at by the Gestapo escort, and his mother was killed. The little boy–I don't know how he found the strength–ran through the forest until he got to Tomaszow, and from there, to his aunt Ettl in Krasnobrod. He refused to eat a thing before *davening*. I don't know how old the child was, but he was very smart. He picked up a *siddur* and began to *daven*...

Shmuel Tentser and his family

Ettl Schlegel's two sweet children knew Hebrew as well as German. They studied with my sister Shoshe Hoz's boy, Velvele. We had two teachers, Meir Perele, and a woman teacher from Grodno. We kept on teaching the children the whole time, believing that we would survive the cursed murderers.

We did everything to save the children. They were given to farmers to work as shepherds. The farmers wore them out physically with too much work and not enough food.

One day, Velvele came running back from the *colonia*. "I don't want to be with the goyim anymore!" I begged him to go back to the village so that he might be safe. But he refused. Maybe if I had taken him back with me, I might have been able to save him.

So we all stand there and go on *davening*…

Kaile Friedlender and Etl Shlegel with her children

In the house, there arose a great wailing, everybody certain that we are parting forever, that we are *davening* together for the last time. And so it turned out to be. I never saw my near ones again.

In the evening, Aaron Greenboim left. He argued that he was not afraid for himself.

He had enough money to buy himself out. A *sonderdienst* caught him by Pawlowski's barn and shot him. He tore the clothes off him and sent them to be hidden in the firemen's *remizeh*. He was buried right there.

My parents came to see me at night and begged me, "Go to Shoshke's house and take the children and sneak over to Turzyniec." My brother–in–law, Moshe Hoz, had been in hiding at various Christian locations since the beginning of the *aktion*. I embraced my parents, and said farewell forever. We went to Turzyniec to stay with a Christian whose name I can't remember. We crawled up into an attic with straw, and met my brother–in–law, Moshe. Around two in the night, we heard the sounds of machine guns. My cousin, the engineer, Jungman, was also with me. So Moshe said, "Let's get out of here." I did not agree. Moshe and the children went to another attic. I found a large wheat barrel and my cousin and I hid in it.

At daybreak, the farmer climbed up to the attic and began to search. He found my sister and drove her out. So she left, wrapped in a shawl, to Szur, to a *goyeh* she knew. She was spotted on the way and pursued. But she escaped from their sight by hiding in the nearby forest. She spent the night with a goyeh in the Tarnawatka forest, near the village of Zielone.

Around two a.m., Moshe came and called to us softly. I heard his voice and we descended from the attic. I told him I did not know where Shoshka ended up. He left the children with a farmer in Antonowka, and we went together up to the Risker forest. There we separated. He went back to the children and I went with my cousin to Hutkow. I never saw him again.

On the third night in Hutkow, my sister Shoshke unexpectedly showed up. She had spent the whole night in a field. At daybreak she went to the farmer where we were hiding in the hay in the attic.

I told her about Moshe and the children. The farmer came up and apologized that he could not hide such a large group. So my sister got up, and went out to the fields. I found out, that at night, she had met up with Moshe. I never saw her again. It was the last time I would be with my one and only sister.

The tragic end

As Sunday turned to Monday on the 26th of October 1942, the German murderers finished with the Jews of our shtetl, Krasnobrod.

They rounded up all the Jews, young and old, herded them into Itche Fuchs's unfinished bakery building, and murdered them all there.

The farmers reported that the Germans immediately set to burying the victims, the living and wounded along with the dead. Their cries and wailing carried through the whole neighborhood. Groans and movement in the earth of the mass grave continued for days. The few remaining Jews were put on wagons, and were driven by the Germans to Izbica. Among them–my parents.

Firok, the farmer from Turzyniec, told me that the Nazis had spared some Jews, because the Gestapo at the cloister needed tradesmen. These were: Yakov Hersh Kreiden, the tailor, and his second wife; R' Yosef Edelstein, or as he was called Yosel Tveed from Hutkow; a *kamashenshteper*; a girl, Rivkah Freiman, Shmuel Rind's granddaughter; and, I think, Hershl Gross, a shoemaker and his wife; and Hershl Shuch, Elem Glaser, in total, about 6–7 people.

Those escaping from the slaughter were: Moshe–Yosef Goldberg and his wife, Taubele; Laizer Gartler, The "*Yetchakhe*" and her son Leibl Bleichman, and a few others.

The farmers helped the Germans in their hunt for Jews. They caught Moshe–Yosef Goldberg and Taubele in the Risker forest. He pleaded with them to shoot him in the back. He and Taubele had vowed not to be taken to the Gestapo. So they "did them a favor," and shot them. The farmers caught Leizke Gurtler also in the Risker forest. They brought him to the *gemineh* to shoot him. From great fear he lost his ability to speak, and could only utter wild cries. They shot him by the *gemineh*. The *goyim* caught the "*Yetchakhe*" in Majdan. She was also shot by the *gemineh*. Yakov Schneider and his wife and little girl were caught and killed in Hutkow. Their older daughter, Leah, was hidden by a farmer and she survived. Today, she is in the United States.

I heard from farmers that many of the escaped later gave themselves up to the Gestapo, and begged to be shot.

I was distraught worrying about my sister and her children and husband. So I sent the Beltsher with a letter to the place I knew they had to be at. He brought back the news that they were alive. But he had not talked to them.

On the third of December 1942, *Motzi Shabos*, I went into town to find something to sell. When I got there, Teofil Kozinowski told me that my sister, Shoshke, and her husband, Moshe Hoz, and their two children, Velvele, and Yeshiahu, were captured in the village of Klocowka. They were taken to the jail in Krynica. They probably knew where they were going and what awaited them there. They were all shot there, and buried by the mill. A farmer told me about this. He happened to be passing by there and saw the killings.

Our bitter life continued. The farmer from Hutkow was afraid to keep sheltering us. He proposed to us that we should go to a man called Monastyrskow. We had no choice but to transfer over.

In December, a Gestapo officer accused Hershl Shuch of having contacts with the Polish partisans. He was taken to the nearby forest and shot. Later, in celebration, he ordered Yakov Hersh Kreidan, the tailor, to marry Yosef Eldstein to Rivkah Freiman. They did get married and lived together until they were deported.

In February 1943, captured were: Yakov–Hersh Kreidan and his wife, the cobbler and his wife, and Yosef Eldstein and Rivkah Freiman. They were all shot together on Todzik Szpiro's property and were buried there.

With this last killing, the Germans succeeded in completely wiping out the Jewish community of Krasnobrod.

* * *

In 1940, a peasant woman who lived behind the cloister bought a kilo of flour from Nathan Lifsh. She then went to the Gestapo to report this. The Gestapo first got a wooden board, and wrote on it that the "*verfluchte Jude*" had cheated a "Polish woman," and that he deserves to be beaten and killed. They nailed it to a pole. A German then brought Nathan to the Gestapo. There, they beat him and jailed him. After a few days, he was released. His skin was black and blue from the blows.

In December 1942, in Teofil Kazinowski's yard, I met Abraham–Yakov Freind. He pleaded with me to lend him some money. I told him that I was supposed to get some money on Saturday evening from Kazinowski. We agreed to meet later. When I arrived at the appointed time to give him the money, he got frightened, didn't recognize me, and ran away. I never saw him again. I found out later that he was murdered by the peasants in Hutkow forest.

Velvl Giter and his family

That same month, they caught Itchele Rodoshcher while he was riding a wagon. He was hiding in a village there. They took him to the police station in Potoczow. The Gestapo forced him to dig a grave. He begged them to shoot him from behind. They buried him in the grave he himself had dug.

The Pole, Pakula, caught Liba Eilboim, Yonah, the shoemaker's daughter, Yehoshua Babad and his family, and Malka Babad. They brought them to the Gestapo and shot them. They caught others after, but I can't recall their names.

At the same time, Velvel Giter sent his young son to buy some bread. The farmers caught him and locked him in a stall. Overcome with fear, Velvel Giter hung himself.

This is what I could find about how all these people met their end.

Wandering

We stayed with the Christian woman, Monastyrska, for a few weeks. She used to inform us about the Jews caught and killed by the Germans, sometimes with the help of the peasants. She began to be afraid of hiding us. "Go in good health, I am afraid for my life."

So we moved to the Hutkow forest, and came to the village to buy bread. We continued like this until the month of January 1943.

Later, we went into the town to meet Janek Lubiesz and offered to pay him 30 Zlotys a day. He took us in and hid us for two weeks. He too became afraid, and asked us to leave his house. We wandered around in the Vilker forest and in other areas, wherever we could. We were exhausted, starved and worn out.

One night, in February 1943, we went into the stall where the city scale was kept, owned by Franek Maruszek. It was filled with hay. On entering, we had the feeling that someone was sleeping here. We got very frightened. But because of the cold that gripped us, we decided to take a chance. Once lying in the hay, it became clear to us that the "someone" was afraid to expose himself to us. It was Feige Fuchs. She had heard us speaking Yiddish, and came out of her hiding place. We were overjoyed to see her. We were with her for two days, then we separated. Where she went, we did not know.

In the Vilker forest where we wandered, we came across a search party of the German army, and Poles helping them. They were hunting partisans. From our hide–out, we could hear them going by and speaking in Polish. It was only by a miracle that we did not fall into the hands of the murderers.

The next day, we went to Stach Fiele and begged for bread. Stunned, he said to us, "What's wrong with you? Right next to me lives a Polish policeman, and you are wandering around…I am very afraid." But pity forced him to hide us in the barn loft. He brought us food. We stayed there hidden for almost two weeks. I paid him money for this.

In the meantime, the Poles were now being rounded up. They were sent off to Germany to work. Every day, more and more Poles began to leave their homes and hide so that we almost intermixed with them.

Hannah Giter arrived from Majdan and also came to Fiele. He immediately brought her to us. We were very happy to see her. We asked her where she had been. She said that she was in Majdan Wielki and some peasants were hiding her. The peasants are now fearful of the Germans themselves. Every day, they are rounded–up and sent to Germany.

Hannah Giter soon left us. We asked her if it was possible for us to move over there. She agreed.

A few nights later we took to the road. When we crossed the Hutkow bridge, we heard the loud baying of dogs. We turned back. It turned out that God was guarding our every step. Hannah Giter was indeed killed there.

In the meantime, a revolt against the Germans broke out in the village of Dzeranze. The peasants and the partisans who were active in that area, were attacking the Germans. They were close to taking Tomaszow. The battles went on for several days.

At the time, we were leaving Krasnobrod at night for the fields of Hutkow. One night it was very bright. The snow squeaked under our feet… Suddenly we heard footsteps, and immediately after, shots. We instantly began to run and kept going until Hutkow.

We went into the first peasant hut we saw. The peasant was happy to see us and asked where we were coming from. He asked us to stay with him in his house.

Throughout the day, his friends kept coming and asking "where the guests are coming from?…" For us, the frequent visits were not so comfortable. We sat there in some anxiety. But we did not dare to show our fear.

The next day, the peasant told us that the Germans had crushed the revolt. Now the Germans intended to initiate *aktion*s against the Poles. As a result, we had to leave the house. We had to go back to the forest.

And thus the days dragged on until summer 1943.

When the wheat began to grow in the fields, we hid there. At night we would steal out to a village to beg for food. Or we would go to the Grabnik, to Borakovitch and the nearby farmers.

One time, we had been to Borakovitch and were leaving with some bread. We heard someone running away from us, stopping and listening–and he recognized us. It was Isrulke Zitser. He asked us where we were hiding, and when we replied that there's plenty of place in the fields, he asked us to take him with. He ran to get his father, Ephraim Zitser, and we left together for the fields.

We were staying in a field where peas grew. Sometimes we were together, sometimes separate. We often snuck out at night to pick turnips from farms where we knew the farmers had been deported to Germany. My cousin found Feige Fuchs in the pea fields. She told him that Ruchele Rotheiser and her children were also here. That's the last we heard from her. She was later killed.

When the peas were ripe, on a Sunday, we discussed the possibility that the farmers might begin harvesting them tomorrow. And that's what happened. Monday morning, hidden among the plants, we heard movement. Before we could react, the farmers and their oxen appeared before us. There were: Stach Hacze, Franek Maraszek, and some other Krasnobrod farmers. They were in good spirits, and told us the news that Italy had surrendered to the allies. It won't be long before the Germans suffer defeat. "We just have to survive," they encouraged us, "and the war will end."

Ephraim Zitser did not want to stay here any longer. He believed that we should leave this place. We explained to him that we had nowhere to go. If he wanted to leave, he could go in good health, and if he should find a spot that would also be good for us, he could let us know.

More time passed. Once we were on the Grabnik on our way to get some bread from the house of a farmer and we heard the sound of someone running away. It frightened us too and we ran back to the fields. A little while later, we heard someone calling us in our agreed– upon Polish names, so we knew it was Ephraim Zitser. He gave us two moldy loaves of bread, and broke into tears because he had no place to stay.

We did not see each other again until liberation.

We continued to wander around in various places. We met Ruchele Rotheiser and her children, and, for a time, we hid together in a potato field in bunkers next to each other. When the farmers began to dig up the potatoes, we found ourselves with nowhere else to go.

One night I went out to the new village, to Lubiesz's, to beg for some bread, and I noticed an unfinished house, locked up everywhere. It had belonged to Wilczinski from the *hoif*. So we, that is my cousin and I, decided to get in there and stay as long as possible. We pried out a board covering the window, and we got up to the attic. The attic was empty. We closed ourselves in so that no one could know we were there, rested and slept. At night, we would creep into the village to get some bread. It would have to last us for half a week, or sometimes, a whole week. We stayed there until winter arrived and it began to snow. It was almost December and we were suffering from the severe cold. Furthermore, we could not get any food now. Our footsteps would be seen in the snow.

My cousin had a female cousin who was hiding in Warsaw as a Christian. She was trying to find out what was happening to us. She wrote a letter to Berbeckin, from Zagaria. She first asked if he had received any letters from Yuzek and Kube who had been sent away to Germany. When Berbecki, replied that he had, she sent him 1,000 Zlotys. These funds came from the money raised by the underground movement and sent via the lawyer Szwientowski, from Zamosc, to support those running from the Nazis. The lawyer, Szwientowski knew my cousin well.

Berbecki himself was always asking about us. We found out he was living in the guardhouse of the sanitorium.

When we visited him he received us warmly and revealed to us that he had a letter for us from the cousin containing money. But he hadn't claimed the money yet. We asked for an advance, and he gave us 200 Zlotys. We asked him if we could visit again. He gave us a big loaf of bread, around three kilos. He gave us the rest of the money at our second visit. We asked him to send off another letter requesting another 1,000 Zlotys.

In the meantime, I found out that the watchman for the unfinished house was Fztule Juzek from the new village. I went to see him and begged him to let us stay there, explaining that the snow was falling heavily, and it was freezing cold, and we could no longer exist in the forest. He gave his permission. We also asked him to bring us food every second day, and if we could use his name to receive money from Warsaw, to which he agreed.

At first, he brought us food. Very quickly though, he became frightened, and he let us know that if the money arrived, he would pass it on to us but…for now, we had to leave this place. We could come back later.

So we snuck into a potato cellar belonging to Lubiesz. It was dug out of soil in the field and was empty.

We had agreed with Berbecki to meet on Saturday night, the 5th of February 1944. We climbed out of our potato cellar and into a blizzard. The snow was knee–high. I was sick, and passed out in the storm. My cousin barely revived me. We had to postpone our journey. In the morning, we received the news that the sanitorium guardhouse had burned down, and that Hershel–Leibel Briks and his wife and children perished there.

The peasants thought that our continued survival showed the hand of God protecting us from doom.

In about the same month, Ruchele Rotheiser and her daughters, Feige and Frume, were captured by peasants on the Grabnik. They took them to Suchowola, and, there the German murderers killed them.

We went back to Yuzef and begged him to let us back into the attic of the unfinished building. He let us back, and brought us food from time to time, for which we paid him. Sometimes, we snuck out ourselves to find food.

In May 1944, the Germans launched a raid in the new village. Many peasants fled.

Two Germans came to our building, tore open the boards over the window. They peered in, searching with their eyes. We were in the attic shut up so that no one could suspect. "There is nothing here, just stones and wood," said one of them, and soon after they left…

We left the attic on July 22 1944.

Liberation

On Saturday, July 21st, the Germans left. That night there was deafening shooting. In the morning, we saw the Soviet soldiers passing through. Nevertheless, we waited a few more days in our hideout.

On Tuesday, the Germans tried to stop the Soviet assault on Suchowola, and wanted to retake Krasnobrod. But, they collapsed under the fire from the Katyushas…

We were liberated.

Translator's notes:
1. Yiddish name for Szczebrzeszyn, a town about 25 km northwest of Krasnobrod.

———

[Hebrew page 131]

How did I survive?

by Fishl Malka (Haifa)

Translated by Mira Eckhaus

When the Germans first invaded Poland, they immediately turned their anger on us. They expropriated our house with all our belongings, and left us only a small room. The Poles also did not sit quietly, and they made us suffer too. First and foremost is the person who framed my brother Motl, who was arrested by the Gestapo and sent to the prison in Tomaszow. There he was interrogated for a long time, but no one was able to prove anything against him, and he was released after several months. We thought that was the end of the matter, but the Poles wanted to harm him, and could not understand how a Jew got out of trouble. Therefore, they began to look for plots. When he understood this, he began to hide. He succeeded in this for 16 months, during which he lived a life of suffering, without a proper meal and without a place to lay his head, while the fear of the Gestapo who were looking for him hovered over him. Until March 10, 1942, when he was caught and taken to Zamosc. There he was interrogated by a Gestapo man, Foss, who was known for his cruelty. After four months he was taken to Lublin. There he was treated inhumanely. We then received a letter from him, through the son of the police chief, in which he asked us to do everything to save him because he was afraid that he would not withstand the torture they were inflicting on him. But what influence did we have then? We lived the life of those "without rights." No lawyer wanted to represent us regardless of the consideration. We could only hope for the mercy of heaven. From Lublin my brother was taken to Zamosc, and from there, with another shipment of Jews, to Belzec to be burned. On the way to Belzec he managed to escape. A farmer brought him to us half-dead. When he left us, he was a strong and healthy 22-year-old man, but when he returned his condition was uncertain. He was beaten and injured, his face was blackened, and he could hardly stand on his feet. As a result of his suffering in the prisons, his health deteriorated. And we had neither a good and worthy house to live in, nor a doctor, nor medicine, and everyone had to hide because he was an "escaped prisoner." Thus, he lay in the cemetery keeper's cabin, on the floor, and died. Before his death he spoke only of revenge. He wished us all a long life, and wished that we would have the opportunity to avenge his early death. He died on July 28, 1942.

[Hebrew page 132]

We did not have the opportunity to mourn our dead properly. It was the time of the aktions, and the living envied the dead. The last aktion was carried out on 26.10.42 and since then Krasnobrod has been "free of Jews." At the same time, my husband also died, may God avenge him, and I was left with a six-month-old baby. With the baby in my arms, I managed to escape to a village and hid in a haystack. Inside it, I made room for me and my baby, and only at night would I sneak out to get a little food. Several weeks passed. The cold grew and snow covered the ground. I realized that I couldn't continue hiding like this. So, I decided I must do something, and I came out of hiding in the daylight. When the children of the village saw me, they started chasing me and yelling, "Here is a Jewish girl with a baby." I ran away to the forest. The fact that it was starting to get dark assisted me, because the farmers were afraid to go deeper into the forest when it was dark and cold. And so, I managed to escape from them. I sat under one of the trees, and I pressed my baby to my fluttering heart and prayed in my heart that he would not burst into tears, and hand me over to my persecutors. I sat all night frozen from the great cold and did not feel how, slowly and quietly, my child was dying. Only in the morning, when I tried to walk, I saw that his body was dead and frozen. I dug a grave for him in the snow. My heart overflowed with grief, but I did not want to die. Maybe it wasn't the will to live that was strong in me at that moment, but the terror of death. I started wandering in the forest and found another group of refugees, among them were also my mother and my sister Chaya'le. I burst into tears, and the three of us began to cry over the great disaster that had befallen us. We also started talking about the rest of the dead and mentioned, besides my brother, my husband and children, also my sister Sarahleh, who was caught on 1.10.42 by the police and shot, and also my sister Marsa who was caught and shot three weeks later. And when will the trouble come to an end?

I decided not to stay in the forest and headed to Belzec, looking for a way to hide. I searched for many days and in the end, I returned to the same pile of hay in the field where I had hidden with my baby, because I couldn't find another place to stay. In the evening, I went out to look for my sister and mother in the forest, and suddenly I heard a scream. I recognized my mother's voice. She had apparently come out of the thick of the forest, and was captured. I started to run towards her, but a gentile came towards me and stopped me. I started struggling with him, breaking away and running, but he tried to dissuade me: "Where are you running? Do you really think you can save her? You are running towards your death; you are running straight to the mouth of a wolf. Come with me and I'll hide you in my house, maybe you'll be able to save your life." And after all, for days upon days I had been looking for a hiding place because I was afraid of death. And actually, his words were words of wisdom. That's how my mother was killed on December 5, 1942, and I stayed with that gentile until January, until he came and told me that he was also afraid for his life. I left him one evening, and while I was wandering, I encountered my sister Chaya'le, who I didn't even know was still alive. She was also without a place to stay. We sold the rest of our belongings, and I paid a gentile to hide her until everything would calm down. He agreed, but when he realized that she had no more money, he took her outside on 20.3.43 and shot her. I learned about it from a gentile whose house I arrived at another gentile's house when I was looking for a hiding place. He then ordered me to go up and hide in the hay in the attic.

[Hebrew page 133]

After several weeks, the Germans organized a hunt for bandits and among other things, they arrested my sister's killer and his entire family. "My" gentile told me about it the next day, with an expression of satisfaction on his face. He said to me: "As you can see, there is a God in heaven, your sister's death has also been avenged and you have one less enemy in the world."

I stayed with this gentile, who was a Righteous Gentile, until the end of the war. Two weeks later, I stopped hiding. I was naive to believe that there was no need to hide anymore. The gentiles I met shared in my sorrow, apparently, and wept with me. And through tears, the question which froze my blood arose again and again: "Look at her, how are you still alive?" And the tone in which this question was asked revealed what those who cried with me really thought and felt. On that night, a group of Poles came to the one who rescued me and demanded that he hand over the "Jewish girl." He crossed himself and swore that there was no Jewish woman in his house. They started searching the whole house and also looked in the attic. I dug myself into the hay and the searchers came close to me but didn't notice me. To this day I don't understand why I had the right to be saved. At dawn I left the village and went to Tomaszow. The horror of the last "rescue" still lingered in my bones and my strength was running out. Close to the city, I met a Polish woman I knew. She took pity on me and persuaded her son to take me to the city with his cart. I was in a state of exhaustion and the gentile brought me to the hospital. I entered the office and found the manager, a nun, dressed in black. I told her what had happened to me, and asked for medical help because I was sick and I didn't have a house or any money. Her answer was: "How wonderful, another Jewish woman remained alive." I burst into bitter tears: "Has the world come to an end? That there is no hospital that helps a sick person, and the nun is brimming with venom and hatred. After all, they are always going on about love!" And here the doctor came in and asked me: "Why are you crying?" I explained it to him, and he answered me bitterly: "Don't cry queen of the history of the Jews, everything will be good!" He admitted me to the hospital, where I remained for four weeks until I recovered.

[Hebrew page 134]

I slowly recovered and when I heard that Jews were seen in the city, I got up immediately, and ran quickly, I literally flew, to see their faces, to speak to them in our language, to once again be together with Jews, and to merge with them and never separate from them again.

Since then, there and also here, I live among my people. And I have a prayer in my heart that I will live here until my last day.

[Pages 362-368 - Yiddish] [Page 135-141 - Hebrew]

Chitkov Village—Its Life and Its Death

by A.G. Kupferstein

Translated by Moses Milstein

A. G. Kupferstein – Israeli policeman

Chitkov[1] village lies about four km west of Krasnobrod. Jewish settlement in Chitkov dates from the 19th century. Although the settlement was small in numbers, it still managed to live a full Jewish life interwoven with the Jewish community of Krasnobrod in all its traditions and customs.

Its spiritual nourishment came from Krasnobrod. It always saw itself as an equal member of the Krasnobrod family. It turned there for help with Jewish problems and dilemmas. The Krasnobrod *rav* was our spiritual shepherd too, and answered our questions. For all lesser questions we turned to our resident, the humble and gentle, R' David Wexler, *z"l*—a perfect example of the character of a by-gone generation.

Almost all the Chitkov Jews stemmed from the family of R' Gershon Rendler, *z"l*, who was among the first Jews who settled in Chitkov, and did forced labor for the prince during the feudal period.

The principle form of livelihood was farming and sometimes also the trades and commerce. Peretz Rendler, the oldest son of Gershon Chitkover, was a potter and made clay pots. R' David Wexler had a general store selling everything from candies to textiles, to leather, and grease for wheels. He seemed to prosper. R' Yosef Holz, Gershon Chitkover's son-in-law, was a rich timber merchant and partners with his brother-in-law, R' Moshe-Yakov Rendler, a son of Gershon Chitkover.

R' David Wexler held a *minyan* in his house Shabbat and holidays. People from the surrounding villages would come there to *daven*.

Soon after Word War I, our settlement began to suffer from bandit attacks. During one such attack, Baruch Wexler, the son of David Wexler, *z"l*, was murdered. When Polish antisemitism began to show its bloody Nazi face, the Jews of Chitkov moved to Krasnobrod. Only R' Peretz Rendler and his family stayed, enduring great need.

At the outbreak of World War II, there were a few Jewish families living once more in Chitkov. They were: Peretz Rendler, my father Noah Kupferstein, Yakov Rendler, Eliezer Shtemer—the son-in-law of R' Moshe-Yakov Rendler—and their families.

When the Germans occupied our region, our situation was terribly difficult. Making our situation even worse was the cold of the first winter. On the 7th day of Adar, R' Peretz Rendler, *z"l*, died of hunger and cold, and was buried in the Krasnobrod cemetery.

In 1940, the Nazis carried out a census of all Jews. Our village belonged to Krasnobrod administratively, and we went there to be registered. No one knew why they were doing this. All kinds of rumours and theories were spread, one more fantastic than the next, but no clear premonition of their satanic plans did we have.

After some time passed, the Germans began to catch Krasnobrod Jews and send them for forced labor to Belzec on the Soviet border. Many Jews fled to Chitkov to escape the raids and hid with the local Jews.

The Germans endlessly decreed prohibitions. They stole freedom from the Jews bit by bit. They leveed huge monetary fines on the Krasnobrod Jews, and sucked out the last of the possessions still in Jewish hands. The situation in Chitkov was no better than in the shtetl. The Germans used to come to our village and beat us mercilessly. During one such "search", Yakov Rendler, a son of Petetz Rendler, was beaten bloody. On the 14th of Nisan, 1942, he died of his wounds and was buried in the Krasnobrod cemetery.

Shavuot, 1942, the Germans surrounded the shtetl and demanded a certain number of men from the *Judenrat*. Their devilish plan was clear, and the *Judenrat* refused to carry out the order. Yosef Goldstein, a member of the *Judenrat*, went to the Gestapo and declared that they could have him, but he would not give them a single one of his Jewish brothers. His brave response infuriated the Gestapo. Like savage beasts they fell on him and murdered him and others of the *Judenrat*.

This was a signal for the bloody slaughter of the Jewish community of Krasnobrod. They murdered without mercy anyone they captured. Only a few Jews managed to escape to the forests. Broken, like twigs in a storm, they returned to the shtetl after the pogrom where they waited in great fear for the end of the bloody play.

Freedom of movement of Jews was forbidden. Leaving the shtetl without permission was punished by being shot on the spot. There was no food available and people were dying of hunger. Even worse off were the Jews who were sent here from the west of Poland. Urged on by hunger, we would sneak out to the villages to look for a morsel of food. The Polish police sniffed around like bloodhounds in the area, and every captured Jew was instantly killed. These Polish murderers were true servants to Hitler and his plans for the extermination of Jews.

In August, 1942, the Germans set fire to the remaining Jewish houses and burned all the inhabitants alive. The Jews still alive were imprisoned in the barracks of Moshe-Leibs building. The only ones left in Chitkov were just our family, Eliezer Shtimmer and his family, and Raizl Rendler. In the neighboring village of Suchowola lived the following families: Berl Wexler and his family; Shmuel Wexler and his mother, Gitl; Yakov Malash and family; his sister, Mirl and her family; Itche Ber and family; Pinchas Krelman and his family. A few Krasnobrod Jews were hiding in the Chitkov forests. Among them were: Mordechai Kopel, Yosele Suchowoler's son, with his family and his sister-in-law. In October, 1942, they were captured by Chitkov farmers and taken to the police in Potochek, where they were all shot. Mordechai escaped and fled. A Chitkov *shaygetz* pursued him and hit him in the head with an axe, killing him on the spot. The next day, a farmer found Mordechai's three year old child wandering around. How the child got there is unknown. Ephraim Kopel and his son, Yosef, were hiding in the colony near Chitkov. In May, 1943, Ephraim was hiding in an attic in the colony. The farmer who was hiding him betrayed him to the Germans. He was tied to a wagon and forced to run with it while enduring blows all the way to Krasnobrod. There he was tortured and finally shot. Two months later, the Chitkov farmers caught Yosef and killed him with an axe. The Chitkov farmers also captured a whole bunch of other Jews and took them to Potochek where they were shot. Among the captured: Itche Ber's daughters, Feige and Chava; Israel Radashtcher 's son-in-law with his seven-year-old son, and Bertshe Gurtler and his family.

One day, Berl Wexler received news that the Germans and the Polish police were preparing to kill all the Jews in both villages. We immediately ran to the forests to hide. When the murderers arrived, in their anger, they destroyed everything we had. They gave to the farmers everything that had value to them. And what does not have value to a peasant? Before leaving, the Germans left an order with the village magistrate that we had to report to Krasnobrod. My family was taken to the barracks. Eliezer Shtemer was imprisoned in the bathhouse, and Chana-Raizel went to her daughter.

Life in the barracks was horribly filthy and cramped. People were swollen from starvation. Fear of tomorrow was unrelenting and threw people into despair. We endured this for two months, up to the final slaughter, the fifteenth day of Cheshvan, 5702[2].

At dawn, the Germans surrounded the shtetl, especially the barracks where the Jews lived. They took everyone to a building under construction. Then the Germans began to shoot into the densely packed mass of people, and threw grenades in through the windows. Who can describe in words the horror of the slaughter? The worst descriptions of hell pale next to the hell the Germans conceived for us. The terrible cries of the wounded were stifled under the bodies of the dead. The murder of infants took place amidst the murder of their mothers, and their blood sprayed on the walls of their "grave." The fingers of the dying clutched convulsively at the throats of the living and strangled them. The groans and the wailing mixed in with the sadistic barking of the two-legged German dogs. The few left alive were taken to Izbica where they were killed.

On that day, my parents, my father Noah, my mother, Dina, and my sister, Chaya, were killed, may God avenge their blood. The Chitkovers who were outside the barracks managed to flee to the forests. Among them were: Chana-Raizel and her daughter, Gitl, and son-in-law, Yosef Edelstein; Yakov and his sister, Miriam Malash; Berl and Shmuel Wexler and their mother, Gitl; Itche-Ber and his family, and my sister, Esther, and I. We hid along with other Jews in a canal not far from Chitkov. During the day, we went out to the villages to look for food, and at night, we lay on the wet and icy earth, shivering from fear and cold. It went on like this for a whole week, until the farmers found us and reported us to the Germans. When the murderers arrived, most of the men saved themselves by running. The captured Jews, mostly women and children, were forced to lie face down on the ground and were killed by a shot to the neck.

Children were killed by smashing in their heads with rifle butts. Killed in this way were: Chana-Raizel and her daughter, Gitl, and her children; Miriam, Ephraim's wife, and her children, and other Jews from Krasnobrod. Murdered in the Sochowol forest were Berl Wexler and his family; Shmuel Wexler and his mother, Gitl, and Itche-Ber and his family.

Alone and starving, my sister, Miriam, and I, dragged ourselves through the forest looking for other hidden Jews. After two weeks in the forest, we met, roasting potatoes at a fire, Yakov Malash and his family, and his sister, Miriam with her family.

The first snows began to fall and the cold tortured us mercilessly. We spent the days in the forest, and at night, we slept at various farmers, for which they were well paid. This dragged on for about a month, until our money ran out. Then the farmers decided to get rid of the Jews. One night they caught everyone, tied them up with ropes, and took them to Krasnobrod. There, they were all shot.

My sister and I hid in Chitkov. The winter and its cold and snow severely weakened us. We would sleep at a different place every night, and took great care not to be captured by the Germans, who were lurking around the villages. It went on like this until they began to settle Germans in the Polish villages. The whole region became filled with Germans. Just one village in the Zamosc area, Feliksowka, remained purely Polish. It was there that I went, and found a good-hearted farmer. He hid me with him until the Red Army arrived. My sister, Miriam, also survived in this neighborhood, and lived to see the day of our liberation.

Translator's notes:

    1.   Possibly today's village of Hutki
    2.   Nov. 5, 1941

————————

[Pages 369-381]

On the Aryan Side

by Malka Babad
(A granddaughter of Itzhak Babad)

Translated by Moses Milstein

The tribulations of Polish Jewry began immediately with the beginning of the war in September 1939. I was living with my parents, my husband, my brother, with near and far relations, in a large extended family that is no more.

Only my six–month–old child and I escaped from the bloody flood.

The arrival of the Germans in our town filled us with great fear. They began with forcing people into labor, searching for merchandise in Jewish homes, beating and shooting for any little thing.

I witnessed a scene in the street that congealed the blood in my veins. I thought then that that was the worst that we could expect from the cursed Germans. I couldn't imagine that this was only an introduction, a prelude to their bloody deeds and monstrous outrages. A young man passed an SS man on the street. The German turned around and called the boy back, and proceeded to slap him. The boy stood there with his hands at his side, and did not react. Then the SS man slapped his hat off, ordered him to pick it up, then to put it back on, and salute him. The story made its way with lightening speed among the frightened Jews. It was concluded that you had to doff your hat when meeting a German. However, they were beaten anyway by another SS who shouted, "What, are you my comrade that you dare to greet me?"

The Poles were happy. Hitler, they said, should have come here long ago. We saw that it was not for nothing that Hitler chose Poland to exterminate us. He found fertile soil here, and loyal assistants.

In 1940 we were segregated in a ghetto, where we suffered a lot. The men were taken for unbearable forced labor. They were beaten with rubber batons. They were not given any food, just water. When I tried to give them some bread along with the water, I met with hard blows from a rubber baton.

It was a bitter and hard enough existence for us up to the German attack on Russia, on June 22, 1941, but it became harder and more horrid still when the Germans perceived that things were not going as well as Hitler had believed they would…They took out their anger on us.

In November, 1941, a decree was issued forbidding the wearing of furs, and even fur collars. The judenrat ordered all the furs to be brought to them. A rush ensued of people bringing in their furs. That very same day, the Germans shot two women and a man for wearing coats with fur collars.

The fear was indescribable.

The darkest and most horrible year was 1942 when the *aktions* began, and the Germans transported our nearest and dearest to Beljec in sealed, overcrowded train cars that were "disinfected" with lime and chlorine, where they would be gassed and incinerated. You cannot imagine what the town looked like on the day of the *aktion*. There could be no talk of defiance. We were held in a vice–like trap, designed to sate the bloodthirstiness of the murderers, and vent their sadistic desires. At that time, I was hidden by a Christian woman, a doctor. There were others there, but because I was always afraid that my child's crying would give us away, I was always alone, separate. In this way, my Berele and I made it out alive from all these *aktions*.

On the 18th of October 1942, the Germans drove us, under the barrels of their machineguns, on foot, to Izbica. They told us that it was going to be a Jewish city. In Izbica, we met Jews who had been expelled from Lublin and Zamosc. But the Germans did not set up a Jewish city or a ghetto.

Monday, October 22nd, the shtetl and the nearby neighborhoods were surrounded by camps of Germans, Volksdeutsche, Ukrainians, Lithuanians, Estonians, and Poles as if for a decisive battle between hostile armies…

Panic spread among the few surviving Jews. They didn't know what to do. The first thought was to find a hiding place. My parents hid themselves in the attic with the others in the house we were at. My child and I–he was now three years old–had to go find another hiding place. I went out and stole into an abandoned house from which the people had already been taken. Around 4:00 pm I heard Yiddish being spoken outside the door. I opened the door and saw people among whom was the owner of the house. He told us that the Germans had loaded the Jews into railroad cars. They released several men. Those who didn't want to leave their wives and children were either shot, or forced into the railroad cars. I wanted to go see my parents, but they were not there. A woman who had hidden under a bed told me that the murderers had forced everyone out of the attic and taken them away.

I was now alone and continued to live with the others who had hidden from the *aktion*.

About two weeks later, November 3rd, there was again a panic. At 5:00 am, shooting began. It was Monday, an awful Monday. The people I was hiding with removed three wooden slats from the ceiling, and we climbed up into the attic. Then we fitted the slats back in place. We were without food or water for three days. On the third day, at around five o'clock, the Poles discovered us and forced us out. They took us to the movie theater plaza in Izbica. There the remainder of the Lublin Jews were assembled waiting for the railroad cars. Around 11 o'clock, unobserved by anybody, I took my child and fled from there. I crept on all fours up to an abandoned Jewish house and spent the night there.

In the morning, I left the hiding place and went on with my child. I saw the Germans and their helpers, running around like poisoned rats, with axes in their hands. I quickly snuck into another lane and found a house. I entered and found a Polish woman alone there. I told her I had fled and asked for food for my child. She gave him some bread and milk and allowed me to wash and comb my hair. Then I begged her to allow me to stay the night. She agreed on condition I give her 1000 Zlotys. She led us into a field. It was raining, so she covered us with a blanket. We stayed like that until 6:00 pm. I gave her the thousand Zlotys and she led us to the train, bought tickets, and took us up to Zavoda. I travelled to Zamosc, because my husband, *A"H*, was in a camp there.

At 9:00 o'clock at night, unobserved by the guards, I stole into the camp. In the camp, there were also my father's brother, Chaim Babad, *A"H*, and other acquaintances. They hid me in a closet where I remained for five days with my child. We could not stay there longer. Every day, the Germans shot people who stole into the camp. My husband made an agreement with a Christian he knew to take us to his house. I was there for two weeks. Then I went to a second place, then a third...until the Jews in the camp were taken to Majdanek.

I decided to go to Warsaw. I went there without documents, without knowing anyone, filled with fear, and yet with great faith. In spite of all the hardships, the will to live was very great. Not for life itself, but in order to live to see Hitler's downfall, something in which I strongly believed.

On December 20th, 1942, at six in the morning, I went to the train station dressed as a village Christian. We arrived in Warsaw at 2:00 am at the Eastern terminus. All the passengers had to wait at the station until 5:00 o'clock. When the tramways began to run, they all went their way, and the station emptied out...only my child and I had nowhere to go. We spent the whole day at the station. It was becoming increasingly dangerous for me. Around 5:00 pm, a Pole and a woman approached. They looked us up and down. Terror ran through me. I took the child and went outside. They both followed me. The Pole asked me where I was from, and whether there wasn't a ghetto there...He said I was Jewish and demanded to see my documents...I told him that I had documents, but I would not show them to him as he had no right to see them. So he turned to my son and asked him his name. My Berele answered him: Bolaslav Adamczik. And what is your mother's name? Helena Adamczik, he answered. And your father?–Zygmunt Adamczik...Where is your father? he inquired further. My father, Zygmunt Adamczik is a prisoner in Germany. I taught my Berele all this in our last hiding place and warned him to remember all these *goyishe* names that I had made up. Before, he had never wanted to repeat all these foreign names, but now, a miracle happened. He answered all the questions accurately, without hesitation. The Pole, the extortionist, began to laugh: "Your mother managed to teach you all this in such a short time?..." And he and the woman left. I figured they were going to go to the Gestapo or to other Polish extortionists. I went back into the station, took my bag and quickly went back out again. Fortunately, a *droshky* pulled up and we got in and I told him to go to Chmielna 1. I had no idea who lived there...But we went...When we got there, I stood outside the house, not knowing what to do with myself. And again a miracle happened. While I was standing by the gate, on the other side of the street, I saw a Christian couple from my town. They had been living in Warsaw since 1941. I immediately ran over to them. They did not recognize me. I told them who I was, and they took me into their house. The lucky coincidence was that they lived nearby on this very street. They immediately began to try to figure out how to get documents for me. They asked me if I had any money because it would cost 10,000 Zlotys. I gave them the money. They brought me a questionnaire where I gave the name that I had crowned myself with: Adamczik, as well as the names of my parents, and where I was from. I swore that my family was pure Aryan, and that there was no Jewish blood in my family. The papers along with three photographs were submitted to the German bureau at Three Crosses Square. [1] I had to come in person to collect the ID card.

Malke's Aryan ID card

I went to pick up the ID card on January 18, 1943. They fingerprinted me, and had me sign. I received my ID card, and left the place with my heart racing, looking around to see if anyone was spying on me. I had the card and my life was now dependent on it. I came back to my child.

During the time we spent in Warsaw, my son forgot his past. He only remembered what I told him and taught him. This was also fortunate.

On January 20, 1943, my rescuers found me a small room with an old Christian woman in Marymont. With that, their friendship ended. I never saw them again. They were understandably afraid that if I were captured, they might be implicated. Thus, I was alone with my small son in the big city, in danger at every step of the way.

Now my bitter wandering began on the Aryan side.

I left the house every day punctually at eight o'clock, saying that I worked for a baker in Prage. At 6:00 pm I returned, made something to eat and went to sleep, so I would not have to talk with the landlady. A month passed like this.

The old lady discovered that my Berele was Jewish, so we left for another place, where there was a woman with no husband and three children. I also told them that I was working, and every morning I left the house and wandered aimlessly around the streets of Warsaw. I visited the ghetto often. The large Warsaw ghetto had already been liquidated, and the remaining Jews in the small ghetto were driven in columns every day to forced labor renovating the destroyed houses in the large ghetto. The Polish street hawkers followed the Jews on the way to work in order to get bargains from them, clothing, jewelry. With my child by my side, I also followed along. I longed to see a Jewish face, to speak a Yiddish word, so I surreptitiously spoke to them. I bemoaned my problems, and wept. I did not notice that the son of my second landlady had overheard me speaking Yiddish and crying. Because of my carelessness, I had to leave my second accommodation. I was afraid that I would get into trouble, so that same day, I rented another room with an old janitor woman.

I was in Warsaw for six months, and lived in six different places. Everywhere they found out my son was Jewish. Our saving grace was that the poles had no power over us…

The uprising in the ghetto began in April, 1943. The Germans suffered big losses at the beginning. Soon though, using incendiary bombs, they conquered the ghetto. Terrible fires broke out which I could see from Marymont. Terrible was the scene and more terrible was what the Poles reported–that the Jews were burned alive. Men and women were throwing themselves off balconies. I forgot about my own troubles. I wanted to get away as soon as possible.

On May 15th, I left Warsaw with twenty Zlotys in my pocket. In the preceding six months, I had used up all my money. I arrived at the train station just as a train was leaving for Naleczow. The region was in a particularly anti–Semitic mood. The Poles constantly harangued against the Jews. This was their favorite topic. "Hitler really gave it to the Jews." The goyim would receive 500 Zlotys or 50 kg of sugar per Jewish head. Like bloodhounds, the Poles would chase Jews and turn them in. I was terrified and I got off the train shaken. I began wandering again with my Berele by my side. I travelled through *shtetlach* and villages. We spent the day in one place, and the night in another. During the day we wandered in the fields and forests. At night, I would approach a small village house and beg to spend the night. Thanks to my ID card, I could go among the Poles and spend the night with them. I endured a long journey. I travelled through the Janow and Pilawa regions, and the villages surrounding Krasnik and Lublin. Everywhere I went I encountered anti–Semites who rejoiced in the downfall of the Jews. I would listen to their words with trepidation and fear. I fought hard with myself not to cry out or weep. I went from house to house. I sewed, knitted, spun thread. Once I had learned village work, it became easier for me. Christians from Warsaw and Lublin came to the villages to trade or look for work. I also passed myself off as a Christian looking for work. I did not stay at one place longer than eight days. I could not bear hearing the poisonous hatred of the Poles. In the villages, Berele was not recognized as a Jew. He could speak Polish well, and knew the Polish prayers.

It is noteworthy that in all my wandering, I was not stopped by a single German. The Poles, on the other hand, frequently stopped me and demanded my documents. They were hunting Jews.

Once, in the winter of 1944, as we were wandering hungry, exhausted from cold and fear, a young Pole stopped me and asked me where I was going. I mentioned a village I was familiar with. So he said, "It's such a long way and you don't seem to be hurrying much." He demanded my documents. Being afraid he would steal my documents, I declined to obey him. He called over another Pole, and they both took me to another village. At the edge of the forest stood a peasant hut. They led me in there. I later realized that this was a gathering place for the A.K. (Armia Krajowa) partisans. They demanded to see my papers. I handed my ID card to the commandant, who looked it over carefully. He gave it back to me, squeezing my hand, and said, "Have no fear, you are a Polish woman. Go where you need to go."

I couldn't believe the great miracle. It is impossible to describe…I had been in the jaws of the wolf, and my child too, and we got away alive. As I left the village, I begged God to give me strength to live to survive these bitter times, and for me and my child to live to see Hitler's downfall.

The winter of 1944 was terrible for me. But with the arrival of spring, new winds began to blow around the world. A flicker of hope began to grow in me, and my heart told me that salvation was not far off. In May, I came to a village near Lublin called Niedrzwica. I went to see an old rich landlord to ask about work. I said I had come from Warsaw. He was, fortunately, looking for a worker. I immediately went to work in the garden. They were very happy with me, and the family was very fond of my Bolosz, as I called him. I was able to relax a little. Fear gradually left me. I began to feel a little freer. After two weeks had passed there, the landlady heard me speaking in Yiddish in my sleep…I had seen my parents, *A"H*, in a dream. They had accompanied me all along my wandering in my dreams. When she told me that she had heard me calling out in my sleep, "Mamenyu, tatenyu," I admitted I was Jewish. I thanked her for everything, and prepared to leave her house. But she told me that I could stay in her house, because no one in her house or in the village knew about my origins. I stayed with her for three months, until liberation, on the 17th of July, 1944, when the Red Army entered the village.

My heart was liberated when I saw the Russians driving masses of Germans along and confiscating their vehicles and weapons. I immediately began to look for Jews. I heard that several hidden Jews had survived in Zolkiewka, and I went over there on foot. From there I left for Zamosc.

In Zamosc, there was a house on Peretz Street where Jews who had returned from their hiding places and from the forests had gathered. Jews from Krasnobrod, Zamosc, Izbica, and Komorow. Altogether about 20 people. My Berele was the only Jewish child in the whole area.

The Poles behaved very badly toward the surviving Jews. When they encountered a Jew, they said, "You're still alive?" They threw rocks and grenades at the house and threatened us with death if we did not leave. They proclaimed that "those who Hitler had not managed to kill, we will finish off. Hitler had written that the Jews would celebrate no Purims, and we will fulfill his prophecy." And they carried out their threats. Whoever travelled to Komorow or to a nearby village did not return.

I felt that we could not stay here any longer in the poisonous Polish air, where every step we took was on soil stained with Jewish blood. In my difficult wanderings, I had dreamt of my child and I coming to Eretz Israel. Now, after the liberation, I was intent on making my dream a reality. It was, as yet, impossible to go there. The war had not yet ended.

Peace arrived on May 8th, 1945. Jews, sick, bloated, physically and spiritually broken, were liberated form the concentration camps, and from their hiding places,. A mad flight to Germany began, in the hope that from there they could go to Eretz Israel.

I travelled to Germany and ended up in a DP camp. The Joint wanted to send my child to America. But I would not give my consent. As I said, I was determined to go to our holy land with my child.

It is painful for me to relive the memories of the nightmarish Hitler years, to remember the agonizing road I had travelled with my child. My consolation and encouragement are in finding my dream a reality. We are in our own land. My son, who is now sixteen years old, knows and understands that this is his homeland where he will live and contribute as a proud and free Jew.

Translator's note:
    1.   Square in the central district of Warsaw

[Pages 382-394 - Yiddish] [Page 142-150 - Hebrew]

The Decline and Fall of Krasnobrod

by Esther Levinson-Lerner (Kfar Ata)

Translated by Moses Milstein

Esther Levinson-Lerner

I will forever remember the day of September 1, 1939, the day the Nazis attacked Poland, and the storm broke out that wiped out the Jewish community in Poland, and with it, my shtetl, Krasnobrod.

Krasnobrod was a small shtetl. It was hard to find on a map of Poland. Why did all this have to happen to it?

Even though Krasnobrod was home to only a few hundred Jewish families, it bubbled with life. It had organizations of various parties—mostly Zionist—philanthropic institutions, and so on. Everything was vibrant and full of life.

On December 14th, as the battles drew nearer, the shtetl started burning, and the deaths began. People were unable to save themselves, because of the danger from bullets coming, without cease, from the front. Among those burned to death in the fire were: Shmuel-Ozer Kupiec, Leibish Kramer, Moishe Fuchs, Shmelke, and others. The Germans entered the city. And thus began the chain of sorrow and persecution, which did not slacken while a Jew still breathed.

As soon as they entered the shtetl, they began to rampage and loot. The local Christian population joined in enthusiastically. They stole whatever came to hand. They burned *sefer torahs*, and prayer books. People were captured "for work," and in the meantime their beards were cut off for sport. Those captured were forced to do hard labor, without food or drink. An edict quickly came out that Jews were prohibited from living with *goyim*. The Poles were forewarned to make sure that we fulfilled the orders, and to help stifle the Jewish population.

One day, in the month of December of the same year, a group of Nazis appeared at Berl Shok's house and demanded that a Judenrat be established. Berl Shok got together a few prominent Jews and they made a list of candidates. The Germans took down the names and left. In February, an edict was issued that all Jews from 10 years of age, must wear an armband with a yellow Star of David on a white background, 15 cm wide. Judenrat members had to wear an armband, 20 cm wide, with a Blue star, and the word, "Judenrat."

We felt terribly humiliated when we had to put on the armband, but we got used to it. Women tried to hide it under their kerchiefs. The Poles and the *shkootsim* ran after us calling us "*verfluchte Juden*," their taunts pricking us like needles.

We had to wear the armband day and night. Whoever was found without the armband, even in his own yard, was threatened with death. If you were lucky, you were just beaten murderously. To all that was added the hell of "*revisyes*." The Gestapo from the district were frequent guests in the shtetl. With the help of the local *goyim,* who knew everybody, and knew how to "find" things, they would break into Jewish homes, turn everything upside down and search… What were they looking for? They were looking to heap troubles on our heads, to beat up everyone in their sight, to laugh and to mock us, to bathe in our blood.

At our house, we used to have at least two such "*revisyes*" a week. During one *revisye* they started on my father: Where had he hidden his merchandise? My father tried to explain that he had nothing hidden. Some of the merchandise had been burned, and the rest was stolen. A German shouted out, "Who are the robbers? The poor populace just took back what was theirs. You are the robbers who robbed them year after year!"

After this, the contributions began in fantastic sums and short terms. The slightest late payment threatened death. People would have given the shirt off their backs to save their lives. But even this did not help.

On *Tisha B'Av* night, the shtetl was surrounded by the murderers, and the hunt for Jews began. People began frantically running around. Germans broke into our house and ordered my father to get dressed. While he was doing this, they asked him where he had hidden the Jews. My father pleaded with them and swore that he had hidden no one. They began to beat him and kick him. Finally, they took him away. Together with thousands of others he was taken to Beljec, where they were beginning to build the crematoria. Every morning they would round up Jews and take them away for work. They forced them to sing the whole way. From time to time they were ordered to run long distances or to throw themselves on the ground. Whoever could not keep up, or who passed out, was shot on the spot.

It wasn't until *Rosh Hashana* that we were able to rescue our father from this prison labor. We ransomed him for a large sum of money and brought him home. We could hardly recognize him.

Around winter an edict came out ordering Jews to surrender all furs: fur coats, collars, and hats. But only those who had been reported by the Poles gave them up. Whoever was not frightened would have been better off burning them and thinking: "Maybe we'll have the honor to live to see those to whom this was to go, burning as well."

In February, the Zamosc Judenrat sent a couple of hundred families that had been expelled from those areas that had gone to the Third Reich. It was forbidden for Jews to live there. They arrived sick and broken, half dead. When they looked around and saw how small the place was and how impoverished the local population was, they understood that this was no place for them. They appealed to the Judenrat to help them get back to Zamosc.

In the morning, three Germans from Zamosc showed up unexpectedly at the Judenrat, and without a word, beat up everyone there. The "oldest" received 75 lashes. My father, Hirsch Shoch, and Berl Shok received 50. Then they went out to the street and attacked anyone they saw. They finished this little bit of work—and they left. My father came home black and blue from the beating, and lay in bed with compresses for several days. But that was not all. A few days later, they sent us twice the number of refugees. The close confinement in Krasnobrod was unbearable.

The *Aktion*

The first *aktion* took place on *Shavuot*. At dawn, vehicles carrying Germans arrived and surrounded the shtetl. On the agreed-upon signal, they began to shoot and murder whomever they came across. Panic ensued. People began running to the forest. Those who succeeded in escaping or in hiding, waited—for the next *aktion*…Those who didn't were either shot, or dragged off to the Beljec crematoria.

The second *aktion* took place in July. It did not come off as well planned as the previous one. On the way in, the lieutenant saw a Jew and tried to shoot him. Luckily, his rifle jammed and the Jew escaped. The lieutenant became enraged, fixed his rifle, and not waiting for the agreed-upon signal, started shooting into the houses and throwing in incendiary bombs. Whoever ran out was shot on the spot. The houses began to burn with the people in them. Among the dead, Baruch-Eliyahu Broder and his entire family, Chaim Faker and his family, Nathan Lipsz and his family, and Itche Fuks and his family. Later, we endured several smaller *aktion* until, on October 26th, Krasnobrod became "*Judenrein.*"

Baruch-Eliyahu Broder and his family

We were the living dead. No one knew what tomorrow would bring. The "quiet" days were just a brief pause before the death that would certainly come, a day early or a day late. The Poles, our "neighbors," poured salt in our wounds. They would go around to the houses and offer to buy this or that. In that way, they gave us to understand that

"You don't really need all this anymore. Sooner or later, you're all going to be killed. Why wouldn't you want to sell it? If I come back with the Germans, I'll get it cheaper anyway."

I will forever remember the last Shabbos with my father at home. A *minyan* of Jews came to us to celebrate *Kabbalat Shabbat*. A *minyan* of broken Jews with the fear of death in their eyes, and with deep despair in their hearts. Father put on his *tallit*, and stood before the assembled. When he began to chant *Lechu Neranena*, he broke down weeping, and so did the whole group of Jews. And the next morning, at *Shachrit*, everyone was crying. The walls wept too for the destruction and misfortunes that befell us only because we were Jewish.

Itzchak Fuchs and his family

After Shabbos, my mother snuck out of the shtetl with my youngest sister, Shoshe, who was five. They left for Hitek, a nearby village. Me and my older sister stayed home with our father. We knew that the last *aktion* would come in the next few days. We spent sleepless nights waiting for the killers who could, at any moment, come and take us to our death.

After one such sleepless night, father said, "Listen, my children. Why do you sit here and wait for death? You are young. Leave, like others have done. Maybe you will live and be witness for what they have done to us here. Who knows? Maybe you will have the honor of taking revenge on the spilling of our innocent blood! I can't go with you. I am not strong enough. Besides, maybe we can buy ourselves out of these murderers' hands. I must stay with those who are still here. I can't forsake them." He rushed over to us and began kissing us and crying. Our farewells could have moved a stone. And so, we parted, forever.

On that very Sunday, at dawn, the last *aktion* began. The Germans went house-to-house, peering into every nook-and-cranny, from the cellar to the attic. The captured were sent to the *Umschlagplatz*. At the slightest sign of resistance, you were shot on the spot.

They carried out this bloody work with German precision and thoroughness. The Poles nearly jumped out of their skin in their eagerness to expose the hidden. For one hidden Jew, they were paid a kilo of sugar, or naphtha, and even got the shoes after the Jew was shot. My father had been hiding with about ten other Jews. The Poles found them, and turned them over to the Germans. They were all shot. Five days later, my mother was handed over to the Germans. They took her to Krasnobrod and shot her.

My older sister, Chana, and I, and a few others, succeeded in getting to the forest. We lay in hiding during the day, and at night, we went out to the nearby villages to find food. In this way, it became known that there were Jews hiding in the forest. Such an "injustice," the Poles couldn't stand. Within a few days, they encircled the forest and began shooting from all directions. My sister, Chana, was felled by a bullet. A wild stampede began, accompanied by the wild screams of the bandits, the agonized cries of the wounded, the wailing of the women, and the cries of the children. I began to run not knowing where I was going. When I came to myself, I found myself near a road not far from a village. Devora Goldstein was with me. We quickly saw that this place was dangerous for us, and we went back into the forest.

Restless days

We stayed hiding in the forest for three days. In the bushes, wandering lost, we came on Devorah's mother, Rachel Goldstein. Later, they were both killed when they tried to leave the forest to go to their place to dig out some of their valuables. They were taken to Krasnobrod and shot.

I went deeper into the forest in the hope of finding a survivor. After a day of stumbling around, I came on a group of Jews. A sad picture. These Jews had lost their human appearance. They were like wild, frightened animals. They were sitting around a fire where potatoes were roasting. Among them were Israel Dichterman and Tsipe Krelman and their families. Despite the biting cold, they had no proper clothing or shoes. Stricken by hunger and cold, with no will to live, but full of fear of dying, they wandered lost in the forest, aimlessly, without a spark of faith in mankind. The "man" they were likely to meet was a German, a killer. Or a Pole who had sold his conscience to the German for a kilo of sugar. Your years-old Polish neighbor now saw in you a kilo of sugar—and nothing else.

I was still, it seems, a little naïve, but I didn't have many options. I went to the Stempinskis, who lived not far away. They actually received me very well. So well, that I was at first ready to believe them, in spite of everything I had lived through. But as time went by, I learned that they thought I had saved valuables from home. Their "love," and their "loyalty" lasted only as long as they believed I had something of value. Meanwhile, Mrs. Stempiniski used to give me "suitable literature" to read, as, for example, a Dmowski novel, or his writings. Or, holy scripture where the torture and death of Jesus was described in detail, where he cursed the Jews, "My holy blood will fall on your heads." I often heard the Stempinskis telling each other that, "In any case, the Jews will disappear like smoke."

I was sitting in the attic, but it couldn't be said that my "protectors" cared about what they said in front of me. They had long ago made their plans. In this way, I learned that Motl Dichterman was caught and murdered in March.

On April 11, Stempiniski came up to the attic and told me to go with him. Motl Dichterman wanted to see me…I quickly understood what he meant. But I thought, maybe he mixed things up and someone else sent him to me. The yearning to see another Jew was so strong, that I allowed myself to go with him. But as we left the yard and he started heading for the forest, I took off running. But I went back to Stempinski's property by another route, and hid in the cellar. The only one who knew was the farmhand. He secretly threw in a few dried potatoes. I was there for two weeks. But, I became afraid of the *shegets*, and a better place came my way.

I fled to Belfant, to the Jaszenows. Mrs. Jaszenow received me very warmly and hid me in the loft over the stable. I was weak and exhausted and I crawled into the hay and quickly fell asleep. In my dreams I saw my mother, and my father, and my grandmother, Leah. They approach me, look at me with pity—and grandmother says, "Do not be afraid, my child. We will fight for you to survive the war." At that moment, I heard Mrs. Jaszenow calling the chickens. I woke up. I felt a ray of hope open in me.

I stayed at the Jaszenows for sixteen months, until July 22, 1944 when the Red Army arrived. I began to breath more freely. I stayed there for another two weeks. The danger for Jews was not lessened. New victims fell every day among those who had come out from their hiding places. The Poles couldn't reconcile the fact that their efforts to help Hitler wipe out the Jews had not completely succeeded. They continued to murder Jews whenever they had the chance.

But more than two weeks, I could not wait. The sword that was hanging over us had been shattered. So I began to think…to do a little personal appraisal. I wept for my lost family, for my father, mother, my sisters, who died as martyrs and did not live to see the victory over our tormentors. I wept for being alone, without a relative, without a protector. I felt a yearning to see a Jewish face, to hear a Jewish word, to weep and mourn together with Jews for the great tragedy that had befallen us all.

I parted from the Jaszenows with tears in my eyes. Mrs. Jaszenow's eyes were wet too. "Keep God in your heart," she begged. "Don't, God forbid, tell anyone that I helped you. They will kill me!" But I still believed then that, when the happy day of liberation comes, we would be able to testify before the whole world about these unique, precious people, these *Chasidei Omot Haolam*, who put their own lives in danger in order to save others. Their goodness and conscience shone like lonely flickers in the dense darkness, in a sea of racism and bloodshed. The Poles continued to try to fulfill the mass murderer, Hitler's, bloody work. On the threshold of liberation, Hersh Leibel Briks, and his entire family were killed by Polish partisans under the leadership of his close friend, Barbecki.

I left the Jaszenows and headed for Krasnobrod. I wanted to see my hometown one more time, the streets and squares, the house I grew up in and left in such tragic circumstances.

Arriving in town, and seeing the devastation, I felt an overwhelming sadness gripping my heart. I was blinded by tears. Every rock glared like a tombstone on an unknown grave from which the innocent spilled blood shouted to heaven. Every street echoed in my heart with the sounds of that life, a life that was extinguished with not a trace remaining. There was actually life on the streets, but a foreign life. *Goyim*, local and from elsewhere, who had forgotten, or who even did not know that Jews had lived here, were living in Jewish houses. A Christian was living in my father's house. He stared with astonishment at this unknown "*Zhidovke*" who had come onto "his" property. Near the park, papers were blowing around, holy pages. The wind blew a page to me, and I saw the title page of a *Gemara*. In an upper corner I recognized my father's handwriting.

I went to the cemetery. No trace of the holy place remained. The whole area was planted with potatoes. The surrounding farmers used the tombstones to pave their pathways and gardens.

And as the place of my birth drew me back before, now it was pushing me away. I felt I had to get far, very far, away from this place. I had to leave for a new country, find a new life where I would not be persecuted by the memories of my tragic experiences under Hitler's rule.

I swore to myself that I would never forget the near and dear ones who perished along with the six million other Jews.

[Pages 395-402 - Yiddish] [Page 162-167 - Hebrew]

In Hell

by Miriam Kopel-Blumental (Ber Yakov)

Translated by Moses Milstein

Miriam Kopel-Blumenthal

At first, when war broke out in 1939, the town remained relatively quiet. There were alarming stories from here and there about German atrocities. We were worried about the future, but we had no idea of the terrible days that awaited us.

One night, we suddenly heard the sounds of shooting. All the neighbors began to flee. We quickly got out of bed. We hardly had time to get some clothes on our backs, and, under fire, we ran in the direction of the "new village." There were 9 of us: me, my parents, sisters, brothers, and grandmother. We ran and fell, picked ourselves up, and kept running. Thanks to the thick fog, we got out unobserved, and made it to the village of Grabnik. There we were shocked to discover that grandmother was not with us. She was the first sacrifice in our family.

Exhausted and broken, a farmer we knew took us in to his hut. In the morning, my parents sent me to find out what the Germans had done with the Jews who had stayed in town. I was 7 years old and looked like a Christian girl. I found out from a *goyeh* that the Germans had shot all the Jews who had stayed in town. I came upon a horrible picture: the shtetl burned to the ground, burning embers still visible. I heard the cries of children who had lost their families wandering around lost and hungry.

In the forest, on the way back to my family, I met my uncle Velvel Tentser, my aunt Sheindel and their children. They were hiding in the forest and were too afraid to leave. Not long after, the Germans attacked the forest, and shot all the Jews hiding there, among them, my uncle and his whole family. Later, I was passing by the forest and the farmers were plowing the land. In the process, they unearthed human limbs, including a hand with a golden ring. By this, I was able to identify my aunt's hand. They were not even buried, but left to lie there for the wolves and the crows.

The farmer where we were staying ordered us to leave his house. He was afraid he would be reported to the Germans for hiding Jews. At that moment, the first chapter in the story of our wandering began.

My father had a large sum of money with him. He entrusted my 3-year-old sister, Ettel, to a *goy*, and every week, he went and paid him for her upkeep. The rest of us lived in an attic belonging to a farmer. For miserable rations, my father paid the farmer a very high price. One day my parents and my brother, Shloime, and sister, Tsiporah, went to see Ettel. While walking through the forest, they were spotted by Polish woodchoppers who took off after them. Shloime and Tsiporah managed to escape, but the blood-thirsty dogs caught my parents, took all their money, and handed them over to the Germans.

The Germans tortured my parents cruelly. They ordered my mother to take off all her clothes. When she refused to obey them, they beat her mercilessly. My father was unable to bear it, and he fell on the German, tore his gun from him, and shot him like a rabid dog. In the commotion, my father, dressed only in his underwear, managed to escape. My mother was murdered in a beastly fashion. My father, wounded in the head, managed to get to a *goy* he knew. He promised to hide him. When my father, exhausted by the terrible events, fell asleep in the barn, the *goy* left and came back with the Germans. It is impossible to put into words the horrible tortures he underwent until he died. I heard it all when they told this to my 15-year-old brother, Shloime. I could not even cry. I could not comprehend how it was possible that my father, the strong one, the invincible one, as I saw him through my childish eyes, who was always laughing, is no more, that I would never see him again.

When the farmer who had taken my sister, Ettel, learned that my parents were dead, and that there was no one to pay for her, he took her to the woods, stripped her clothes off, and left her naked and alone in the forest. It was a Friday. It rained heavily all day. Puddles accumulated. In one of those puddles sat a small child and helplessly cried, and called for her mother. It was my little sister, Etteleh, with her golden curls. She was condemned to death. A Jewish girl, who was hiding in the same village, and sewed for the farmers, heard the cries of a child in the forest. She went to investigate, and found my sister, naked, blue with cold and almost unconscious. She took the child with her and brought her back to the village. The Poles forbad her to take the child in with her, and ordered her to bring her to the "*soltis*." We found out about this, and my brother and I went to the *soltis* and tearfully pleaded with him not to hand her over to the Germans. He replied that no one was willing to take her, and he had no choice. The Germans immediately shot her. We were helpless. We couldn't save her.

We had no more money to pay the farmers, and they threw us out. We wandered from village to village, trying to earn a piece of bread. It was easier in the summer. My brother worked, and I herded cows. At night, we would sneak into a barn to sleep. The coming of winter brought worse misery. We had no warm clothes and we were barefoot. I used to steal into the pigpens and eat the leftovers. At night we would hide in the Hutki forest and snuggle together for warmth. One day, after such a night, my 5-year-old brother, Berele, did not get up. My sister sent me to the village to get a shovel, and with my own hands, I dug a grave for him. We then decided to separate, everyone to go a different way. We could no longer go around together among the *goyim*, and maybe this way, we might find a way to save ourselves. My brother went to Suchowola, my sister with the smallest brother, Yosef, stayed in Hutkow, and I went to Zaboreczno, my mother's birthplace.

As I was passing over the bridge, I heard my sister and little brother crying that the goyim had caught them, and were bringing them to the Germans. In panic, I began to run, the cries of my loved ones following me. I didn't question why I ran away from them. It was the instinct for self-preservation that guided me away from death. Exhausted from running without rest, my feet lacerated, and my fingers frozen, running in the snow, I made it to Zaboreczno. I begged the *goyim* to let me in, promising them I would do any work for them.

Every day I was in another house. For a stale piece of bread and a place in the barn, I would haul water from wells, help with the washing, herd the cows. The Polish children would taunt me, call me "*Parszywy Zhidowa*." (Mangy

Jewess). My emaciated body was being eaten by lice. I could not take any more suffering. A *goy* advised me to go to another village where no one would know I was a Jewish child.

In my new place, the owner used me for hard labor. He would beat me with his boots when my work displeased him. I was always starving. I had to steal a piece of bread. His two daughters would report to him if I took a potato out of the oven, or a piece of bread that I had hidden under a pillow. His wife suffered from epilepsy, and I had to pick her up and put her to bed. I was afraid to sleep at night, picturing nightmarish scenes of her lying there with foam growing on her lips. I got so used to the blows that they ceased to bother me, they were as natural as the piece of bread they gave me. During the Christian holidays, I went along to church to pray. I knew the prayers well, and more than once, that saved me from death.

One day, instead of going to church, I ran back to Hutkow. I can't remember how long I travelled, a day or two, not even knowing the way. It seems that an unseen hand directed me through the dense forest on the right way. When I got out of the forest, and could see village houses in the distance, I heard a noise and saw a carriage with two horses harnessed approaching. I scarcely had time to conceal myself when the carriage stopped at a house. A farmer woman came out and seated herself in the carriage and drove off to a field of rye. Two Germans got out of the carriage and began to search the rye, the woman pointing out where. A few minutes later, they led out my uncle Ephraim Kopel and tied him to the carriage. I had heard that my uncle Ephraim was alive and hiding somewhere. He was so close to me yet so far, a distance impossible to breach. The Germans whipped the horses to a wild gallop with my uncle tied to the carriage. He quickly fell and his body was dragged along the road, leaving dark trails of blood. I bit my lips until they bled so that I would not cry out for fear of being heard by the woman who was standing on the road, and watching with sadistic satisfaction the horror show.

I began to search for my brother in the hope that he might help me to endure my suffering. He was after all, older than me! I learned that my brother was in a ruined abandoned hut, half a day from the village. I set off, hungry, to find him. It is hard to describe the joy of our reunion, but it was not to last. In the hut there were about 10 Jews in hiding. The night after I got there, we were attacked by *shkootsim* armed with axes and spades. They stole watches, money, penknives, everything was valuable to them, and, he who had nothing, received a beating. Among the *shkootsim* was the son of the *soltis* who knew us from before the war. My brother began begging him to, at least, leave me alive. I was crying, and I called out that I wanted to go together with him. The *shegets* promised that he would save us both. They loaded everyone on carts, and he pushed me behind a wall, and told my brother to get up in the attic with him. After the carts drove off, I went back into the hut and called my brother, Shloime, to come down from the attic. Nobody replied. In tears, I ran in the direction of the carts. As I was running, I heard the sound of shooting and machine guns. I knew that the Polish animals had murdered the group of Jews, and my brother, Shloime.

And so I was alone in the world. A young girl whom fate was punishing without mercy. I dragged myself from place to place, from house to house. I myself do not know how I stayed alive, how I survived the hard labor, the hunger and cold. But I lived to see the day of liberation.

When the war ended, I was still in the village. There was no one to care about me or to help me find a way out. One day, a *shikse* I had become friends with, came and said to me, "Manye, run away, because the boys (*shkootsim*) want to kill you today. They are afraid that you will tell the Russians who betrayed your family to the Germans." In panic, I took off running. I ran through swamps and forests until I fell exhausted. I don't know how I got to the Russians. I was sick, feverish, calling for my mother, hallucinating and begging to be hidden. The Russians helped me a lot, and later they brought me to Zamosc. There I was taken in by Ephraim Zitser, through the efforts of Moshe Fishel.

After a while, they put me in an orphanage in Lublin, and from there I was transferred with other children to Chazhaw. I was there for over a year while my lungs were healing. I went to school. There I also learned about our land, about the Jewish settlement in Eretz Israel, and the struggle for *aliyah*. I came to the borders of the land in the illegal *aliyah*, but was torn away from there by force, and taken to Cyprus, to a camp encircled by barbed wire.

I lived to be able to come to our free country, to feel the joy of a full Jewish life that will no longer be captive to the whims of mad men.

I find the consolation for the hell I went through, in the circle of my little family, in my own home.

[Pages 403-406]

With the Partisans

by Hersh Gurtler (Haifa)

Translated by Moses Milstein

Hersh Gurtler

As soon as the Germans invaded our shtetl, my father, Moshe ben Zainvel, gathered the whole family together, and we left Krasnobrod.

Along the way, not far from Hrubieszow, we were attacked by peasants who tried to rob us. Fortunately, we were armed, and we drove them off.

From Hrubieszow we went to Kipetchov where my brother Falik was living at the time. While there, my father was accused of engaging in commerce. He was soon arrested by the Soviet authorities and sentenced to 8 years in prison. On the way to jail, my brother, Abraham, and I tore him away from the guards. We all hid out at our townsman, Nachum Lefler's. He lived in the forest near the shtetl, Treuchenbrod. My father stayed there for a whole year. My brother and I parted. I went to Vilitsk, and Abraham to Rowne.

In 1941, when the German bandits invaded the Ukraine, I went back to Kipetchov. I only travelled by night. Ukrainians intent on murdering me, on more than one occasion, attacked me. It was only through a miracle that I was able to save myself from them. After ten days, in the middle of the night, I reached Kipetchov, and tearfully fell into my mother's room.

In the morning, early Thursday, I left to find my brother, Falik. While I was sitting there in his house, the door opened and a neighbor woman came in. She told us that a bunch of killers were sitting in her restaurant getting ready to come over here and murder me. I immediately ran away and hid in the fields. Friday, at dawn, I went to say good–bye to my mother, and I left for the Psianara forest. I wandered around lost in the forest for several days, and on Saturday morning, I came upon a group of Jews *davening*. They gathered around me and asked me where I was from and what news there was.

I left for Ludmir that same day. I was accompanied by a Ludmir Jew with the family name of Laizerovitch. As we were travelling through the forest, we were attacked by two Ukrainian bandits armed with one revolver. They took our valuables and let us go. As we were getting ready to go on our way, one of the bandits came over to me, gun in hand, and demanded the golden ring he had seen on my finger. I suddenly threw myself at him, and wrenched the revolver from his hand, and wounded him badly. The other bandit ran away, and we too took off running deeper into the forest.

We got to Ludmir in the evening of the following day. I spent the night at Laizerovitch's and left early the next morning to search for people I knew.

As I was visiting one of my friends, a group of Germans and Ukrainians came in and took me away. I worked for them for several days, and then they let me go. On my way, I noticed placards posted in the streets ordering that all the Jews must present themselves at the plaza by the *shul*. So I went to the designated place. And there I saw young storm troopers murdering Jews, and rivers of Jewish blood flowing. I immediately began to try to find a way to escape, and I was successful. I got out of there, got my revolver out of its hiding place, and looked for a way to get to the partisans in the forest.

After wandering around in the forest for several months, I came to a place where a partisan group had organized itself. There were 25 of us with weapons. Since I only had a revolver, the commander ordered me to get a rifle. I headed for for the military barracks at Ludmir. I concealed myself and tracked the movements of the watchman. At the right moment, I jumped him, tore the rifle away from him, and ran away into the forest to my squad.

With time, our group enlarged, and we began to carry out attacks, and various diversion activities against the Germans.

One day, I stole into the Ludmir ghetto, took several families out, and got them settled somewhere safer. One family is in America today, and still others are in Israel. I also saved the two Friedling sisters, of Zamosc, from certain death.

The second time I went into the ghetto, I was surrounded by about 20 Jewish policemen who wanted to turn me over to the Germans as the one guilty of freeing the Jews. The Germans had demanded a reckoning for the escapes from the Jewish police and the judenrat. As the ghetto police had no weapons, and I did, I started shooting, and in the commotion, I escaped. I hid in a well. I don't know how I got out of there alive, other than through a miracle from heaven.

There were several Krasnobrod families in the ghetto, of which I can only remember Hersh ben Shmuel Gertler and his wife. Unfortunately, they did not heed my pleading for them to join the other families I had rescued from the ghetto. They shared the fate of the Ludmir Jews and perished in the various *aktions*.

Some time after the first *aktion*, I went into the ghetto again. This time a terrible picture of despair greeted me. Jews were standing ready to be slaughtered and could only cry, "Shema Israel!" I shouted out, "Jews, come with me and let us save ourselves!" Twenty people rallied to me. We succeeded in escaping the ghetto and fleeing to the surrounding forests. One of the group, Nachum Weissman, lives in Ramla today. The next day small groups of Jews tried to escape the ghetto, but this time, the Germans responded with fierce firepower, and they fell dead or wounded.

A while later, I left the partisan troop, and set out for Kipetchov to find my parents. But I came too late. My parents, brothers, and sisters perished with all the Kipetchovers in the shtetele, Azreian near Kipetchov.

May their memory be for a blessing.

[Pages 407-423 - Yiddish] [Page 151-161 - Hebrew]

And I Was Left Alone

by Rivka Lamm–Burstein (Ber Sheva)

Translated by Moses Milstein

Rivka Lamm–Burstein

The year, 1939, brought the Second World War, and the beginning of our tragedy.

The Jewish population of Western Poland fled to the Eastern regions of Poland. They fled from fear of the German army and Hitler's rule.

At the time, we were living in Lublin. During the first German bomb attack on Lublin, our wood shed was burned. Mother immediately sent us off to Krasnobrod where our grandparents, and uncles and aunts lived. We were not the only ones. Many other refugees also fled there. German airplanes followed us. A few days later, they bombed the shtetl because the Polish army had been concentrating its defensive forces there. We fled the shtetl under the fire of both battling sides to hide on St. Roch Mountain. There we learned that the shtetl was on fire and no one dared to try to fight it.

The battles did not last long, and the Germans entered the shtetl.

Soon after their arrival, the Polish Christian population, with the help of the Germans, enthusiastically took part in looting Jewish possessions. Some entertained themselves by cutting off beards and *payes*, and mocking the Jews when they bent under savage beating.

They forced men to dig graves to bury the horses that had fallen in the battles. They forced them to undress and to bury their clothes under the horses. After a couple of hours, they ordered them to dig up the graves and put on the putrid clothing.

A few days later, the German army left and the Soviet army came in. We went to my uncle Motl, in Zamosc, with the idea of returning to Lublin.

Two weeks later the Russians retreated to Rava–Ruska, and the Germans re–entered Krasnobrod.

Some of the Krasnobroder Jews whose houses had been burnt had nowhere to go. They had had an early taste of Nazi rule, and decided to leave with the Russian army. Thus, the Krasnobrod fire was an indirect cause of their survival. Without that, no sign of Krasnobroder Jewish existence would have survived.

My father did not want to, nor was he able to, abandon everything he had, so we returned to Lublin.

At first, we lived as well as was possible. But, after a few months, the Germans confiscated our apartment and furniture and exiled us to the Jewish street. There we decided to return to Krasnobrod because life was easier there at the time. Because of the fire, the Jews were crammed together in the few remaining houses, for example, Unzug's house, Chaim Bronstein (the baker's) house, or in the "*tcherinaske*." Others lived with the *goyim*. We stayed with Kwarcziani until they left the forest for Zolav. We had stayed there for almost a year in reasonable peace, until the *aktions* began, and put an end to the few Jews in Krasnobrod.

The first *aktion* took place *yom–tov*, but I don't remember which *yom–tov* it was. As the Jews were returning from shul, the Gestapo and SS suddenly appeared and opened fire on the Jews. In a blink of an eye, the street emptied out. Only Chaim Stringler remained lying shot on the ground. After that, people fled in frightened panic whenever the murderers showed themselves.

Some time later, a transport of refugees from Zamosc arrived. They were Jews from Western Poland who had been "*ausgeziedelt*" when the western regions were apportioned to the Third Reich. They had been driven from one place to another until they ended up in Zamosc, and from there to us.

But the shtetl was destroyed by fire and the inhabitants had no place either. My father proposed that we move them into the public bathhouse after we renovate it a bit to make it suitable for people. The proposal pleased neither the refugees nor the shtetl residents. The latter gave the refugees to understand that there was no place for them here, and the best thing to do was to return to Zamosc.

We paid dearly later for my father's mixing in. As the refugees were returning, the Germans accosted them, and out of fear, one of them said that a man called Lamm had ordered them to turn back. (It so happened to be that just my father's name came to his mind).

A few days later we were visited by an important person–the well–known Gestapo officer, Forst–accompanied by his three henchmen. Fortunately, my father managed to escape at the last minute, and only we women were left. They immediately began to poke around and look for trouble. They found my school identification card and demanded that

I tell them what it was. I explained to them it was school identification and that I didn't belong to any organization. Then they found an electric cord from an iron and began clamoring to know where the radio was hidden. Fortunately, we had a certificate stating that we had surrendered our radio in Lublin. Then they asked me how old I was. When I told them, they began to hector me about why I wasn't wearing the yellow Star of David. I told them that I was not required to wear it in the house. In response, I received a whip across the face, the handle cutting into my cheek. I was so scared, I didn't feel the pain. When they saw the *mezuzot*, they made my mother take them down and explain what the writing meant. Then they took my brother's *tefillin*, and ordered us to put them on, and enjoyed themselves greatly humiliating us.

When they had had a good laugh, they ordered my mother and I into another room and ordered me to lie down on the bed and gave the whip to my mother and told her to beat me. She refused, so they exchanged our roles. I, obviously, also did not want to beat my mother. So they grabbed my arm, and hit her with my arm. I tore myself out of their hands and fell across my mother. They began beating me with the whip. Then they exploded a gas bomb in the house and fled outside and looked in at the window to see us suffocating from the gas.

Finally, they came back into the house and promised another visit in eight days. They took me with them when they left. I thought they were taking me to jail, but I was mistaken. They brought me to the bathhouse. There they ordered me to take off all my clothes and go into the *mikveh*. They stood around me and ogled my body, black and blue from the blows. When they tired of the show, they ordered me to get dressed and to go right home. I ran with the last of my strength. But my strength failed and I passed out. Fortunately, my grandmother had been following me all along. She helped me up and led me home. I was broken physically and spiritually, from the beatings and from shame. But when I entered the house and saw my mother lying unconscious on the bed, I bit my lips and said nothing. She was in bed for a couple of days with the doctor at her side throughout.

A few days later, the refugees from Zamosc returned for good. They arrived in the company of the Gestapo. About 10 families were brought to our house. We squeezed them into the largest room. This was also the day of their promised second visit. Mother and I went to Stanka's where my father used to spend the night.

As we were sitting in father's room, we saw three *Volksdeutche* come up. We quickly got out of father's room and went over to Stanka where we sat around as if we were "guests" so that they would not suspect anyone of hiding here. Stanka also said we had just arrived as her guests.

They brought us back home, and the same scene of a week ago was replayed. They beat mother and me with no mercy. This time, my little sister, Zisele, was also beaten. By chance, Zisel Mozes happened to be there. But she managed to quickly escape. And again they promised that they would return. But they would not find us again. We left our home and went to the forest to the *gajowa*,[1] Kaniya. There a new period in our life in the forest began.

After a while, we got used to life in the forest. On one beautiful, wonderful, summer day, as I was out in the forest picking blueberries, an oppressive feeling suddeny came over me. I grabbed my sister and pulled her home. As we approached the ranger's house, I saw my parents and my grandmother and my aunt standing outside, waiting impatiently for us, ready to flee. It turned out that Yosef Goldstein had learned from the *hoif* that they were looking for father. He learned it from the mayor who had telephoned the *hoif* to see if he was there. Before we could turn around, the mayor arrived with a Gestapo man. The ranger was not at home. They began to question his family about us. The ranger's wife categorically denied everything. Suddenly, the ranger's eldest daughter mixed in and began to talk back. The mayor kicked her and declared to the Gestapo man that not only was she lying, but with chutzpah too. It was lucky that the German did not speak a word of Polish. They both got back on the carriage and drove away. A few hours later, the ranger's dog, who had become very attached to mother, brought my uncle David. He told us we could now return.

We did indeed return, but our peaceful interlude was over. We were afraid to sleep in the house, so we slept in the stable in our clothes. Father kept guard while we slept. At around 3 am, he heard the sound of a car approaching the forest, and then getting stuck on the sandy road. He woke us up and we fled, taking the dog with us. In the forest there was a valley ahead. We had planned to take the upper road. But the dog began to pull toward the valley. We followed him. When we got deeper into the woods, we heard the police car again. It was travelling on the upper road. And so we were saved yet again. The killers had surrounded the whole area. They were certain they were going to capture us. It did not occur to them that the noise of the car would alert us.

Since father spent most of his time in the forest, he was also accused of having ties to the partisans. We had to leave the ranger's, so we went to Olszewski. Father hid in an attic in Zaguza. He had to hide not only from the Germans, but also from the Poles. Mother often snuck out to him. We kids would ostensibly be going to pick berries, and we would hang around the house. Sometimes I would go with my brother, Maniek, sometimes Zisele and Berele, and father would see us through the cracks in his hiding place. We were not allowed to see him. My father stayed in hiding until the Germans sent a secret–agent, a Jew, and he did sniff something out, and telephoned to Zamosc. But my father found out, and found another place.

The next day, the Gestapo arrived. They surrounded the village, mounted machine guns, even dug a grave, and began the search. Hersh–Leib Briks was also hiding in Zaguza at the time. They found his wife and interrogated her, but she knew nothing. She couldn't tell them anything even when they brutally beat her. My father's cup of suffering and misery was not full enough it seems. He had to endure much before his death. They looked everywhere but where he was hidden, and they left without achieving their goal. But they put a price on his head.

My father was still consoling himself with the thought that he had escaped certain death, when news came about a new *aktion*. We also got news about the *aktions* in Zamosc that had wiped out that community. My father now saw the senselessness of the game of hide–and–seek that he was playing with the Germans. What kind of thing is capable of coming one fine day and wiping out an entire community of Jews, old and young, big and small. He decided to leave hiding and come and live with us. If, God forbid, it is fated that we all die, then it will be together, not alone. And maybe, who knows? Maybe it is fated that we all live?

We became aware of the possibility of getting "Aryan documents." We decided to try to get the documents, and we began to prepare for our roles. I was sent to Stempinski. One day as I was sitting and learning a Polish prayer, I heard Esther Lerner's voice. She was describing how, on St. Roch Mountain, they had found my parents hiding place. I went straight out to her, and when she saw me, she became rattled. Later, she tried to calm me down by saying that she had not seen it with her own eyes, but she had only heard about it. People talk. I did however, know that my parents were there, and I could not calm myself. I quickly set out with her to discover their fate. Along the way, some farmers told us that Esther's mother and sister had been arrested. She wanted to run to them, but I held her back. As we arrived in town, we saw them sitting in a horse–drawn carriage guarded by police. When the carriage departed, we took off running back to the woods, calling for a few armed Jewish boys to intercept them. But as we entered the forest, we heard two volleys coming from the direction the carriage had gone. We knew that there was nothing to run after anymore. It also made no sense to return to the shtetl and certain death, so we entered the forest and wandered around lost. In the evening, we found a group of Jews. Later, I met my uncle, Laizer, who tried to reassure me about my parents, and promised that he would unite me with them. At two o'clock that night, Yosef, Laizer's son, came and led me to a hiding place between piles of branches where I waited a whole 24 hours.

Czech Sokolowski came and took me to my parents. I met my grandmother on the way. She was half crazed from hunger and deprivation. She didn't recognize or understand me. She could only mumble grandfather's last words. "I am dying before my time… but I do not envy you your life." I took her with me and begged Mrs. Sokolowska to give her something to eat and allow her to sleep in the stable. She agreed at first, but later she threw her out. Finally, my grandmother, starving, exhausted, resigned, could not endure any more. She went to the shtetl, and begged them to kill her. And so did many others who had been hiding in the forest. The Poles had stopped selling them food, and they could no longer endure the hunger and the misery without a roof over their heads. They could not, and no longer wanted to, live like this.

The reunion with my parents was short. I received my document and the address where I was to meet Zisel and my brother, Berl. I said farewell to my father, my mother and my little brother, Maniek. I did not know then that we were saying farewell forever.

I went away from them with a new name into a world that wanted people like me dead, where if I, God forbid, revealed the secret–that I am a Jewish daughter.

And so I entered the Aryan side, a foreign world, as Felicia Lotz, as my document confirmed. It was not so easy, however, to travel from one place to another. The Germans were carrying out the latest *aktions* in the area, and every station was carefully watched. They pried into every little corner, maybe a Jew had succeeded in saving himself. I did not fool myself into relying too much on my document. I continued to hide and scurry from place to place. It was clear that practically any Pole would recognize me. I was also not so experienced in my new role. It was not hard to uncover my secret when they saw my reaction to what I had witnessed. And if I still had any doubts, I soon had the chance to change my mind.

I was standing in the station in Zwierzyniec and witnessed the deportation of the Jews of Bilgoraj. I had until then endured something, but such a horror I would not have believed, had I not seen it with my own eyes. The Germans were driving the people like a herd of sheep, driving them along with wild, bloodthirsty dogs that were well trained and attacked anyone who strayed out of line, or old people who were lagging. And should they be attacked, they would not get out alive. And this all took place under the eyes of the SS who walked on beside them with bayonets mounted, on which hung the heads of dead Jewish children.

My eyes could not believe what they were seeing. My body was numb. It must have been seen in my face, as a Pole quickly came and arrested me. It turned out, however, that the *pshadavnik* knew my father, and after a long sermon, he let me go. I had to, however, give him my medallion, a remembrance of my mother.

I finally got to Wilkoloz where Zisele and Berele were. When day dawned, we set out, the three of us. Just as we got to the station, we were told Jews were being hunted. Nevertheless, we took the train and got to Lublin. At the station, again the same thing. Secret–agents and spies were running around looking at everyone. We saw that Berl was, for understandable reasons, in greater danger of being exposed, and we too as a consequence. We agreed to separate. I later learned that Berl returned to Krasnobrod and hid near our parents and Maniek. He could not be with them in order not to arouse suspicion. At the end, some farmers caught him near the *hoif*, and brought him to the Germans. The Gestapo came and tried to get him to reveal where our parents were. They tortured him terribly, crushed his hand between millstones. But he told them nothing. Finally, one of the betrayers couldn't stand it anymore, and begged them to shoot him. The German agreed out of "good–heartedness," but he did not do a complete job. When my brother was buried, he was still alive. He was buried near the mill in the *hoif*.

Chava and Yosef Lamm – Rivke's parents

A while later, my parents met their tragic end. After years of pain and fear of death, of vegetating in their hiding places, after they were drained of every *groschen*, they perished at the hands of their "friends" who they had depended on for help, whose holy oaths they had foolishly believed.

In Lublin station, I lost track of Zisel. I found her a few days later in the "*arbeitsamt*." We couldn't find any work in Lublin. The danger of being exposed was greater here too. We decided to go further away, the further the safer. We signed up for labor in Germany. We registered and we went off to the "*umschlagplatz*" on Krochmalna 1. A few days later, we were sent to Germany.

Slavery

We worked for 6 month in an aluminum factory. On the day we had planned to escape with a French woman to France, the police showed up and arrested 18 girls, including us. Apparently, someone betrayed us.

We were dragged from prison to prison. We went through: Bitterfeld, Halela, Leipzig and Dresden. Finally, on a dark and rainy night, we arrived at Auschwitz. It was pouring buckets. Our greeters were dead drunk. Zisele wanted to make a move to escape, but I prevented her. They brought us to the guards at the entrance and told them they were bringing another pack of dogs. We were soaking wet and they brought us to a barrack that was stuffed with people who had arrived before us. During the night, a new transport of Greek Jews arrived.

The Germans quickly got to work tattooing numbers on our arms. Zisele got the number 39938, and mine was 39939. In the morning, they shaved our heads and took us to the baths. This was on April 4, 1943. Snow was still on the ground and it was bitter cold. They forced us to go outside naked and lie down in the snow and mud, then back into the cold baths. After the "washing," they gave us filthy soldier uniforms. I got the uniform of a Red Army soldier. When I was dressed, I went outside, and Zisel was shocked to see a Red Army soldier coming straight at her. But when I began to talk, she recognized my voice.

We got sick 3 months later. I got Typhus and went through 2 operations. Zisel got the Grippe and dysentery. Because of the different nature of our illnesses, we were separated. It was not easy to get together. After my illness, I was sent to the munitions factory, and Zisel to the death division. With a lot of effort, I was able to get her out of there and into the shoemaking division. But she fell sick again. This time she got a lung infection and a frozen foot. She stopped eating, and couldn't stand on her feet. She was transferred to Block 25. From there they would go to the gas chamber. On the day they came to take people to the gas chamber, someone from the administration came and took a few people off the list including Zisel. Once spared, she looked for a way to let me know. Thus, I had another chance to see Zisel again.

Those who had been taken off the gas chamber list were sent to the hospital. A few days later, instead of going back to my barrack, I went to the other camp to look for her at the hospital. If I were discovered, I would go straight to Block 25. But if you spend each day under the ever–smoking chimneys, not knowing if today, or tomorrow you will become smoke too, you look at danger differently. I finally found Zisel. Her face had the look of a dead person. Only her black eyes glistened and I could see it was she. She begged me for a spoonful of potato soup, but who could get such a thing?

She went through two more "selections" without trouble. But she could not endure much longer. On February 16, 1944, she gave up her soul. And I knew nothing about it, going that day, like everyday, to be with her. It was late because it was "*shpere*" at the barrack and I couldn't get away. So I went ostensibly to the doctor and then snuck into the hospital. I could not find her anywhere. I asked the sister and she pointed to a pile of bodies in the yard. I did not want to believe it, and I began to feverishly search through the bodies, hoping I wouldn't find her. Then I found, off to the side, an arm with the number, 39938, a number that was burned into my heart. Yes, it was Zisele's body from which the *tselem elohim* had long ago left. Her black eyes were shut. As if they no longer wanted to see this depraved world, this world that allowed her to wither before she had bloomed. I felt a stab of envy deep in my heart that she was done with her suffering. Who knows what still awaited me? I had done everything I could to be with my dearest ones. What kind of a so–called life did I have? But, out of spite, death spared me.

I got out of Auschwitz on the last transport. They drove us to Ravensbruck. There they gave us hardly anything to eat. Whoever could not "arrange" something, died of hunger. Then they sent us to Malchow and from there to Taucha. On the way to Hamburg, the railroad line was heavily bombed. Most of the cars were damaged. I somehow arrived in Taucha in one piece. The Germans already felt they were doomed, but they couldn't bring themselves to let us go.

We weren't even in a camp, but were driven from village to village. They didn't know what to do with us. All we got to get through the day was a raw potato or an onion. Once, when I left the ranks to go pick a turnip in the field, bullets whizzed by my head. And another time, for the same reason, I was hit so hard by the guard that I almost passed out.

We could see no end to this. So a Dutch girl and I agreed to escape together. We crawled on our knees for a kilometer and a half before we dared to get up and run. This was on May 3, 1945. I later learned that in a few more days all the Aryan women would be released, but they would continue to drag the Jewish women around. That same day, they shot 10 of them.

Further away, I began to feel free. I decided to go to the front, closer to "home." Maybe, maybe, God had shown some mercy and I would find someone alive. I walked for two days and came to Afala. From there I took the train to Czestochowa, and from there to Lublin, and finally Zamosc. I wanted to travel to Krasnobrod, but I couldn't find a ride. I didn't yet know that every *goy* who recognized me would consider it a *mitzvah* to kill me. I went to the new city to see if maybe someone from my uncle, Motl's, family was left. He was my mother's full brother. But I found no one there. Someone brought me to Moshe Fishel's, and there I learned who was still alive. From our large, extended family, I was the only one left, alone and forlorn. Like a stone in a field.

Sometime later, I joined a kibbutz in Krakow. That same year, we set off to make *aliyah*. Czechoslovakia, Austria, and finally the sadly famous port of La Spezia.

On May 19, 1946, I arrived in the port of Haifa.

Translator's note:
    1.   Forest ranger

[Pages 424-432 - Yiddish] [Page 168-174 - Hebrew]

A Slaughtered Family

by Shlomo Untzig, Tel-Aviv

Translated by Moses Milstein

In the little shtetl of Krasnobrod, the Untzigs, a broadly extended family, made up a good fifteen percent of the population.

Who did not know Shimon Untzig, the Gerer Chasid, who used to tell wonderful stories, Saturday evenings at the *melave malkas,* about the Bal Shem Tov, about the Barditsher R' Levi-Itzhak, and other rabbis. Everybody would come to hear his stories.

This large family lived quietly and happily. All the children, except for me, were married and lived in Krasnobrod. Come a Saturday or a holiday, the sons and daughters and their children would get together at father's house. We were happy in each other's company. Mother would pass out presents to her grandchildren…And in this way, we lived peacefully, until the year 1939 arrived, and World War II broke out.

With the arrival of the Germans, the population fled to the forests on Mt. St. Roch. My father and I, and a few other older Jews, locked ourselves in our house. We sat and recited psalms. We begged God for a quick end to the war. Then, we heard banging on the door. I opened it, and several Germans entered shouting, "Jude, get out fast, or you'll burn with your house." We fled straight to the *lonke,* to Yankele Gareler. We threw ourselves down on the ground. It was night already, but bright as day. The city was on fire. I heard a shot, and Eli Liebel fell dead. We lay on the ground, we didn't dare to look up, our lives were in peril. I held my *siddur* and prayed to God, father pleaded with God, loudly, to have pity on His few Jews and put an end to their sorrows.

The fire grew, the shul burned down, and the fire moved on until a miracle occurred. The fire stopped at Natan Lipschitz's house and at ours. The houses remained intact. Father thanked God for His help. His house was not burned. He did not know that, because his house was spared, it would become the cause of the destruction of our entire family.

Father said, " I will take all the children in to live with me. Why should I run to Russia, when I don't know if I will ever come back?" …

Nevertheless, I went to Rawa-Ruska. After a few months there, I became homesick for my parents. I got ready to return home. It meant stealing over the border… I took with me Feige, Arele Untzig's daughter. We staggered through the forests in deep snow. Feige's feet froze. She couldn't walk. I practically had to carry her on my shoulders until we got over the border. (She later, unfortunately, was killed by the Germans).

I managed to get to Krasnobrod in peace. It is impossible to describe my parent's joy…

One day, I went out and saw a horrible scene. A German was driving Natan Lipschitz through the streets and beating him. *Shkotsim* followed them, the German shouting, "He deserves to be punished. He charged a Christian more than the goods are worth." Natan lay in bed all Shabbos from the blows. On seeing this, I resolved to go back to Rawa-Ruska immediately. Early Sunday, Yekutiel Kupiec and I headed for the border. My dear mother accompanied me and cried bitterly on our parting. It did not occur to me then that I was leaving my parents and my sisters and brothers forever…

I stayed in Rawa-Ruska for a few weeks, and then I became the first sacrifice: I was arrested in the street, and sent to Siberia. I will not dwell on the years I spent in Russia. Whoever has been there, knows full well how life was…

As the end of the war approached, I wrote two letters to Krasnobrod. One to our neighbor, Pavlovsky, and the other to Shitkowisk with the question as to whether any of my family still lived. To my great sorrow, I received the news that my parents were dead. I cried long at these tragic tidings. Nevertheless, a spark glimmered in me. I hoped, that if I could leave Russia for Poland, I could get to Krasnobrod and see if anyone was still alive from the huge family that we had.

And I lived to see the day when I arrived in Szczecin, Poland. From there, I left for Lublin. And on that very night, traveling to Lublin, another disaster struck, the Kielce pogrom. The Poles were determined to finish what Hitler could not—the annihilation of the Jews. In Lublin I met Moshe-Eli Untzig and Moshe Fishl. They would not allow me to travel to Krasnobrod. Moshe Fishl told me all about the great tragedy that had happened there. I decided not to travel there for the time being.

It took a year, but Moshe-Eli Untzig and I got permission from the Zamosc authorities to exhume our relatives' bodies. We requested an escort from the Zamosc police. But they refused to send any of their men. It seems that, in broad daylight, the police in Krasnobrod had been taken out of their station and shot. This was done by the bandits of the A. K.[1] Nevertheless, we were determined to go there and carry out the exhumations. No one can feel or comprehend the great calamity of someone who has to go around looking for the bones of his parents, his sisters and brothers. No writer in the world could understand it adequately in order to describe what I went through. Once in Krasnobrod, Moshe-Eli and I went to the village Szur. Under a tree in Szur, Moshe-Eli's mother, Matl Untzig, lay buried. We were led there by a Christian who identified the grave by the name of the interred. We began to shovel and dig. We quickly uncovered some bones and a head. We gathered the bones and transported them to the cemetery and buried them there. Now I turned to the hunt for the remains of my own family. I wanted to know how and in what circumstances the Nazi murderers killed my parents, sisters, brothers and their children.

My family had hidden themselves in an attic, concealed by planks. At night, one person would steal out to find food for everyone. A Christian lived in the house, but he did not know that there were Jews sheltering in the attic. The coming of winter brought cold and greater hunger. One day, a child was crying, and a passing *sheygitz* heard and quickly ran to bring the Germans. They were all brought down from the attic, taken to Sziskowski's wall, that was

Shmuel Ozer's place, and shot. Many Christians stood around and calmly looked on as the last Jews of Krasnobrod were eliminated…Who did not know Janek Zomb? He went around removing the boots and shoes from everyone. He dug out a large grave and buried everyone in it. I was told that my dear brother, Henoch Untzig, refused to turn his head to the wall, so they shot him first…

It was not easy to find a *goy* who would help me dig up the bones. I had to resort to the same Janek Zomb (Jaszek Kaszkales). With great enthusiasm, and for a good fee, he agreed to help me with the work of disinterring the same people he had buried there with his own hands. I went with him to Milniczik at the sawmill, bought some boards and built two coffins. I then went to work opening the grave. Rivers of tears fell from my eyes. From a whole city if Jews only I am left to do this holy duty. I had just begun to dig the earth when in only a couple of shovelfuls, I came on bones with children's heads… --Dear, innocent children, why did you have to be taken from the world! I placed the remains in a coffin and continued to dig. I began to find larger skulls. I couldn't tell if it was mother or a sister or brother. I placed these in the second coffin. And then I unearthed a head which was so dear and familiar, as if alive. It was my father's head with the blond hair in his beard. And Zomb, my assistant adds: "This is your father, who I hid here four years ago." My wails reached the sky. It was indeed my father's beard… there was a curious group of goyim standing around and they added their agreement, "This is your father, Shimon."

I had to steel myself and stop crying so that I could keep removing the bones, and put them in the coffins with a little earth. I accompanied my holy family to the cemetery. I met many Christians along the way. I could see that they were laughing at me. With lowered head and constricted heart, I brought the martyrs to a Jewish burial ground.

The cemetery was also destroyed and in ruins. The tombstones had been torn out. At the very entrance, at the end, the ground was sown with wheat. The tombstones had been removed by the Germans to pave the roads. I looked for a spot deep in the cemetery. There was a large rock near a tree. Here I ordered a grave be dug. I lowered the two coffins, filled in the graves, and left a mound of earth on top. For a tombstone I placed a large board between stones and inscribed the names. I quietly recited Kaddish, and said good-bye to them forever.

It is hard to imagine how strong a person can be, how hardened he can become in times like this…There was one small consolation; I was able to do one last deed for them after their death…

On the way back to the shtetl, I passed the new bakery in the building that Itche Mendele's had begun. And, in this very place, I was told, lay the buried bodies of the children. One hundred and twenty seven perished here. Here too lies my brother Itzhak-Moshe. They were taking his children away and he went with them to their death. The Germans used grenades to kill them. The blood of the children flowed through the streets.

I came to my house and found the Christian, Zob, living there. Jusef Kazenowski lived in my brother's house. Everything was familiar to me. The same shutters hung that I used to close every evening. I saw my name written on the wall and various invoices my father had written for shingles for the *goyim*. I crawled up to the attic. Tattered *siddurs* and *chumashes* lay around. I picked everything up. It was all infinitely dear to me, because mother and father had held them and prayed to God…

Back down again I looked around. In this room my quiet uncle, Israel-Leib Untzig, had lived. He perished in Belzec. And here is the house where my uncle Henoch and aunt Sarah Untzig, Aharon Gershon Kleiner, and Chaim Untzig had lived. He was shot in the middle of the day on Shavuot. The house of Hershele Untzig remained. I found out that my aunt Malkah Gross and her children perished. They had come here from Siedlce. The entire family of Hersh Untzig perished, his children Itche Untzig, and his family. Shia Untzig, and his family, Yechazkiel Untzig, and his family. My uncle, Aharon Shmuel Mintz, and his children. No one was left from Chaim Bronstein, and Yankele Gurtler's families. Only the empty place where their houses once stood. Now the town hall stood here. On Shmuel Levenfuss's place a wooden house now stood, a gentile one…

I went further and saw the place where my brother, Henoch Untzig, had lived. A little further on—Shlomo Glomb. Every day, I used to get the paper at Yonah Glomb's. All these places have been built up with small wooden farm style houses. The lots of Pesach Helfman and Itzhak Untzig held houses now. Farther toward the bridge, there had lived Baruch Eli Broder. We used to *daven* together at the Gerer *shtiebl*. A little further on, Shmuel Gurtler's place has houses on it…Jewish life was torn out by its roots and extinguished by the Germans with the help of the Krasnobrod Polish population. Every foot of earth is saturated with Jewish blood. My sister-in-law, Surele Zimmerman lies in the Zielone forests. A *shaygets* killed her with a club.

Shlomo Zeltzer and I unburied the remains of his sister, Kaile Soshtchak, and buried them in a Jewish cemetery. Jews, in the hundreds, lie buried along the roads, in yards. Cattle and horses tread over their graves.

There is one Christian I stayed with whose memory I must laud. That is Felek Kozenowski. He kept with him in his house for a long time Yankele Laizer's grandson. Later, afraid of the neighbors, he sent him to his sister. But death was not eluded; he was killed with her on the way.

It is impossible for me to describe everything I heard while in Krasnobrod. Day and night I asked everyone about how and where people had died. They told me about how they dragged Hersh Leibl Briks and his wife from the sanatorium and shot them. I could not tear myself away from Krasnobrod. Time after time I went to the cemetery to say farewell to my nearest and dearest, and to all the martyrs of Krasnobrod. When I came to Israel and met my brother, Shmuel, my burdened lessened somewhat. I could at least tell it all to him.

Translator's note:
    1.   *Armia Krajowa*, Polish Home Army

[Page 433 - Yiddish] [Page 162 - Hebrew]

****

by Moshe Eliyahu Untzig (Tel Aviv)

Translated by Moses Milstein

I inscribe here the names of the martyrs of the Untzig family who perished in Krasnobrod. May their names be memorialized in this book.

The dead are:
Itzhak Untzig, and my mother, Matel Untzig. The oldest sister, Tsirl, and her husband Itzhak Zilberstein, and their two children. The next oldest sister, Roize, and her husband, Yosef Lam, and one child. The third sister, Aidel Kimmer, and her child. The fourth sister, Sarah Untzig, 16 years of age. The fifth child, Meir Untzig, 14 years old. The sixth child, Etl Untzig, 11 years old. And the seventh child, Sheindl Untzig, was 10 years old.

Those are the ones who died in my family!

Now I will list the family of Yehoshua Untzig and his wife, Elke, and their three children, two girls, Etl and Shaindl, and a son, Chaim Untzig.

The family of Yechezkel Untzig, his wife, Baile, and their five children: Chanaleh, Shlomo, Chaim, Leah, and Perl. All killed!

I was repatriated to Poland from Russia in 1946, and I went to Lublin. From there, I wrote to Krasnobrod inquiring as to the fate of my family. I received an answer that 20 members of my family were taken from Shimon Untzig's attic and shot. They had had to first dig a mass grave on Shmuel–Ozer Kupic's land.

That was the atonement.

Soon after that, I travelled to Zamosc, with Shlomo Untzig who had also arrived from Russia, to acquire permission to perform an exhumation in Krasnobrod. When we got there, in the course of about 8 days, we dug up the remains in the mass grave, and buried them in the Jewish cemetery in Krasnobrod. It consists of one family grave near the rebbe's tombstone which has remained intact to this day.

In that grave lie Shimon Untzig and his wife, Sheva, and their children: Henoch, Avramke, with his wife and their children, and Itche Moshe Untzig and his family.

While in Krasnobrod, I learned that my mother, Matl had been killed in the village of Szur, and she was buried on the village magistrate's property. So Shlomo and I travelled to the magistrate in Szur. We made a coffin, opened the grave and transferred the remains of my holy mother. Her clothes were still intact…We put everything into the coffin and buried her according to Jewish law. This was on May 29, 1947.

For the few days we spent in Krasnobrod, we stayed with Michal Macikewicz. He told us that during the last liquidation in Krasnobrod, the old people and children were assembled in the unfinished bakery, shot and buried there. The *soltis* from near the church, Klisz, told us that Fishl Shlegel was called to the *gemina* and shot there.

[Page 435 - Yiddish] [Page 177 - Hebrew]

Yakov Lederman's Story

By Shabtai Barg

Translated by Moses Milstein

Yakov Lederman

The trials and survival of Yakov Lederman, a son of Yosl and Hindeh Lederman, who finds himself in Poland today, are here described by his friend, Shabtai Barg. While he was in Poland, Shabtai Barg discovered that Yakov was alive. He tracked him down and met him in 1946. Here he passes on what he was told by Yakov.

* * *

In 1946, I found myself in Szczecin, Poland. By chance, I met Shlomo Untzig. He told me that my cousin, Yankel Lederman, had managed to save himself from the Nazi murderers. He was now living in a village among *goyim*. He gave me an address with a Christian name, Jan Malinowski. He got the address during his last visit to Krasnobrod.

I was strongly moved by the news that my cousin, the always happy and cheerful, Yankel Lederman, was still alive, and I quickly sent off a postcard. I waited impatiently for a reply. After several days of anxious waiting, he arrived. But I was stunned and shocked by his appearance! His clothes – tattered; his feet wrapped in rags. Truly naked and barefoot. He looked greatly aged and worn out. I found it hard to believe that this was the same Yankel. I could not take in the idea that a man in the bloom of his youth, who had always been so happy and full of life, could become like this at the age of 32.

After we had well and truly cried, and talked about what had happened to our families – relatives, brothers and sisters, fathers and mothers, who had been martyred by the murderous Nazis – I wanted to know how he had survived and why he was in such a deplorable state. I tried to hearten him and encouraged him to talk as much as I could. I must add that the city also had made a strong impression on him, seeing how life there was more or less normal, and that it was possible for Jews to meet. He was certain that there were no Jews left in Poland.

– What should I tell you, Shefsel, he began, and where should I begin, since each day was its own separate tragedy…You never knew what the day, or the night would bring. No one had an inkling of when his fate would be sealed: today or tomorrow. There was no food. We were swollen from starvation. Death was always staring us in the face.

– Tell me, Yankel, I urged him – How did you save yourself and where did you last see your mother and your sisters, your uncle, Melech, and his family, and your aunt, Blumeh, and her family?

– When Krasnobrod was burned down at the outbreak of the war – he went on – all of us, meaning our family, uncle Abraham Itche and his family, and later also uncle Melech and his family, we all went to Shumsk, to aunt Blumeh. She had lived there before. Shumsk was under Russian occupation. Grandmother, Baile, mother, Etl, and her two little children, aunt Tsetl and her family, uncle Volvish, and his family, and my brother, Nachum, and his family, all remained behind in Krasnobrod. Uncle Shmuel, and aunt Sarah Riva and their two little children stayed in Shebreshin.[1] In Shumsk, we soon found work. I got work in a Christian bakery. My sister, Gitl, worked in a pharmacy. We planned on sitting out the war here, and then returning to Krasnobrod.

Uncle Abraham Itche, and all of his children, could not wait, and they registered to return to Krasnobrod…But instead of Krasnobrod, they, along with many others, were sent deep into Russia. They envied us our staying behind and not having to wander who knows where…We did not want to register ourselves, and were preoccupied with figuring out how to return to the burnt – out houses we had left. So we kept on waiting…until the fire came to us.

As soon as the Germans, may their names be cursed, took the shtetl of Shumsk, they set up a ghetto, and packed all the Jews in there. All our families and myself were in the ghetto. The younger people were led out every day, under heavily armed guard, to various kinds of labor. They were brought back at night. I was also among them.

I worked in the same bakery where they baked bread for the Christian population. I got along well with the Christian workers. Among them, there was also a Christian girl, Stefa, who had a special affection for me. She tried to cheer me up in any way she could. She knew that I had a mother and sister in the ghetto. She would bring me all kinds of news, what was going on in the shtetl, what the word was about the war. One day, she told me that they were going to liquidate the ghetto. – "What do you mean, liquidate the ghetto?" I asked her. "Maybe they are going to set us free?" She was silent for a moment and then said quite clearly, "It means, liquidating the Jews." I wanted to know how she knew such things, and where she had heard this. "It was heard," she said, "from drunken Gestapo mouths. If you want you and your family to be saved," she advised me, "you have to escape from the ghetto before it's too late. I will show you a place you can hide."

When I returned to the ghetto and told my mother and uncle, Melech, they refused to believe it. "It's not possible," they said, "that they would kill all the Jews, and we mustn't risk it by running." It wasn't long before, on a certain morning, they shut up the ghetto and surrounded it with soldiers. No one was let out of the ghetto, not even those who had been taken out to work before. We saw that we were lost. Stefa had been right. She wanted to save us and we had not believed her. Now it was too late. What to do? We were hopeless and in shock. Our blood congealed in our veins. We looked at each other with deathly fear. We saw each other as dead already. There was no hope or salvation. Some tried to console themselves, "Is it really possible that they would simply just kill us, slaughter us like sheep?"… People hid, crammed themselves into any hole, in order not to see the face of the murderers.

Outside it was pouring rain, as if God were weeping at our fate. Night fell, and the killers did not enter the ghetto. Perhaps the rain hindered them.

Hinde Lederman with her children
On the right, Yakov Lederman

We sat pressed together, in despair and trembling, our hearts pounding. At such a tragic moment, when we were facing death, my dear mother found some courage and said, "If we were all too late to escape, maybe, my son, it is not too late for you. The darkness of the night and the rain will help you. Jump over the fence." I will never forget the deep sorrow I saw in my mother's eyes. That look still accompanies me wherever I go. I will never forget how she pressed me to her heart,

[Page 436]

"Go, my son, save yourself. Maybe we will see each other again." I could not oppose my mother's will. We quietly said our goodbyes. We had to restrain our feelings in order not to attract attention. With a prayer on my lips that we should someday be reunited, I left the house, and all those dear to me.

When the rain got stronger, I jumped over the fence and took off running. But after running only a few tens of steps, a hail of bullets suddenly fell on me. I thought it would never end. I didn't know if they were shooting at me or at the ghetto. I quickly dropped to the ground. The swamp covered me almost completely. Each time the shooting increased, I dug my face deeper into the mud to shield myself from the bullets. I lay there like that for hours on end. My face was covered in cold sweat, and my life shimmered before my eyes. The shooting finally stopped. I started crawling on my belly, on all fours. When I passed my hands over my face and my head, my hair came off in my hands… I was struck with fear. I didn't understand what had just happened to me. I began to feel my head: Maybe I was wounded and was too full of fear to know it? No, I was not wounded. My hair fell out by the roots from pure fear – Is it a surprise for you to see me as I am? – Slowly I made my way back to Stefa before daylight.

Here, a new chapter of my sad story, with new sorrows, of a life lived in a dark cellar, begins.

* * *

No one could know about me in Stefa's house, not her brothers or sisters; it had to be kept a secret from them. Hiding a Jew was punishable by death. But Stefa, with her devotion, kept me from strangers' eyes. She hid me, as I said, in the cellar of their home. I sat in a large sauerkraut vat beneath another vat. Stefa cared for me like for a small child. She brought me food that she stole from the house, and carried away my things. She told me about the terrible disaster in the ghetto. About my dear mother and my young sweet, sisters. They sent me away to save myself, and they are here no more. The vat was wet with my tears. – What is the point of living? Stefa told me how heroically my uncle, Melech Tentser, defended Jewish honor. When he and his household, and other Jews were being led from the ghetto to be shot, he threw himself on a German murderer, tore the rifle from him, and shot him, calling out, "Jews, save yourselves!" But no one came to his aid, and he was shot there with his two little children. And that's how the murderers finished with the Jews of the shtetl.

Melach Tentser and his wife and child. Hy"d.

Stefa's parents noticed that bread was missing in the house. Bread was treasure in those days. Her father snooped around so long – until he found me sitting in the cellar…

[Page 437]

This created a terrible situation. He did not want me to be there any longer. Stefa defended me, and first of all, begged him not to betray me to anyone. He agreed, but on the condition that I leave his house. Stefa promised him, and took to finding me a new hiding place. After much running around, she managed to find a place at a friend's house, but only for a short time, until she was could find another place. She went off to a village to look for a hiding place. In the meantime, she heard that the Germans were registering farmers for work in Germany. She reasoned that the two of us should register so that we could get away from here. She doubted she could keep me here safely much longer. The plan appealed to me. That way, I could have a chance to breathe fresh air, and see the sun again, and not have to creep around in darkness afraid of the slightest sound.

But for me, it wouldn't be so easy. All those who were registered for work had to be examined by a medical committee, naked, to see if they were healthy. How could I do this? They would immediately know that I was a Jew. But clever Stefa had an idea. She found someone who, for a certain amount of money, presented himself to the medial committee and went through all the formalities. With these documents, I applied for transport. My name was Jan Malinowski.

Stefa was very happy that I was able to walk about in the free air. But I – how could I be happy when everyone was so cruelly murdered. How could one forget what the murdering bands did to our sisters and brothers, and I, a lone Jew, left to wander on the earth? Oh, how horrible this is. But I owe Stefa a lot. She is my guardian angel; she placed her life in danger for me. She left her home, her parents, her whole family, in order to save me.

Our transport carried us to Germany like cattle. They drove us to some small town, to the marketplace. Surrounded by villagers, we waited wondering what the bandits were going to do with us, where they were going to send us. They made us assemble in rows, and gave everyone a number, pinned to our lapels. My number was F854. Then, the Gestapo announced that they had brought "slaves for sale." They allocated a price for each number according to age and physical strength.

The "buyers" were already waiting for the "merchandise." First, they busied themselves examining us, feeling our muscles, pushing us to see if we would stagger, and then, they began to haggle over the prices. And that was the meaning of "they're taking us to Germany for work…" And that was how, exactly like the army, or maybe even much worse and brutal, in the year 1943, they sold us for slaves.

Stefa and I were bought by a farmer, a brutal person, to work his land. They treated us exactly like cattle, harrying us, cursing us "Faster, faster…,verfluchte untertanen!" Food was never enough. We worked and we starved, always living in fear, sundered from the world, with the horrible knowledge that all my near ones are long gone. And us – how long will we endure? Will it ever end?

Remark: Here I temporarily ended my talk with Yankel. I saw that he was too exhausted to continue telling me about his terrible experiences. We postponed it for another time. Regrettably, we did not meet again, because I left Poland shortly thereafter.

I only know that when the war ended, he travelled back to Poland with Stefa, settled in a village and lived there. He was certain that there were no more Jews left in Poland.

He did go to Krasnobrod to see if maybe, someone was still alive. But he could not even find any graves. He left his address with a goy who was once his neighbor in case some survivor would inquire about him and want to look him up. That was how I got his address.

Today, Yankel is in Sczczecin, Poland.

A letter from Yankel

Dear aunt Gitl!

I have been saved from the claws of a monster, the likes of which the world has never seen – from Hitler.

…The battle for my poor life was very, very difficult. My bitter lot, my constant anxieties, and what I had lived through in the war, and what I had afterward seen in Krasnobrod, saw and heard – I say to you, that for me, it was not worth the struggle. It would have been better if I had perished along with my sisters and my mother.

…The Hitler sadists, along with the Polish people, destroyed, in the cruelest way, all the best and dearest that we possessed. We have no one left. Our shtetl Krasnobrod has been erased. Even the cemetery was not spared, the tombstones broken. The earth – plowed…

Your nephew, Yakov Lederman.

Translator's note:
    1.   Szczebrzeszyn

[Page 445]

Yizkor

By Shlomo Sonnstein (New York)

Translated by Moses Milstein

For the exaltation of the holy souls of the Krasnobrod martyrs; all those who fell and perished for the honor of the Jewish people, for the exaltation of the Jewish faith, Yizkor!

May these lines that I write be a ray of light in the *ner – tamid* that burns in our hearts. May it light the mass grave of the holy congregation, a congregation that was exterminated by a cursed, stupid, murderous, beastly people.

May the holy Jewish letters in this book shine clearly and by their light reveal the greatness of Jewish life, and the mighty courage of the Jewish *Kiddush Hashem*.

May our children and grandchildren read these words written in blood about our diaspora life; may they know what a bloody price we paid. May they understand how to cherish freedom and independence of Jewish life in our dear, free Jewish state. May they gain strength and courage from Jewish martyrology to fight for our freedom. May it be the consolation for our sorrow at the lives that were cut off before their time, for the community that was mercilessly annihilated before the eyes of the non – Jewish world.

Fate decreed that I, an unburned remnant of the holy Krasnobrod community, should be a living eyewitness to the fire that consumed the Jewish community. Thus fate punished me so that I would see with my own eyes, the first burnt sacrifices under the ruins of Jewish homes.

Krasnobrod was the first of the burned – out Jewish communities in Poland. It was the first of the sacrifices to be consumed by the flames of the worldwide fire. We were the first to be crushed by Nazi boots in their bloody march over the soil of Poland.

[Page 446]

Among the first victims were Shmuel – Ozer Kupiec and his son Mechl. Their faces were burned beyond recognition. We recognized the father by his *tallit katan*, which miraculously survived the flames. It was like a holy sign, and a symbol that the Jewish body can burn, but the spirit will survive any fire.

We found other burned bodies in the ruins. Unfortunately, we could not identify them, most were refugees from other Jewish communities.

On the same day, the Nazis shot: Leibish Kramer, Shmuel (Shmelke) Shtemer, and the mentally ill, Reuven.

That was only the beginning, the beginning of the end. The fire that consumed our shtetl, took a third of our people. It dried up the spiritual wells of Jewish life, and destroyed the generations – long, settled and deeply rooted, Jewish communities in Europe.

The murderous hands of the oppressors also did not spare the Krasnobroders who fled to the cursed soil of the Ukraine. There they shared the tragic fate of the Jews from Breilov.

The Germans carried out their murderous actions with meticulousness and precision. First, they murdered those who either had no trade, or had a trade that was not needed by the murderers. The tradesmen were then murdered after they were of no use anymore for slave labor.

Between one action and the next, people tried to find a way to escape the ghetto. In particular, they wanted to get to the areas under Romanian occupation…, in the so – called Transdniester. Although Jews there also lived in ghettos and in prison camps, the mass slaughters that were occurring with the Germans had not yet happened. They risked their lives and reached Zhmerinka and Breilov.

On a clear day at dawn, Romanian soldiers surrounded the ghetto, and drove all the refugees, 300 in number, to the slaughter, halfway between Zhmerinka and Breilov.

Among those driven to death were a Krasnobrod mother with her son and two daughters. They were Mirl Kupiec and her children, Chana, Bina, and Abraham. Chana refused to obey the murderers' order to strip naked; she was tortured to death. But morally she triumphed. She perished in her clothes.

May eternal shame accompany the murderers who wanted to disgrace the honor of this virtuous Jewish daughter, Chana. May the blood she shed be a holy gift for that which decides Jewish fate, and weaves it into the web of history, and soaks foreign soil with Jewish blood.

Yizkor! May the names of the holy martyrs of Krasnobrod be sanctified, may their memories remain forever in our minds, as the sorrow lives in our hearts.

[Page 448]

Addition to the list of the dead

Translated by Moses Milstein

Yonah Berland, Leibche's son, a lad of 20, while serving in the Polish army at the end of the war traveled to Krasnbrod with the hope of finding someone from his family still alive. The goyim caught him in the shtetl, and murdered him.

Feigele Fuchs, Itche Mendeleh's daughter, 18 years old. She survived in the forests until the end of the war. She went to Turzyniec. At the place where her parents had a mill, where she went to beg for some food from some goyim she knew, she was thrown into the water by *shkotzim* and drowned.

Tzipe Krelman, Moshe Krelman's wife and a 16 year old daughter had hidden in the forests near Botshiv. Soon after the war, when the Russians had taken the surrounding cities, they were told by the local farmers that they could return to their home in the town. On the way home, 2 km from the shtetl, at the village of Hutkow, she was seen through the window of the house of a goy who had been learning the shoemaking trade from her husband. He chased them both into the forest and murdered them.

Yosef Rind, Shmuel Rind's son. When the Zhmerinker ghetto was created, he gave all that he possessed to a farmer acquaintance. From time to time, he stole out to the farmer to sell something in order to provide for him and his family. At one such visit, the farmer, "his protector," murdered him.

[Page 449]

There once was a town—it is no more

by Abraham Barg (Tel Aviv)

Translated by Moses Milstein

There was once a town here not long ago. It seems only yesterday that I was there, spoke with everyone, saw everyone—and suddenly, all of this is gone.

A shtetl, like many other shtetls in Poland, settled by peaceful, quiet Jews, citizens for generations—and suddenly, they are all gone.

A shtetl with all kinds of chassidim: Belzer, Radziner, Gerer, and Trisker…They travelled to visit their rebbes, good Jews, bringing petitions, and pleas for prosperity, doing business, wandering around, modest achievements—and suddenly all this is wiped out and gone.

There were scholars, proud of their *Yiddishkeit*, studying Torah day and night, surviving often on only a heel of bread and water, all undertaken for the love of His name—and now they are all gone.

There were businessmen, honest, hard–working people, preoccupied with the burden of making a living, but never forgetting to financially help out a brother, a friend, or the community fund to lend money to a near one, to help a neighbor in need, to visit the sick, and not only grant the *mitzvah* of *bikur cholim*, but also thereby, leave some money under the pillow in secret—and suddenly, all these dear people are no more.

There were the dear blooming youngsters, full of ideals, goals, politically engaged, debating issues, fighting among themselves for a better tomorrow, who thought they would bring salvation to the world, and to the Jews—and now they are all gone.

There once were children, bright, sweet, "*yedder kind mit zein mazel*," as the Yiddish expression goes. There were mothers and fathers with their joys and sorrows, with their hopes. They hoped and strived to live to see a little *naches* from their children, and it is all obliterated and gone.

There are no more little children. There are no more mothers and fathers. There are no longer any hopes or dreams…There are no more sisters or brothers! Oh, dear, goodhearted Jews, I see you all, you are all around me. Here I see you in the days before Passover as you go from house to house collecting *maos chitin*[1], providing wine and matzos for the poor. Now I see you at dawn, still dark out, walking sleepily to *slichot*, carrying big lanterns, woken up by Zalman Ber, the *shammos*, who went from house to house, and with his big wooden hammer banged on the doors and shouted: "Wake up, wake up, holy Jews! Get up for *avodat habora*[2]!"

And now I see you, little children, Lag B'omer, dancing happily on the way to the tall "Mt. Sinai,"[a] carrying bows and little rifles, the mothers at the doors of their houses looking proudly on at their children who will grow up and study Torah, and forge the chain of the Jewish people.

Holy Krasnobroder *Yiddelach*, joyful children, future generations! Where are you now? Where have you gone? Where did the whole shtetl full of Jews go? None of you are left! Everyone killed, murdered; houses and their inhabitants incinerated, young and old dying together! hunted in every little corner, dragged out from all the dark hiding places, accompanied by taunts to the graves where the wild beasts were lurking, and who fell on your exhausted bodies like blood–thirsty animals, tore living pieces from you, threw you alive into your graves, one on top of the other, people covering people. Machine guns and rifles muted your death cries, suffocated your last breaths; your lives were wasted for the smallest things, by any vile creature. Nobody interfered with the murderers. No one asked, "Why?" Everyone was happy that your blood ran like water, the blood of children mixing with their mothers'.

Fathers, mothers, sisters, brothers of Krasnobrod. Who tore you away from us, tortured you to death, starved you, murdered you! Who stole from us our treasure, the youth of Krasnobrod! Daughters of Krasnobrod, gentle, tender, you were dragged by the two–legged beasts to the forests, raped, dishonored, and murdered. Mothers who shielded their children with their own bodies were shot with the same bullet.

Little children of Krasnobrod, little babes torn from their mothers' arms, thrown into the air like toys. Their screams, their sobs, concerned no one. The cries of children were not heard by heaven. Innocent children. Little souls! Why did you merit such a punishment? Who can comprehend it, who can endure such grief, such pain?

Woe to us that we lived to see with our own eyes the great sorrow, the terrible rage that God poured over His people Israel. Is there such a fire in hell? Does the *tochecha* contain such curses, that mothers and children should die such deaths!

Krasnobroder grandfathers, grandmothers, where shall we look for you? Where are your graves, where do your persecuted bones lie, your hands and feet that were tied to wagons and dragged through the streets. Where should we look for you–in the fields, the forests, in the gutters, or in Majdanek, Belzec, Auschwitz, where the German beasts, in the shape of humans, had built modern gas ovens for you? And what were you guilty of?–just being Jewish. And for that reason no one saw or heard the great tragedy. No one felt this great pain. No one wanted to help you. No one heard your cries for help, not in the east, not in the west…Enemies laughed. "Friends" were silent. Perhaps, they thought, we will be rid of the Jews forever.

The call to avenge the six million hangs forever in the air, and warns and demands that we not forget the blood that was spilled. Punish them God, the wicked, the murderers, for our innocent blood. Punish them for making soap of our flesh. Make them pay dearly for the ones they starved to death. May the murderers consume themselves, and tear their children asunder. The Aryan devils wanted to exterminate and obliterate every trace of the ancient line of Israel. May they disappear themselves.

We are left orphaned, perpetual mourners. Who can console us, understand our grief?

The last memorial in Israel. Cheshvan, 15th, 5715

First row from the right, standing: Sh. Babad, F. Dimond, A. Giter
Second row seated: A. Rind, A. Borg, G. Borg, A. Lochfeld
First row from left, standing: Sh. Gurtler, M. Fishl, Sh. Levenfus
Second row, seated: Y. Shlegel, A. Gurtler, A. Untzig, M. Rapoport

Y. Rind, M. Shochet, Z. Ullman, Sh. Lefler, Z. Rind, Z. Krellman, Y. Shtemer, Y. M. Gurtler, A. Y. Tentser, M. Dimond, Z. Appleboim

The first commerotive assembly in Ulm, Germany
Photographed by Hersh Ben Moishe Gurtler

A group of young Zionists in Krasnobrod

Translator's notes:
1.   Charity for the poor on Passover
2.   Service of the Lord

Original footnote:

    a.   On the other side of the river in our shtetl, there was a tall sand hill that the children named "Mt. Sinai."

[Page 455]

People

Translated by Moses Milstein

[Page 455]

[Page 457 - Yiddish] [Page 187 - Hebrew]

Rav Menachem Munish Margalit, HY"D

A. Lochfeld

A descendant of an extensive rabbinical family. His mother was a daughter of the Babad family, the grandchildren of the Tarnopoler "Minchat Chinuch." In 1924 he was hired as rabbi for Krasnobrod.

He was a scholar, an expert in Talmud and poskim. A genius in fields of Talmudic knowledge, knew Jewish history and was a talented speaker. With his first passionate speeches as our rabbi, he won the hearts of everyone.

I was honored to be among the first of his students in Talmud. He would explain the most complex passages with simplicity and clarity, so that they stayed deeply embedded into the mind. My knowledge of Talmud I owe to him. Later, when I embarked on the ways of a more worldly culture, and threw myself into the study of Yiddish literature, he invited me to see him, and he explained that drawing on worldly knowledge does not necessarily have to end in heresy, or denial of Jewish faith. "One can," he said, "read books, learn worldly subjects and still be a faithful and pious Jew."

[Page 458]

His words affected me and that was the approach I took until I left for hachshara[1].

He was a warm-hearted person with an open sensitive heart. He gladly gave to every important project, and saw to it that others also gave. His house was open to everyone. He took part in every philanthropic institution like "Hachnoset Orchim," Gemilut Chasidim," "Bikur Cholim," and others.

He shared the fate of all the Jews in the shtetl, but no one knows where he perished.

Translator's note:
     1.   Agricultural training camp

[Page 458 - Yiddish] [Page 188 - Hebrew]

R' Moishele Soifer z"l

by Abraham Barg

The name, Moishele Soifer, was well known not only in Krasnobrod, but also in many of the surrounding shtetls.

He was a man of average build, already in his elder years. His face was framed by a small white beard. He always walked with slow steps, his pipe in his mouth. With a good-natured smile always on his face, he simply charmed people.

He was held in esteem both by Chasidim and religious functionaries, and by ordinary folks, because he was a Belzer Chasid, and a scribe for religious objects, renowned as an artist in his trade, he was able to converse with anybody. Young and old were happy to be in his company.

[Page 459]

He had a whole collection of pipes, a special one for each holiday. Here a longer one, there a shorter one. A really different one for Purim, so long it almost reached his knees. It was rimmed with many colors. It was a "historic" pipe, an inheritance from a great grandfather.

His gentle eyes shone like a child's, and a special delight spilled over his face when on such days he put his pipe to mouth, and slowly lit it–not with unwarranted pride, God forbid, but with respect for the holiday–and described the history and the origin of the pipe, and when Moishele Soifer was telling a story, everyone listened.

Young and old loved to hear, and enjoyed deeply, the homey, folksy stories he would tell at every opportunity.

Everybody liked him, and he liked everybody. As already mentioned, he was a scribe known beyond the borders of our shtetl Krasnobrod. A pair of tefillin, or a mezuzah from Moishele Soifer, always fetched a higher price than from other scribes. A sefer Torah written by him was a rare prize. But Moishele wrote more for the sake of the mitzvah than for the money, and so he was always poor; one could say, he lived on bread and water. But he was happy with his lot.

There was not a celebration in town where Moishele Soifer was not among the first of the important invitees. Whether it was an engagement party, a wedding, a bris, a pidyon haben–everywhere, Moishele Soifer was invited. He always knew how to amuse the crowds. He had his stories ready in hand to interest and amuse the guests and the in-laws.

If a Jew was engaged in another shtetl, and the wedding took place there, no one attended without Moishele's presence...Moishele Soifer showed a special interest in weddings involving poor Jews that in most cases took place without klezmer. There his talent for entertaining shone greater. So that the parents of the couple should not feel humiliated, he took the place of the klezmer, the badchen, and the dancing audience...In one word, Moishele Soifer was everything, and really knew how to do everything.

Friday evening and the Shabbes prayers was his most enjoyable time. Surrounded at the "table" with chasidim like him, as well as ordinary folk, he felt like a "fish in water." He would gush with chasidic stories and tales of pious Jews. From time to time he would get up and dance with other chasidim. At the end of the celebration, he had his own dance. It was called the "*broigez* dance," the dance of a quarreling couple. The man wants to apologize to his angry wife. But she is stubborn, and does not want under any circumstances to make up. So he gives her various presents. Each time, he takes something different out of his pockets and tries to give it to her, until she finally becomes reconciled, and they make up. Then both start dancing together. The audience applauds and dances along. People stood on tables and chairs to see the couple dancing–and went wild! They used to say in the shtetl that whoever has not seen Moishele Soifer dancing the "broygez dance," does not know what dancing is...

[Page 461]

I believe it is worthwhile relating one of his stories here, as much as I can remember, although my memory may leave some details out.

There was a young man, an orphan who lived in a shtetl. He was very alone and lonely. He got to know a girl who was also a lonely orphan. They both strove to achieve a happy union that would end their lonely, sad life. Unfortunately, they could not attain their goal. They were so poor they did not have any means of establishing and building a nest for themselves. In their desperate situation, they both decided to leave for other places to look for work, and with God's help, to slowly improve their situation, and lead a family life. They would finally be free of the sorrow and torment they had had to endure in their younger years. But as soon as their plans became known, the shtetl raised a ruckus. "What? An unmarried young man and girl will, without supervision, go off into the world? Such a sin, a transgression! Who knows what kind of trouble, God help us, will befall the shtetl... We cannot allow this to happen under any circumstances."

They rushed to the rabbi. The rabbi called together the worthy men of town and they decided that they would marry the pair in conformity with the laws of Moses and Israel, and then they could go wherever they pleased.

And so it came to pass. They held a wedding. The rabbi officiated according to Jewish law. The worthy men gave wedding presents, the shtetl celebrated. It was a double celebration: two orphans were married, and the shtetl averted a big sin.

After the wedding the couple went on their way as they had planned. They went off on foot to establish their new home.

[Page 462]

As soon as they left the shtetl they found themselves in a thickly wooded forest. They lost their way and wandered deeper and deeper into the forest. They could not find a way in or out. Suddenly, they heard the wailing cry of a child. They followed the sound of the voice until they found the child sitting under a tree. By its appearance and its clothing it appeared that the child had Christian parents. But how it came to find itself deep in the forest they could not understand. They picked up the child, calmed it down, and continued blundering around until they finally got out of the forest.

The sun had already set by the time they got out to the open fields, and in the gloom of the evening they saw a light from a house that was quite far away. They set off in that direction.

When they crossed the threshold of the house the residents of the house broke out in joy. They saw two strangers bringing back their lost child. It turned out to be a very well to do household. The people were owners of a large holding of land. One morning they had gone hunting in the forest and brought their child along. While they were hunting, the child got lost. They searched for it all day fruitlessly. Their grief was indescribable. And here the child has suddenly been returned.

When they asked the couple how they had found the child, they told them the whole story of how they were orphans alone, that they had gotten married the day before, how they had set off for unknown places in order to support themselves, and how they had gotten lost in the forest.

[Page 463]

And while they were wandering around tired and worn out, looking for the road, they suddenly heard the cries of a child. They followed the voice until they came to the tree and saw the crying child. "We carried the child in our arms" they added, "calmed it down so it stopped crying, and with God's help, managed to get out of the forest."

--Because you saved my child from perishing in the forest–the father called out with gratitude–I give the forest to you as a gift!

Because you brought my child back alive and healthy to my house–added the mother–I give you the orchard that I inherited from my father, a gift!

The other relatives also gave them many gifts, and the young couple returned with great joy to the shtetl, and told everyone about the incident, and the great good fortune that had befallen them.

Here Moishele Soifer's story ended, and he explained the meaning of the story, that this happy ending happened, because religious Jews did not permit the unmarried pair to go off together, but instead got them married according to the laws of Moses and Israel.

Moishele Soifer also used to have his own sayings:

There are three things, he used to say, that a person does that are not nice, but that don't matter; the first, when a person eats preserves with a spoon. It's not nice but it doesn't matter.
Second, when somebody beats his wife, It's not nice, but it doesn't matter. She gets a few slaps; it actually makes her better.
The third thing is, when an older man gets married to a young girl, it's really not nice, but it doesn't matter.

[Page 464]

As mentioned earlier, Moishele was a pauper, because he did his holy work for the sake of a mitzvah. As was his entertaining people done for its own sake.

[Page 464 - Yiddish] [Page 192 - Hebrew]

R' Moishele Soifer z"l

by A. Rind

A scribe of the old generation. He wrote tefillin, mezuzes, and Torahs. A highly accomplished man with all the virtues. After his death we understood the words of the rebbe's eulogy, "Saints after their death are called living." For the shtetl, he did not die, but lived on in the memories of everyone who knew him.

During his life, he strictly observed and lived the 613 commandments and laws of the Shulchan Aruch, while still finding time for drawing, painting, carving and engraving. He wrote poems, composed melodies, and sang them with feeling. In his later years, it even brought him some money. He carried out various performances, painted signs, sewed, chiseled, etc.

Moishele Soifer was a peacemaker who loved people, and would give up his life to help people. He listened to everybody, kept secrets. He endeavored to make broken families whole, brokered peace between quarrelling sides. He entertained audiences at celebrations especially after cantor Chaim, the city cantor died, and he was invited to every celebration.

He failed to get naches from one thing, and that was his house. It was in a bad state, and low almost to the ground, and cost him his health and brought him a lot of distress. He was able to be of service and aid to everyone except himself and his children.

[Page 465 - Yiddish] [Page 193 - Hebrew]

R' Moishe Leib Barg z"l

by A. Elboim

R' Moishe-Leib was one of those wonderful Jewish types that have become rarer and rarer in Jewish life. He was one of those Jews from the older generation for whom traditional Yiddishkeit and piety were identical with love of fellow man and boundless loyalty to the Jewish people. He was a person who lovingly undertook the burden of Torah and the burden of social leadership carrying love for friend and foe in his heart.

R' Moishe-Leib Barg was born and raised in a chasidic home, and from childhood on, was steeped in the spirit of the Torah and piety. Throughout his life he was among the first to dedicate himself with devotion to each religious action and undertaking. He never refused even the smallest tasks, and of course, accepted every responsible task and mission that was entrusted to him. He was a shtadlan who sacrificed himself for the individual as well as for community issues.

It was he who freed the young men from military service during the Polish-Bolshevik war. And it was he who went from door to door with lulav and etrog in order to allow people to perform a mitzvah. As a member of Chevra Kadisha, he battled to keep the traditional observances in the burial laws, even in times of danger. He did not tire of going from house to house encouraging Jews, and calling on them to give tzedakah. Whether it was the pushke for "*Meir bal Haness*," or Maot Chitin for matzah for the poor, or even the rebuilding of the ruined besmedresh, his energy, initiative and zeal inspired, and brought to success every activity.

[Page 466]

Even though he was himself not wealthy, and sometimes in a difficult situation, he did everything without drawing attention to himself. He was a model of religious faith, and he refused, under any circumstances, to benefit from the help others in need received. In the awful war years, he wandered through Russia. It appears that his past gave him the strength to survive the suffering of homelessness, hunger and privation. From the camps in Germany, he arrived in Israel. In spite of the hardships of the war years, his spirit did not break. His faith became even stronger, and his readiness to engage in social work found, in Israel as well, a wide field of activity.

After three years living in Tel-Aviv, he received a dwelling in shikun Ramat-Yam in Bat- Yam. He quickly began a drive to establish a synagogue in his neighborhood.

In spite of his age and frail health, he threw himself into the task with youthful passion. He did not tire of approaching donors, and he opened their hearts and their pockets. He lived to see the completed synagogue, the fruit of his efforts.

At the age of 73, he was taken up to heaven.

———————

[Page 466 - Yiddish] [Page 194 - Hebrew]

R' Moishe Leib Barg z"l

by A. Rind

Moishe Leib Barg, always happy, smiling and good-natured. He carried a large burden, always busy with hundreds of things on his head. He had *"a sach meluches, un veinik bruches."*[1] He found time to listen to you, and to give advice.

[Page 467]

He knew everybody and everybody knew him. We used to say, "From the day you're born to the day you die, you are in his hands," an allusion to his participation at a bris, family celebrations, or at funerals.

He was by nature compassionate, ready to help, and actually did. The last years, he was overloaded with work and problems. He was administrator for others' money, bill collector for the electric company, and took care of other business for the graf's court. He tended to hold onto the collected money as long as possible and lend it out to storekeepers so they could supply themselves with merchandise for the market, or pay a bill.

Translator's note:
1.   Many businesses and few blessings

[Page 467 - Yiddish] [Page 195 - Hebrew]

R' Shmuel Zeinvl Melamed, z"l

by A. Rind

It us hard to understand how, on our sinful earth, there existed people like R' Shmuel Zeinvl who were far from materialism and everything worldly. Their lives were dedicated to serving God and to be worthy of it. To imagine R' Shmuel Zeinvl it would be enough to take all four books of the Shulchan Aruch, dress them with a kapoteh and belt, boots, a hat with a yarmulke, and you would have before you this very, dear Jew.

"*Pat b'melech tuchal v'mayim bimsorah tishteh v'al ha'aretz tishan*[1]." For whom were those words spoken if not for Shmuel Zeinvl. He took two essential mitzvoth on himself: To surround the shtetl with an eruv, and bikur cholim. Neither mitzvah brought him any satisfaction. The first demanded a lot of work, and the second sometimes brought him into contact with people with embittered hearts who vented their bitterness on him. He confided secretly to me that when he sees some of the sick, from their torments and despair, they begin to complain to God in front of him.

[Page 468]

He conducted his work with love and forgave those who caused him distress.

By his strong piety and love of the Jewish people–and maybe because of this–he was not a fundamentalist in matters of law. He prayed with his whole heart. He did not travel to see any rabbi, and did not hurry to meet them when they visited the shtetl. The reason for it we did not have to ask; we understood it well.

Translator's note:
1.   You shall eat bread with salt, drink small amounts of water, and sleep on the ground.

[Page 468 - Yiddish] [Page 195 - Hebrew]

R' Abraham-Meir Shushtchek z"l

by A. Rind

A Jew, quiet as a mouse. A keen learner, a passionate Radziner chasid. Lived frugally. Always sitting in his store by an open Gemara and studying. When he tore off a piece of paper to wrap something for a customer, it seemed as if he tore a page out of the big Gemara. He had virtually never stopped studying, and didn't get involved in debates, but he could respond quietly and persuasively.

I saw a list posted in the Radziner shtibl of those paying a weekly allowance to the rebbe. When I asked him, "R' Abraham Meir, how can you commit yourself to one Zloty a week for the rebbe?" His answer was, "Why do people undertake to pay for life insurance? Because they are insuring themselves against a tragedy, or for their retirement. Nu, I am doing the same thing."

[Page 468 - Yiddish] [Page 200 - Hebrew]

R' Abraham Yakov Freund hy"d

by A. Rind

I knew R' Abraham Yakov and his parents from my earliest years. He was a Cohen, and that was probably why he was an angry man, quick to get worked up and irate. He quickly regretted it, and tried to make up, and bring back the previous mood.

[Page 469]

He was a good-hearted person, and had good traits. He often made donations anonymously. He was a pious chasid, and loved scholarship. Even a young man that could study well impressed him. He suffered his whole life for not being able to study a page of Gemara with tosafot. He searched for ways to achieve this. He had a glass case full of religious books, the whole Talmud. He spent money and effort so that his children should achieve what he was not able to, and he was not very successful there either.

He observed the "law of Israel," with the parsha Rashi and a chapter of mishnayes. He fasted the 6 winter Fridays–"*Shovivim.*"

Yom Kippur, after Kol Nidrei, he stayed awake all night. Every Shavuot he stayed at his rebbe's. We used to avoid telling him our troubles and worries knowing that he would take it hard. In his later years, after his children got married, he and his wife, Esther, went on a diet. He would invite a guest for Shabbes, and bring him to my mother's restaurant, and pay for his meal.

———————

[Page 469 - Yiddish] [Page 201 - Hebrew]

R' Shmuel Malke's z"l

by A. Rind

Shmuel Rind, or as he was called by us, Shmuel Malke's, was a simple man, who was not well versed in religious studies, only capable of Shabbes davening, and reading the weekly portion. He was a person with a pure, honest Jewish heart. He believed in observant Jews, saints, and rabbis, but he also loved every Jew, and required from others that scholars be respected.

If a preacher, or an author, or simply a guest, came to town, his house was always open to them. He offered the nicest and the best to them, and helped his wife, Yote Malke's, to prepare meals for the guests. If a poor man showed up after the meal, there was also no resentment. The table was quickly covered by a tablecloth, bread, cheese, sour cream, butter and a glass of tea, and the guest fed and watered, and bid goodbye with a gift in hand, a prayer for the road, and "*shalom al Israel.*"

[Page 470]

[Page 470 - Yiddish] [Page 197 - Hebrew]

The Duck People

by A. Rind

The Duck people, that's what the old couple, Moishe and Chana Greenboim, were called in the shtetl.

They were an old childless couple that lived by the shul. They were both endlessly pious, and loved to sit together and study. Which one of them knew more was not known. Sometimes it seemed that Moishe was learning from her and sometimes the reverse. Their biggest worry was that after they died, they would have no one to say Kaddish for them. Auntie Chana, as I called her, took to raising as Kaddish sayer her brother's, Itche Fecher's, son, Hersh. He was a motherless orphan who was very smart and knowledgeable. Because of his wild behavior and brains he was called in the shtetl, "Der Meshugener Hersh."

A lot of naches from their kaddish they didn't have. To the extent that they were pious, he was the opposite. He could study a lot, knew the whole Tanach off by heart, knew several foreign languages, and was an expert in scientific studies. But he abandoned the couple in his younger years, and visited them only once a year. He remained an old bachelor, and supported himself giving classes in wealthy Jewish homes in Lublin.

Moishe and Chana took upon themselves the worry of Hachnoset Orchim. Their house was open to all strangers. Provided with cushions, blankets they would prepare beds for any pauper or traveller who came to their house. When too many guests showed up, they took the bedding to the shul, or the Radziner shtibl, and set them up there. More than once they were paid back with trouble. When Auntie Chana would bring the paupers the "*negl vasser*[1]," one of them would steal her last few pennies from under the pillow. Nevertheless, she continued doing her mitzvahs. When R' Moishe complained, she calmed him down, and promised that God would repay the loss.

The lived poorly, made do with little. Washing before eating and the blessings took more time than the whole feast. They made a living from three sources. The primary source was the lime business. Jews and Christians bought their lime because they knew they would get an honest weight. The second business they only pursued in winter when they slaughtered and sold geese. The profit was in the feathers for the poor to stuff cushions with, and sometimes also the giblets for cholent for Shabbes Kodesh. Their third means of earning was kept in a locked box in which there were several bottles of alcohol, and a few dozen cookies of various kinds. This merchandise was off limits to non-Jews, or even Jews who did not say a prayer before eating. Only those who belonged to the shul and the besmedresh could buy them. There were always two notices (Moishe Soifer's work)–the prayers before eating and after eating, so that the customer would not have to exert himself and search for them in the siddur.

If a poor Jew had Yohrzeit and could not afford a bottle of alcohol and some snacks, he could get right there as much as he wanted. A little water mix for the alcohol, he provided himself.

[Page 472]

And a few cookies, broken into little pieces, were enough for the whole minyan. When two Jews had, during the davening, agreed on a business deal, they had a little to eat. When two quarreling Jews made up it was definitely a mitzvah to have a drink and a little dry cookie. A good dream was also a suitable reason. Even the besmedresh boys were fond of snacking on Chana's cookies. If there was no money, they took it on credit. The point was the blessing, so Moishe and Chana could answer, amen.

There were also Shabbes customers. The Chevra Kadisha was of this sort. They would take it on credit and repay. One Shabbes after prayers the Chevra Kadisha wanted to make kiddush. However, Moishe and Chana did not want to extend any more credit. They argued that they were owed a big amount already. But how can you go home without kiddush? When they came by, Chana responded, "Bring some collateral, and I'll give you." So they said, " Nu, chaverim, bring as collateral the *ta'are breyt*![2] A frightened Chana gave it to them on credit, and begged them to repay her after Shabbes so she could buy fresh product.

Translator's notes:
1. Water to wash one's hands before prayers
2. The board on which the body of the deceased is placed for purification before burial

[Page 472 - Yiddish] [Page 196 - Hebrew]

R' Itche Sender hy"d

by A. Rind

Itche Sender's, Lefler, a simple Jew with a pure heart. A faithful chasid who was keen to host his chasidic rabbis, if not the real big ones, at least the little rebbelach. Always gave to charity and saw to it that others gave too. If you were unloading your troubles to him, and shedding a tear in the process, he would weep along with you, and add his troubles to yours.

Itche Sender was no scholar however, but he was not far beneath one. He found his satisfaction in the book of psalms. He was an assiduous student of psalms. He was a corpulent, broad-boned man, who so strongly evoked the simple healthy folksy type–it was fitting that he was called *"Tehillim Yid."*[1] His tehillim reciting was heard around the shtetl and on the roads–travelling to the markets. It seemed as if it floated in the air and filled the air with the songs of David.

[Page 473]

One cloudy, rainy day, Itche Sender's did not go to the market. He came to the besmedresh to get in another barchu with a kedushah. I asked him, "R' Itche, what are you doing here, what's happening with the market?" He replied, "I already, baruch hashem, had a good market today, and I earned more today than a bunch of markets." "How?" I asked him. "I managed to get in a barchu and a kedusheh. This is a more certain return."

Translator's note:
1.   Psalm man

[Page 473 - Yiddish] [Page 199 - Hebrew]

R' Shmuel Gurtler

by A. Rind

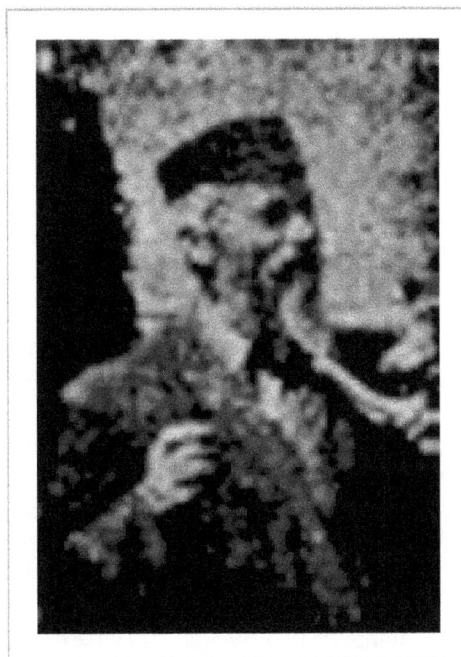

R' Shmuel Gurtler was not a scholar, but it could be said of him as the Mishnah states, "The important thing is the action, not the learning."

He was a chasid, but not a fanatic. He knew and understood life very well, but he understood there are boundaries to action.

He was one of those who always took on himself the burden of public service, and sometimes the public foisted the burden on him against his will. He did not want to become dozor, even though he was the right person for the job. He wanted to remain outside so he could stay objective and independent, and keep the friendliest relations with the community. That's why he was well liked in all circles.

[Page 474]

He had a fiery character, quick to get upset–like his whole family–but never lost his equilibrium, or stopped his activities.

He would give to charity with an open heart: always wanting to be the first and to give the most. Even in hard times, he gave as much as the wealthy. During a charitable appeal, he gave, as an example for others, the largest amount, and assured thereby the success of the campaign.

His house was a center for everything and everybody. As the expression goes: "*Fun rav biz tzum beder.*[1]" His house was always noisy and busy. People came and went, some to get advice from R' Shmuel, and some to discuss their troubled minds. Davening, reciting *slichot*, singing *zmirehs*, carrying out *shalosh-siddes, melave malkes*, and *kidesh-livoneh*, everything took place in and around that house.

There you could encounter the same people in different ways. Shimon Balagoleh during the week, and the Shabbes Shimon; Chaim-Zalman from the butcher shop, and a Chaim-Zalman reading mishnayes. Here, standing by the lectern, with glazed, pious eyes is Meye Mendele's, and next to him stands the Christian administrator of the graf's court waiting until the davening has ended. Here Aharon Gershn sings "*Dror yikra*", and at the same time the phone rings. And a strange harmony of sounds and rings is created not found in any other house in Krasnobrod.

Translator's note:
    1.   From the rabbi to the bathhouse attendant

R' Bunem Melamed hy"d

by A. Rind

Almost all the children in Krasnobrod knew him. He was renowned. Eighty percent of the children studied with him, went through his cheder, a melamed for three generations. Our parents, our children, and us were taught by him…He did not look to be so old.

[Page 475]

He did not have a big family. A father with 2 sons. All three slightly built. Furthermore, they all had one eye. The youngest was completely blind. But that did not interfere with their trade. Bunem Melamed was a big believer, a faithful Jew. He travelled to several rabbis, stayed in contact with them waiting for a remedy for the eyes. He did not hold with any doctors. They could not help him at all. In addition, he had living examples of God's help by virtue of the rabbis.

Like, for example, with his earning a living, or two livings. His wife dealt with fruit. She used to rent orchards, and spent the whole year in the market with apples and pears.

The method of his teaching: children of 5-8 years old. About 30 children sat around one large table. The house was always full of fruit, boxes, troughs, scales, weights, straw, and so on. He was always standing with his twitch in hand. He lashed out right and left.

He had a nickname for every student. Some nicknames stuck permanently. As if it was not enough to suffer him during the week, he also came to hear us out on Shabbes. We could not breath freely. He never missed a *tanis-tsiber*[1], although he would sometimes visit his rebbe then…

He was nevertheless good-hearted. One of his virtues was his antipathy to money. As soon as he got some, he would look for a way to give it away. He needed nothing for himself. He was so proficient in donating his few coins, that he always managed to find the place where his gift was most needed.

[Page 476]

It is worthwhile to recall one other thing. Bunem Melamed, poor as he was, was a big *machnes oyrech*[2]. He seldom sat at his table without a guest for Shabbes. In order to be assured a guest, he had an arrangement with the gabai of the shul, who used to apportion guests for Shabbes or holidays. The deal was that he would get the first guest, meaning that if there were only one in the shul, he would get him.

Permit me to tell a story about Bunem Melamed.

I once met Bunem Melamed at the rebbe's. As is the custom, after Minche-Maariv, a drink is served and a l'chaim made with the rebbe. When it was Bunem's turn, with his glass of whiskey in hand, he took a sip and fell into such a rapture, that he called out, "Rebbe you must help me, and you can help me, to make my son Moishele begin to have some sight, to become sighted like every other person... You can help me. You just have to want to." He yelled loudly, " I will not leave this spot. Help me! If your father could help me, you can help Moishele." And he begins to tell the rebbe the following story.

In 1905, during the Russia-Japan war, Chol Hamoed Sukkot, he and two other chasidim went off to visit the then rabbi, his father. In Zamosc, they encountered a lot of soldiers marching through the city. He was already half blind, and a Cossack on horseback trampled him, and badly wounded his head so that his eyes became bloody, and he became completely blind. The people who had accompanied him wanted to send him back home. But he would not hear of it. He insisted they take him to the rebbe.

[Page 477]

They could not prevail over him. They took him on the long trip to the rebbe. There was no train yet to Rejowiec. With God's help, they arrived at the rebbe's erev Hoshana Raba in the evening. They took the blind Bunem Melamed and led him into the rebbe's house. You can imagine what kind of noisy tumult and throng prevailed erev yom tov at the rebbe's. A crowd of chasidim who came from different cities. They stayed up all night. Bunem sat there blind. He said nothing. He moaned and wept asking to be brought to the rebbe. His crying and lack of sleep made his condition worse.

They brought him to the rebbe. He told him his problems. The rebbe calmed him down and told him to go to bed and get some rest. He argued, " Yes, what will I do in the morning? The davening I know off by heart. But what about all the prayers and *hoyshaynes*[3] that I don't know off by heart. How can I recite them?" The rebbe replied, "Bunem, don't worry. You'll sit next to me. I will recite out loud, and you will recite after me."

Bunem agreed and went to sleep.

It must be added however that the custom of the rebbe was not to stay seated during the prayers and hoyshaynes, but to walk around with the etrog and lulav, making a circuit of the whole synagogue, something no one remembered, including Bunem.

Morning arrived. Bunem made all the preparations for davening. Even blind, he did not fail to go to the mikvah. They began the davening. Bunem sat at the head, near the rebbe. He davened off by heart along with all the chasidim, with tears and great fervor. The rebbe was standing for Shmone Esrei. It was time for him to leave his spot for the hoyshaynes. Suddenly Bunem felt as if someone had stretched out his hand and wiped his eyes with a handkerchief.

[Page 478]

The rebbe left his spot to continue with the prayers–and Bunem's eyes cleared up as if nothing had happened! He was able to daven from the siddur like everyone else, and he had a happy holiday.

This was the story, and Bunem was one hundred percent convinced that if the father was capable then so is the son…He just has to want to…

What the rebbe answered, I don't remember. But one thing I do remember: we tried to change the subject so that Bunem would not interfere with the celebration at the rebbe's.

Translator's notes:
1. Exceptional communal fast day
2. Person who regularly invites the poor to his home, esp. Shabbes or religious holidays.
3. Hymn recited during Sukkot

R' Mordechai Gurtler hy"d

by A. Rind

One could say he was a born social activist. He was involved in community events from his youth onward.

About a decade before WWI, he had already made plans to rebuild the besmedresh that was as old as our shtetl itself.

He rebuilt it, adding another story for "ezres noshim," the woman's shul. He completed it down to the smallest details, and ruled with a strong hand.

The whole time, as I recall, he was the gabai of the besmedresh, or the shul of the Chevra Kadisha. He was also dozor[1]. He was constantly called in to consult with the assessment commission for revenue taxation, because he was well known, and he knew everybody. True, he did not decline any of these honors. But his close friends always nominated him when the need arose. Why? Because Mordechai Gurtler knew his job. He was not a person who compromised. He did what he thought best. He did not even consult his advisors. Thanks to his strictness, he made enemies. But those who knew him best, did not desert him.

[Page 479]

They knew his virtues and good qualities, and his house, which was like his hands, open for anyone in need.

Mordechai Gurtler and his wife, Sheva (Elisheva) were childless. The shtetl was sympathetic, spoke of it with pity. It was said that it was because he had a quarrel with another chasidic sect, and was cursed. His home was never depressing, however, always brightly lit, and noisy with people: guests, gabaim, preachers, emissaries, heads of yeshivas. A bed was always ready for anyone who had to stay overnight.

His wife, Sheveleh, was good-hearted, quiet, friendly, a saint. She was often oblivious of the tumult in the house. She was always reading religious books. She was learned in religious texts and concerned with loftier matters. She would set up the brass samovar for the guests, and re-immerse herself in the spiritual world.

I would see him quite often at meetings and assemblies, and witnessed his integrity. The problem was his inability to compromise. Either yes or no. With this approach of his, his projects sometimes fell through.

I can recall one failure. As gabai of the Chevra Kadisha, he, the Gerer chasid and zealot, disapproved of the behavior of his group. He prepared to do a "housecleaning." But such a thing was unheard of. There was a rule that whoever was a member of the Chevra Kadisha was there for life. He was not even allowed to hint that he would leave.

Mordechai Gurtler informed those he didn't like that they were expelled from the group. But he did it all by himself. At the same time, he informed some young people in town, without consulting them beforehand, that they had been made members of the group. This was viewed poorly. But Mordecahi Gurtler knew everything. He was not afraid, neither of the living, or the dead. When he included me without my knowledge among the new inductees, I asked him why he hadn't first tried to get my permission. He replied, "Your father was inscribed in the Chevra Kadisha, that gives me the right to include you."

When the cheder, Yesodei-HaTorah, was founded in our shtetl, he was also then the "boss" in the shtetl. Of course, everyone in the shtetl knew who was sending their children to the new cheder. Chaim-Leib, the hat maker, a simple man, was not in a hurry to send his two kids to the new cheder. One evening after the market, Chaim-Leib came to the besmedresh to daven. So someone called out, "Chaim-Leib, why don't you send your children to the cheder?" Chaim-Leib answered quite naively, "Why are you making such a big deal about your cheder? If you had founded a cheder where all 70 languages were taught, I would have something to hurry for. But for this cheder–I have time.

Mordecahi Gurtler heard everything. He went over to him. "What?" he said to him. "A cheder with 70 languages you need?" And in the blink of an eye he picked him up and carried him out of the shul–and he lay out there outside. In addition, he threw in, "Now learn 70 languages."

He was just afraid of one person, Hitler, may his name be erased. With Hitler's incursion into Poland, he became so frightened, that I saw him carrying with him all he possessed and his whole family: his tallis and tefillin, and his wife, Shevaleh, who from fear lost the ability to walk. He carried her to the hiding place he knew so well, and where he was always the boss, and where he knew every hidden nook and cranny–the cemetery.

[Page 481]

He also managed to hide and wall up in his cellar 16 Torahs before leaving his house.

Translator's note:
1. Community leader

———

[Page 481 - Yiddish] [Page 202 - Hebrew]

Hersh-Leib Briks hy"d

by A. Rind

Born in 1907, Hersh Leib belonged to the younger generation.

He was raised in a strict religious home. He was watched constantly, not allowed go anywhere without supervision. His mother, a widow, wanted her only son, who was possessed of lots of talent, a good memory, and was an assiduous student, to become a rabbi. She sent him to the finest cheders, and required her second husband, Yoshe Goldberg– who had been a student of the Volozhiner yeshiva–he should study with him. She wanted to see him become a rabbi as quickly as possible.

Hersh Leib had an altogether different view of his future. Early on, he secretly and with zeal, began to read Yiddish literature. He became familiar with Mendele, and Sholem Aleichem. He read Zhitlowsky and Bórochov, internalized the ideology, and became a passionate follower of Labor-Zionism.

His family discovered that Hersh Leib had "left the proper way," and they began to persecute him. He suffered greatly from the fanatic Bergsteins, but was not broken, and energetically took to setting up a branch of Poalei-Zion. The party and its youth movement, Freiheit, grew quickly. Hersh Leib was the animating spirit of the movement. Very well liked by the youth, he was made the spokesman of Poalei-Zion in the shtetl. He addressed lectures, held interesting readings, and was at the head of every activity. He was not inclined to compromise, but he nevertheless found a way for agreement with every party.

[Page 482]

He threw himself into business as well, with enthusiasm and energy. He became quickly rich in 1931–but during the big economic crisis–he became greatly impoverished. He took up the lumber business and quickly became one of the richest people in town. He became inactive in the party, and was satisfied with an occasional appearance.

He perished along with his wife and two children.

[Page 482 - Yiddish] [Page 203 - Hebrew]

Avraham and Yehoshua Shnur

by A. Rind

Avraham Shnur was a Jew of the older generation. By trade he was a shoemaker. An honest shoemaker as was said in the city, trying to please his clients.

His trade, such as it was, was not inherited from his parents. Zalman-Ber, the shammes, once told me that he learned the shoemaking trade with him. (And he really was better at it than his teacher).

He had two good qualities: he liked learned men–although he himself was not a scholar–and his trade. It seems that he strongly abided by the Mishneh, "Eem ein kemach, ein Torah; v'eem ein Torah, ein kemach.[1]" In the besmedresh, after work, he always loved to listen in on the studying. He respected the scholars. On the other hand, he didn't keep his sons or daughters very long in cheder like other faithful Jews. He made them all learn a trade.

[Page 483]

When Avraham Shnur was looking for a match for his daughter, he sought a son-in-law in keeping with the above-mentioned mishneh. The daughter, in this case, agreed with the father. It did not happen so quickly. But ultimately God sent him Getzl Ehrlich, the hat maker, a young man, religious, a believing soul, a Belzer chasid. He had a little scholarly knowledge and the rest he achieved through good deeds. Avraham Shnur was overjoyed at God's gift.

The founder of the Bund, Yehoshua Shnur, hy"d

It is however interesting to mention one of his sons. Yehoshua Shnur was born in 1901. As was the custom, Yehoshua was only taught by the *dardeke melamdim*[2], and was sent to learn a trade at an early age. But Yehoshua was not an ordinary child. He strove to something higher. From an early age, he took to education and absorbed learning like a sponge. I was frankly astonished when we got together. He was then working as an apprentice for Hanoch Glickman. When we went for walks in the evening, or when we met at various debates, Yehoshua knew how to respond to any questions, and was aware of things beyond his years.

In 1921 he served in the Polish army and returned a Bundist. All we heard from him then was the Bund, Medem, Michailovitch, Victor Alter…

Yehoshua was not satisfied with just carrying on discussions. He set on creating a Bund party in the shtetl. He attracted friends, Ruben Kramer, Yakov Geistat, and others. They also founded a "*Skif*" division and a "*Zukunft*" organization. Yehoshua was the head of the work.

Around 1930, on a nice Saturday morning, about 9:00 o'clock in the morning, when the Jews were in the besmedreshes, they went out demonstrating around town with banners, red flags, and songs. The pious, Sabbath Jews could not abide such a thing, and a fight broke out. There were wounded and bloodied participants. The Polish police now had the best excuse to mix in and disperse the "celebration." But Yehoshua Shnur continued to lead his party with a firm hand. He taught students in his methods. He later married Moishe-Leib Borg's daughter. He was killed by the Nazis along with his wife and children.

Translator's notes:
1. If there is no flour, there is no Torah; and if there is no Torah, there is no flour.
2. Teacher of the youngest children

[Page 484 - Yiddish] [Page 205 - Hebrew]

Reuven Kramer hy"d

by A. Rind

Reuven Kramer was a barber and the son of a barber. His grandfather was a barber, and he was called Itche Roife. His father was called Leibish Itche Roife's, and he himself was called Reuven Itche Roife's.

He was an interesting person, graced with a noble character and organizational talent. Aside from the fact that he was the leader of the Bund, he was beloved by the youth of all circles and his house was always full of young people.

He was one of the founders of the library.

[Page 485]

When the Gemiles Chasidim was founded, he was one of the first of the founders, and contributed money from his own pocket. He was also a member of the Chevra Kadisha, and thus won the sympathy of the religious bloc.

In later years, before the war, he was elected as dozor on the artisans list. He was very active, took part in all meetings, brought in various proposals and fought to see them realized. He showed much understanding of religious needs, and often promoted the interests of the rabbi for whom he had a personal liking.

When the war broke out, he escaped with his family to the Caucasus. Unfortunately, the Nazi beasts tracked him down there, and cut short his life of creativity.

––––––––

[Page 485 - Yiddish] [Page 205 - Hebrew]

Various personalities

by A. Rind

Unfortunately, it is difficult for me to enumerate and describe separately examples from the gallery of people and types who would need to be included in this book of memory. I will just have to content myself to mentioning a group of people, who with all their hearts, were loyal to the ideals of Zionism, each according to his ability: R' Baruch Glustman, Mendl Rozner (today in Argentina), Itzchak Babad, Yosef Lederman, Baruch Ze'ev Kupiec, Nachum Lederman (today in America), Meir Laizer Melamed, who was always thinking of aliyah to Eretz Israel, Leibish Lerner, the first to rent a hall for Zionist meetings and was persecuted for it, Israel Babad, Eliezer Gurtler, Meir Kerer, and Pesach Helfman, a pious Gerer Chasid who was the first to send his children to the Yavne school, and later to high school in Zamosc.

I'd like to pass along an episode that I heard from Leibish Arele's (Lerner).

[Page 486]

After his bar mitzvah, Leibish studied for a couple of years in Belz. After, up until he got married, he studied in the besmedresh in Krasnobrod. One day he went over to the bookcase and took out a book. He was astonished to find it was a heretical work by Yakov Reifman of Shebreshin,[1] near Zamosc. (The teacher of Y. L. Peretz, and Dr. Gelibter). In the meantime, R' Isrulish Gurtler came in. He glanced at the book, and seeing what it was, he tore it out of Leibish's hands, and threw it into the burning oven, and gave Leibish a stinging chasidic slap.

Translator's note:
    1.   Polish name Szczebrzeszyn

[Page 486 - Yiddish] [Page 206 - Hebrew]

My Father Chanoch Untzig hy"d

by Tuvieh

Who in Krasnobrod did not know Henoch and his children? Although not a rich man, he was always happy with his lot, and did not envy those who had more.

His greatest pleasure was to travel to Ger for Shabbes and listen to the Torah straight from the rebbe's mouth.

When the war broke out, and the city burned, our house remained intact. The joy, that we would not have to sleep in the streets, was great. But it did not last long, because we quickly began to feel the brutality of the Nazi murderers, ym"sh.

[Page 487]

When the Russians left the shtetl, my father also left for Rawa-Ruska. Coming to the border, he was tormented by the thoughts of his wife and family at home, and he returned, a broken man, and there he was murdered.

Yakov Zimmerman

by A. Diamant

His external appearance, and the way he treated others, indicated that he possessed an inborn gentleness. In the worst, most strained social situations, he was never heard to raise his voice. His every observation was well thought out. He dealt with every crisis with stoic calm, and knew how to get out of them. His face always shone with happiness in spite of the fact that his closest most intimate friends knew very well that he suffered much at home. But he never told anyone about his problems.

He was among the first in the shtetl to organize culture clubs and discussion evenings.

[Page 488]

He founded a chess club, which later evolved into a political club of General-Zionism.

He led the club on his own. Being such an affable person, he was always able to resolve differences of opinion between comrades in any area, and thanks to him there was always peaceful relations among the activists of the various parties. If our shtetl had a good Keren Kayemet L'Israel committee that successfully raised money for Eretz Israel, it was chiefly the work of Yakov Zimmerman who gave his heart and soul to it.

How much he was beloved by the residents of the shtetl was seen when he fell ill. At first, it was a light illness, but later, because of a fatal misdiagnosis by the doctor, the life of this gentle and hard-working young man, came to an end. There was not one house where the question was not on everyone's lips, "How is Yankel, what does the doctor say?" When he was transferred to the neighboring city of Zamosc, he was accompanied by a whole host of people. While he was in the hospital we set up a reporting point that updated news about his condition every two hours. (There was no telephone yet in the shtetl). The news quickly spread from house to house.

When the news reached the shtetl about his premature death, there was grieving not only among his family and near ones, but everybody in town without exception was affected. His funeral, organized by his comrades and friends, was transformed into an imposing mourning demonstration of people who felt that the loss was a heavy one for the town in general, and his family in particular.

[Page 489]

Mendl Farber hy"d

by A. Diamant

He was originally from the neighboring shtetl of Tarnogrod. He came to Krasnobrod as a young bachelor, got married here, and became a family man. But he was unsuccessful both in his family life and in his business life. On the other hand, he was very successful in his social and cultural activities.

He was always in a happy mood. (He was called the happy pauper). He never got upset at all his problems. There were times when he simply had no bread to feed his children, but he didn't lose heart, and his cheerful mood did not forsake him. Thanks to these qualities, he was never broken, and overcame the hard times and reached better ones.

His first steps into social-cultural work were the establishment of Hebrew classes for children and adults. At the same time, he began to organize political clubs that, with time, evolved into a General Zionist organization whose chairman he was the whole time.

He helped organize and took part in cultural events. These undertakings helped many of the youth to find their way from the old-fashioned Chasidic shtiblach to the political parties and culture clubs. As time passed, some of these young people's talents became noticeable. They later stood at the head of the youth organizations that were created.

For Mendl Farber there was no work that was not done purely for spiritual reasons. He did everything unselfishly, dedicating his heart and soul to his ideas. There was no task that he could not accomplish.

[Page 490]

No sooner had the work been decided upon than it was fulfilled. If others did not do it, he would roll up his sleeves and get it done.

I had the honor of working with him for ten years, day in and day out, when he was chairman and I was secretary, and in Keren Kayemet and Keren HaYesod committees. I can, with clear conscience, state that none of the activists and coworkers showed as much devotion to the work as Mendl Farber.

Naturally his social work did not always go to his satisfaction. He was the first martyr to be besmirched by the older generation of Jews, from the chasidim and fanatics in the shtetl. More than once, the parents of young people in the organisations attacked him with curses and insults, and created scandals. He, as was his wont, took everything with a smile–and continued his work, but with even more ardor and energy.

His weakness was chess. He would sit for hours without a break engrossed in the game, foregoing lunch and sometimes supper.

He worked for some time as an insurance agent, and he would be absent from the shtetl for a week at a time. When he would come home for Shabbes, he would bring along a couple of new songs from the movement, and teach them to us.

[Page 491]

Yehoshua Babad hy"d

by A. Diamant

Yehoshua Babad was one of a kind, an enigma that puzzled many. He was a bachelor without particular education who practically never left the shtetl, and had very little contact with the outside world. He did not gain any knowledge sitting at other tables–and yet–what talent did he not possess? From early on he could play the violin. He produced and led a troupe of actors. He founded a choir and put on performances that were organized by him alone, without anyone's help. There was no cultural or political activity where you would not find him at work. He had to be everywhere. It was simply impossible to imagine any social activity without him.

One can state with certainty: if Poalei-Zion had any success in Krasnobrod, it was due to Yehoshua Babad.

Aside from this alone, he was a cheerful and modest person. He was not arrogant. He had time for everybody, young and old, helping in any way he could, sometimes with advice, sometimes with material means. He helped others even when his own situation was difficult. It was common knowledge among many that if they were in need of material help, Yehoshua Babad was the right address. He would immediately organize and gather together the required sums. Nobody ever refused him, or asked who the money was for. They knew that if Yehoshua requested money, you had to give–and they gave.

Finding yourself in his company meant enjoying a pleasant and comfortable time. Often after stormy meetings or assemblies he would gather us together, comrades as well as opponents, and teach us songs. This was his favorite pastime. He could sit with us until 2-3 o'clock in the morning. He had already established a group of selected young singers. Among them was Esther Kamm (now Glickman) who had a very nice voice.

[Page 492]

He was personally modest, but as a Jew, he was proud with a warm Jewish heart. When a Jew was insulted by his antisemitic neighbors, it was for him a real tragedy. He regularly actively reacted against every kind of antisemitic wrong and statement. In such cases he would agitate for the organization of a self-defense squad, rather than wait for help from the police, antisemites in uniform.

I can recall an incident where he almost lost his life defending Jewish honor. Military maneuvers were taking place in the shtetl. Some Polish soldiers were making fun of Jews. Yehoshua happened to be walking by and noticed this. He reacted, as was his wont, by physically attacking them. It looked like it would become a horrible adventure. Were it not for the intervention of the superior officers, he would certainly have paid with his life.

He was beloved by everyone. Anyone who was associated with him, whether friend or opponent, revered him for his boundless devotion and abilities, for his prodigious diligence, in the furtherance of his idealism.

Even during the bloody Hitler years, he did not lose his pride or his dignity as a Jew.

[Page 493 - Yiddish] [Page 206 - Hebrew]

Grune Gurtler–Lochfeld a"h

by Ben

A child of poor parents, as a young girl she worked as a seamstress making men's pants in order to help out her family.

After a twelve hour day bent over a sewing machine, she found the time and the energy to be active in the Poalei Zion party, took part in all the activities, and in the performances of the drama club.

In 1932 she joined HeChalutz HaKlali and went to the Krasnobroder kibbutz. There, she performed hard physical labor in the sawmill, sawing wood by hand. She endured whatever difficulties arose with patience. She was an example of diligence and discipline. In 1933 she was sent over to the Dror kibbutz in Cracow where she worked until her aliyah in 1936.

Here in Israel she was one of the founders of the kibbutz, Ein Hayam, near Atlit (today Ein HaCarmel). She endured all the hardship of the occupied land. She worked in various capacities, was happy with the achievements of the kibbutz, and hoped to bring her family over. In 1938 she left the kibbutz for health reasons, and settled in Haifa.

When the war broke out and the first news about the fate of the Jews under Nazi rule came out, she wept day and night for her parents, brothers, and sisters who had remained behind in Krasnobrod. In 1943, when it became known that all the Jews there had been murdered, she became very ill from grief, took to her bed for two years, underwent great sorrow. She could not reconcile herself to the great tragedy, and ended her life in 1945, not having lived to see the establishment of the state of Israel she had dreamed of for years in her short and creative life.

[Page 494 - Yiddish] [Page 209 - Hebrew]

From the Publishers

by A. Lochfeld

After much effort and work and the participation of a group of comrades and friends, we succeeded in gathering together all this material, memories, photos and evidence about Krasnobrod's existence and destruction.

As we hand over the book to the Krasnobrod she'erit hapletah, it is with the feeling that we created something out of nothing. We took all the separate threads and wove them into the web that became this book of memory.

Permit me to express my heartfelt thanks to all those who contributed their donations and work in the bringing out of this book. I especially want to thank my friends, Eliyahu Rind, Pinchas Diamant, Gitl and Avraham Barg who dedicated their time and energy to this important task.

I extend my heartiest thanks to the editor, Mordechai Kroshnitz, who showed us how to begin the project, agreed to edit the accumulated material, and gave us much of his time, energy and talent.

We hope that the Krasnobrod survivors will feel the spirit of the old home in this book. They will return to the bygone years of their youth, relive the tension of a meeting with generations that have vanished, and absorb the deep, unappeased sorrow of the great catastrophe that befell us.

Our younger generation will recognize in this book the "golden chain" of their noble origins, and will with pride remember their grandfathers and grandmothers.

This book will remind us all that we are an orphaned family that has a shared yohrzeit day–the day of *tet vav* Cheshvan.

[Page 496]

Martyrs of the Holocaust

The candle of G-d is the soul of a person

[Page 497]

Words of Eulogy and Esteem

by Rabbi Yitzchak Halevi Shulzinger of Haifa, author of *Imrot Yitzchak*

Translated by Jerrold Landau

"I will render vengeance to Mine adversaries, and will recompense them that hate Me. 42 I will make Mine arrows drunk with blood, and My sword shall devour flesh; with the blood of the slain and the captives, from the long-haired heads of the enemy. 43 Sing aloud, O ye nations, of His people; for He doth avenge the blood of His servants, and doth render vengeance to His adversaries, and doth make expiation for the land of His people." (Deuteronomy 32)[1]

"For he doth avenge the blood of his servants, and doth render vengeance" – two acts of vengeance: "vengeance for the blood and vengeance for the violence." (*Yalkut Shimoni*, 247 946)

The heart is oppressed, the soul is mournful, the hand trembles, and the eyes shed tears as I take the pen in my hand to record an eyewitness memory for our children and grandchildren, until the end of days, about what happened to the communities of Israel in all the lands of Europe at the hands of the Nazi murderers, the accursed Germans, may their names be blotted out. Regarding this, the sweet singer of Israel said (Psalm 79)[2] "Pour out Your wrath on the gentiles who do not know You, and on the kingdoms who do not call in Your name, for thy have consumed Jacob and laid waste his habitation."

"Consumed Jacob" – more than six million, a sizable portion of the Nation of Israel, from the cream of the crop of Jewry, youths and babies, pure and holy, righteous people and Torah greats, elderly and children, men and women were annihilated with harsh torture and unusual deaths.

"And have laid waste his habitation" – they murdered and pillaged in accordance with the verse "Have you killed and also taken possession"[3].

Standing on the blessing shall be my friend Reb Eliyahu Moshe the son of Reb Avigdor Halevi Rund, and Reb Efraim Ben-Zion the son of Reb Aharon Tzvi Luchfeld, who were among those active to make an eternal memorial, to put the thoughts into a book as a perpetual memorial, to perpetuate the dear souls, the holy, pure community, the holy and faithful Jews who went up at the stake, who were suffocated, killed, and burnt in sanctification of the Divine Name, of the Torah, and of Israel in the important city of Krasnobród, Zamość district, Lublin region in the country of Poland.

Krasnobród, which was renowned and splendorous in Israel, was influenced by the Torah and wisdom of Chachmei Lublin…

Lublin was famous already from the time of the Mahara'm of Lublin[4]. He would use the expression *Makshin Haolam* [difficulties of the world] in his novellae and commentaries on the Talmud. It is asked:

[Page 498]

And is the world difficult, and does the world have something more difficult than the statements of the Talmud? For only the people of the House of the Talmud, the people of the study halls, the studiers, who toil and weary themselves to understand and know the words of Torah in general, and the Talmud in particular. They have questions and difficulties in their studies. They respond to questions and break apart problems to ascertain the text properly. So, is there any place for the expression "difficulties of the world"? Does this have any connection to reality?

However, the Mahara'm of Lublin of blessed memory expressed in this manner his great and broad opinion of the people of Israel in general: That the world of Torah, the studies of Torah and those that fulfil its commandments are indeed the world. The world is founded and based on them, as it is written: "In the beginning created" [Genesis 1:1]. Rashi states there: This verse demands explanation, as our sages of blessed memory have written, "For the sake of the Torah that is called 'the beginning of His way', as is said (Proverbs 8): The L-rd made me the beginning of his way; and for the sake of the righteous who are called 'the first' as is said (Jeremiah 2): Israel is holy to G-d, the first of its produce, everyone who consumes it will be guilty, evil will befall them, thus says G-d. For them, the world was created, and in their merit it exists. Had Israel not accepted the Torah at Sinai, the world would have reverted to unformed and void, as before creation."

We agree completely that the gentiles who did not want to receive the Torah at Sinai perpetrate deeds of ruin and destruction, evil and corruption, even though they possess wisdom, as it is written (Lamentations 2) "Their kings and princes among the nations have no Torah." The Midrash states there: "If they tell you that there is wisdom in Edom, believe it, but that there is Torah in Edom, do not believe it." We were present, and have studied with clear knowledge that wisdom that is not the wisdom of the Torah is wisdom that will bring evil, and the culture of the gentiles is the culture of sinners. How much evil did the Edomites perpetrate with their "wisdom." How did they raise their impure hands to beat the holy flock with their evil fists. In this, they continue the ways of their father Esau, as is written "And I will kill my brother Jacob" (*Toldot*) [Genesis 27:41]. The wicked in their anger have killed infants and suckling babes, women and men, the old and the children, the righteous and the pious, greats in Torah and people of virtuous deeds.

It is fitting to recite the dirge [*kina*] of Jeremiah the prophet, who lamented the destruction of the Temple: "Would it be that my head was water, and my eyes were a source of tears, I would weep day and night for the victims of the daughter of my nation." (Jeremiah 8). "For death has come up to our windows, and has entered our palaces, to cut off infants outside, and youths from the streets." (Jeremiah 9).

Woe is me for my hurt! My wound is grievous; but I said: "This is but a sickness, and I must bear it." (Jeremiah 10[5]). The community of Krasnobród was an important community within Polish Jewry. It was based on faithful principles and holy foundations, upon Torah, the commandments, and the traditions of the fathers. Rabbis who were great in Torah served there. They prayed and poured out their supplications in the synagogues and Hassidic houses, as they communed with the Holy One Blessed Be He. In addition, there were also those who frequented the *Beis Midrash* and studied Torah alone or in public, in all subjects of Torah – Tanach, Mishna, Gemara, Midrash, and Jewish law – each according to their ability and understanding.

[Page 499]

The city consisted of many streams of Hassidism. There were Hassidic prayer houses for Belz, Radzyn, Gur, and Trisk.

Krasnobród was close to the city of Izbica, where the honorable Admor, the Tzadik Rabbi Mordechai Yosef, may the memory of the righteous and holy be a blessing, the founder of the Izbica-Radzyn dynasty, lived. His grandson, the Admor and Tzadik Rabbi Gershon Henech, may the memory of the righteous be a blessing, authored a book on *techelet*[6], and reinstated the use of *techelet* in *tzitzit*.

Regarding the commandment of *tzitzit* in general, it is said (Torah portion of *Shlach*) [Numbers 15:40]: "So that you will remember and do all of My commandments, and be holy to your G-d." The Gemara states (*Menachot* 43): "This commandment is equal to all of the commandments." The Gemara continues there: "How is *techelet* different from all other colors? Because *techelet* is similar to the sea, and the sea is similar to the firmament, and the firmament to the Throne of Honor." The *Yalkut* (*Shlach*, 247 950) states: "The Torah says that anyone who fulfils the commandment of *tzitzit* is considered as if he welcomed the face of the Divine Presence, for *techelet* is compared to the sea, and the sea is compared to the firmament, and the firmament is compared to the Throne of Honor, as is said (Ezekiel 1), "And above the firmament is like the appearance of sapphire stone."

The commandment of *tzitzit*, which is considered as equal and important as all the commandments of the Torah, with the addition of the commandment of *techelet*, reminds one that it has the power to raise man in the trait of faith in the Blessed Creator, to the sublime point of uniting with the Throne of Honor, as is written (Hosea 2): "And I shall betroth you in faith, and you shall know G-d."

That which Jacob saw in a dream "And behold there was a ladder planted on the ground with its head reaching the skies, and angels of G-d were ascending and descending upon it." (*Vayeitzei*). According to the simple meaning, it is referring to the angel of above, angles from heaven, as it says (*Vayishlach*): "And Jacob sent messengers." Rashi says there: "literally angels." But there is another intention to angels going up and down. Our sages have said (*Vayikra Rabba*, chapter 1): "The prophets are referred to as angels, as it says" (Numbers 20): "And he sent an angel and took us out of Egypt." And was it an angel of G-d? Was it not Moses? Why is he called an angel? From here we learn that the prophets are called angels."

[Page 500]

However, it is not only prophets who are called angels. The Admor, the holy and righteous Gaon Rabbi Yehuda Aryeh Leib, may the memory of the righteous and holy be blessed, of Gur, says in his book, *Sfat Emet*, on the Torah (*Vayikra*, year 5631 [1871]): "In truth, every person of Israel sent into the world to do the will of Our Father In Heaven is called a messenger and an angel, for an angel has nothing other than its mission… If a person watches himself to refrain from doing any deed that does not fulfil the desire of The Blessed One… then he is indeed called an angel." The Admor, the righteous Gaon Rabbi Avraham may the memory of the righteous and holy be a blessing, the Magid Meisharim of Trisk, says in his book, *Magen Avraham*, on the five books of the Torah (*Vayeitzei*, page 22, folio a): "Ladder" [*sulam*] "is Sinai" for Sl'm [מ"לס] has the same *gematria* [numerical value of the Hebrew letters] as Sinai [י"נים], which is the acronym for *Yosef sod yesod nikra* [Joseph is secretly called the foundation], for his strength was in the rectification of the trait of foundation[7] of a Tzadik, for this is the fundamental foundation in the ways of serving the Blessed G-d. This is what "standing on the ground" means, that is, that even the matter of this service stands upon this earth. However, in truth, "and its head reached the Heavens" for the head of this reaches upward and upward to the heights of the supernal worlds. "And behold, the angels of G-d are ascending and descending upon it." The angels of G-d are going up and down has the *gematria* of the 613 commandments of the Torah, and they are angels of G-d! They are occupied in Torah and in the 613 commandments within the Torah. With all this, the fundamental aspect of their ascent and descent is dependent on this ladder, which hints at the rectification of the foundation of the sign of the covenant. When they sanctify themselves with the holiness of *yesod* [foundation] they ascend to the heights of the upper levels and reach elevated levels. On the other hand, when they do not have this trait, they can still reach the state of descent, Heaven forbid.

Indeed, our father Jacob, peace be upon him, rectified this trait as appropriate. Therefore, he merited a great ascent, and merited that the light of his name will be revealed to him by G-d, as is written: "And behold G-d is standing before him." [Genesis 28:13].

Further there (Portion of Naso, page 42, folio b): "And it says in the Gemara: And on each and every spike, there are heaps of *halachot*. *Halachot* implies "the ways of the world"[8], which means going from step to step from world to world, for on each and every spike there are pathways of ascent, enabling the lowly human to go and pass to all the supernal worlds. Therefore, a wholesome person who walks in the ways of G-d glorifies and strengthens the crown of his blessed kingdom, so to speak – in accordance with the verse "Your right hand, o G-d, is glorious in power" [Exodus 15:6], and as is written "Ascribe strength to G-d" [Psalms 68:35]. Israel adds strength to the Heavenly hosts – through this, he has it in his power to go from world to world, to pass through all the worlds, and to cleave to the essence of his Blessed G-d in the light of the Eternal Blessed Be He and Blessed Be His Name – to awaken from there the continuation of all the positive influences through all the worlds until the lower world, and to influence all of Israel.

[Page 501]

The Admor, the righteous Gaon Rabbi Shalom Rokeach, may the memory of the righteous and the holy be blessed, from Belz, says (brought in the Book Belz by Rabbi Y. M. Gutman, page 46): "And he stood over them under the tree and they ate" [Genesis 18:8]. It is appropriate to understand why at first it says "stood over him" [Genesis 18:2], implying that they [i.e. the angels] were above him [i.e. Abraham], and here it is written "and he stood over them" implying that he is above them.

The explanation: It is known there are several groups of ministering angels. There is a group that is high above other angels, and greater than Israel until the future to come, when they will merit being in front of the ministering angels. Those angels that came to Abraham our forefather, peace be upon him, were of the elevated level. Therefore, it is written about them "stood above him." However, Abraham did not realize they were angels, so it is written "men" "and Abraham ran to greet them." "And he ran" – he did the act of the mitzvah, and then he "greeted them" – literally equal with them, for a man of Israel, through the act of the mitzvot, is able to merit high holiness, and he merits even more of what Israel will ultimately merit in the future to come. This is the meaning of "and he stood above them."

Furthermore, it is said (ibid. page 53): "Then Moses and the Children of Israel sang this song to G-d" [Exodus 15:1]. It is known that if a person of Israel studies and prays, the Holy One Blessed Be He prays along with him. And what is the prayer of the Holy One Blessed Be He? "May it be [My] will that My mercies shall overcome My anger." [Brachot 7a]. Certainly when the Community of Israel sang the song with a pure heart, they caused the Blessed God to also recite the song. This is the explanation of "And then Moses and the Children of Israel sang this song to G-d." ישיר is a causative noun, meaning that Moses and the Children of Israel caused G-d to also sing this song, hinting to G-d that He too recite this song.

From all the holy writings brought down here, we learn that every Jew, through the study of Torah, the fulfilment of the commandments, and prayer can reach the level of an angel, and even higher than that. For the holy song of every Jew wherever he may be connects, blends, and cleaves to the song of the G-d may He be blessed, in accordance with "And thou who cleave to the L-rd your G-d are all alive today." [Deuteronomy 4:4]

The foundational principle of all these matters is faith, as the prophet states (Habakkuk 2)

[Page 502]

"And the righteous shall live by his faith." It is written in the *Yalkut Shimoni* (Hosea innuendo 519) "You find that the exiles are not gathered other than through the reward of faith. As is written (Song of Songs 4): 'Come with me from Lebanon my bride, come with me from Lebanon, peer from the top of Amana'"[9]. Faith is great before He Who Spoke And The World Came To Be, for as a reward for the faith that Israel had, the holy spirit rested upon them and they recited the song, as it says (Exodus 14): "And they believed in G-d and in Moses His servant – then did Moses and the Children of Israel sing." Similarly, it says (ibid. 17): "And Aaron and Hur supported his hands, and his hands were steady"[10]

That which Jacob our forefather saw in a dream was: that the Children of Israel could ascend upward on a ladder planted in the earth, whose head reached the heavens – to the supernal point of uniting with the Throne of Honor. The commandment of *techelet* [blue strings on *tzitzit*], reminiscent of the Throne of Glory, demonstrates this level, and the path to ascent through the House of G-d.

In Krasnobród there was study of Torah, the fulfilment of the commandments with great faith, charity, and virtuous deeds. There were acts of benevolence, tending to guests, visiting the sick, groups who recited Psalms, a burial society [*Chevra Kadisha*], etc.

Destruction then came and destroyed everything. We must always remember this. It is forbidden for us to forget. The Torah commands "Remember that which Amalek did to you on your way when you left Egypt." [Deuteronomy 25:17] If there is a commandment to remember that which Amalek did to us when we left Egypt, how much more so must we remember that which the German murderer, forged from the branch of Amalek, a shoot from its root, did to us at the threshold of the beginning of the redemption, at the threshold of the third and final redemption.

Regarding the war with Amalek, the Torah tells us (Exodus 17): "And Amalek came and fought with Israel at Rephidim." It is said (ibid.): "And Joshua weakened Amalek and his nation with the sword." That means, that in the final reckoning, the Children of Israel achieved the defeat of Amalek. The sin of this murderer was the opening that was opened before all the enemies of Israel, the permit that permitted them to fight with Israel. For until that time, the fear of Israel was upon all the nations who saw the glory of the pride of G-d that was revealed at the Exodus from Egypt, and the splitting of the Sea of Reeds, as the Torah testifies (Exodus 15): "Then were the chiefs of Edom affrighted; the mighty men of Moab, trembling taketh hold upon them; all the inhabitants of Canaan are melted away. Terror and dread falleth upon them; by the greatness of Thine arm they are as still as a stone; till Thy people pass over, O LORD, till the people pass over that Thou hast gotten."[11]

Amalek was the one who breathed into all the nations the evil inclination to fight and to start up with Israel. The spirit of Amalek dampened the fear of Israel and its G-d, as our sages of blessed memory explain regarding the verse: "He met you on the way"[12]. Rashi explains "This is from the language of cold and heat, he cooled you down and tempered your boiling. For all the nations were afraid of fighting against you, and this one came, began, and showed the way for the others. This is like a boiling bath into which no creature could enter. A certain base person comes and jumps in. Even though he is scalded, he cools it down for others."

[Page 503]

There is an opinion that Amalek cut off and killed several Israelites. However, even though he murdered individuals, he did not reach the level of his German descendants, may their names be blotted out, who consumed and annihilated approximately seven million [sic] of the cream of the crop of the nation. This disaster that took place "Before the great and terrible day of the L-rd comes" [Malachi 3:23], is 77 times greater than the war of Amalek against Israel[13], for had those millions who were murdered at the hands of the German Amalekites been living with us today, the State of Israel would be different from end to end by all criteria. We would not be afraid of intruders at night and murderers in the light of the sun. The millions of our faithful, dear brethren would have actively helped and participated in the upbuilding of the land, the sprouting of the desolation, and the returning of this crown of this Holy Land to its former status.

The Holocaust that cut down over our heads during this tumultuous generation was greater in length and essence than the war with Amalek at Rephidim. Therefore, we must remember it and etch it upon the tablet of our hearts with a pen of iron and a point of diamond[14].

In the Song of the Sea, it says: "Then Moses and the Children of Israel sang this song to G-d, saying: I will sing to G-d for he is very exalted, He drowned horse and rider in the sea." [Exodus 15: 1-2]. It says in the Gemara (*Sanhedrin* 91:2); "Rabbi Meir said: it does not say 'sang' but rather 'will sing' – from here is a reference in the Torah to the resurrection of the dead." The song of the sea during the Exodus from Egypt was the beginning of the song of the redemption of Israel, which began with the Exodus from Egypt, the splitting of the Sea of Reeds, and the defeat of the enemies of Israel. However, the song did not cease. It will be continued in the future. The continuation will be after the final eradication of Amalek, "You shall erase the memory of Amalek from under the heavens, do not forget" [Deuteronomy 25:19] – after Israel is saved by G-d with an eternal salvation, a perpetual salvation and redemption from the wellsprings of light and redemption. Then the statement of the prophet will be fulfilled (Isaiah 26:19): "Arise and sing you who dwell in the dust, for your dew is the dew of light, and the land of the shades shall be brought down."

Speedily in our days, Amen.

[Page 504]

Yizkor

May G-d remember the souls of all my relatives, male and female, whether from my father's side or my mother's side, who were murdered, killed, slaughtered, burned, drowned, or asphyxiated in sanctification of the Divine Name, for I pledge charity in memory of their souls. In reward for this, may their souls be bound in the bonds of life with the souls of Abraham our forefather, Isaac, and Jacob, Sarah, Rebecca, Rachel, and Leah, and the rest of the righteous men and women in the Garden of Eden, and let us say Amen.

* * *

G-d full of mercy, the judge of widows and father of orphans, do not be silent and complacent over the blood of Israel that was spilled like water. Grant proper rest under the wings of the Divine Presence in the holy, pure heights, in the splendor of the glorious firmament, to the souls of the martyrs of Krasnobród, men and women, boys and girls, who were murdered, slaughtered, burnt, drowned, asphyxiated, and buried alive in our city of Krasnobród.

All are righteous and pure, among them Gaonim and Tzadikim, Cedars of Lebanon, and mighty ones of Torah. Let their repose be in the Garden of Eden. Therefore, the Master of Mercy shall bind their souls in the bonds of life. G-d is their inheritance. Their martyrdom shall be recalled by us, and their merit shall stand for us and for all of Israel. Earth, do not conceal their blood, and let there not be a limitation to their outcry. The dispersed of Israel shall return to their land, and the righteousness of the martyrs shall be an eternal memory before G-d. May they come to peace, and rest in peace in their repose, and let us say Amen.

Translator's Footnotes:

1.   Deuteronomy 32: 42 (latter half of verse) – 44, from the song of *Haazinu*. Translation of these highly poetic verses courtesy of Mechon Mamre: https://mechon-mamre.org/p/pt/pt0532.htm
2.   I.e., King David. These verses are also recited in the latter part of the Passover Seder [*Shefoch Chamatcha*].
3.   From I Kings 21:19, the words used by Elijah when confronting King Ahab after he had his neighbor Naboth murdered in order to take over his field.
4.   See https://en.wikipedia.org/wiki/Meir_Lublin
5.   Jeremiah 10:19. Translation of this verse was taken from Mechon Mamre: https://mechon-mamre.org/p/pt/pt1110.htm
6.   Strands dyed with a special blue dye used for making the fringes of *tzitzit*. See https://en.wikipedia.org/wiki/Tekhelet
7.   Foundation [*yesod*] is one of the Kabbalistic spheres.
8.   The word *halacha* generally means Jewish law. Its literal translation would be 'ways of walking' or 'paths.'
9.   A play on words, as *Amana* אמנה here literally refers to the Amana Mountains in Lebanon. However, it has almost the same letters and pronunciation as *Emuna* אמונה, meaning faith.
10.   Exodus 17:12. The word used for 'steady' in this verse is the same as the word for faith: *Emuna.*
11.   Exodus 15: 15-16. Translation from Mechon Mamre: https://mechon-mamre.org/p/pt/pt0215.htm
12.   Deuteronomy 25:18. The word for 'met' that is used here, קָרְךָ, has the same root as 'cold.'
13.   A reference from Genesis 4:24.
14.   See Jeremiah 17:1. I based my translation of this difficult portion of the verse from Mechon Mamre: https://mechon-mamre.org/p/pt/pt1117.htm

[Pages 505-525]

List of Holocaust Victims

Transliterated by Ofir Azrilovici

Family name(s)	First name(s)	Gender	Marital status	Father's name	Mother's name	Name of spouse	Additional family	Remarks	Page(s)
א Alef									
ADLER	Moshe	M	married						505
ADLER		F	married			Moshe			505
ADLER	Duvid	M	married			Golda		Family with 5 family members	505
ADLER	Golda	F	married			Duvid		Family with 5 family members	505
ADLER	Leah	F							505
ADLER	Devorah	F							505
ADLER	Leizer	M	married			Gila		Family with 3 family members	505
ADLER	Gila	F	married			Leizer		Family with 3 family members	505
ADLER	Feivel	M	married						505
ADLER		F	married			Feivel			505
ULMAN	Baruch Yakov	M	married			Perl			505
ULMAN	Perl	F	married			Baruch Yakov			505
UNCIG	Yisrael Leib	M	married			Teme			505
UNCIG	Teme	F	married			Yisrael Leib			505
UNCIG	Feiga	F		Aharon					505
UNCIG	Shimon Dov	M	married			Sheva			505
UNCIG	Sheva	F	married			Shimno Dov			505
UNCIG	Yitzchak Moshe	M	married			Sura			505

UNCIG	Sura	F	married			Yitzchak Moshe		505
UNCIG	Yosef	M						505
UNCIG	Shifra	F						505
UNCIG	Avram	M	married			Chana		505
UNCIG	Chana	F	married			Avram		505
UNCIG	Naftaly	M						505
UNCIG	Nana	F						505
UNCIG	Rivka	F						505
UNCIG	Hanoch	M	married			Sura		505
UNCIG	Sura	F	married			Hanoch		505
UNCIG	Eliahu	M						505
UNCIG	Sheindel	F						505
UNCIG	Chaim	M	married			Feiga		505
UNCIG	Feiga	F	married			Chaim		505
UNCIG	Yechiel	M						505
UNCIG	Yissaschar	M						505
UNCIG	Shalom	M						505
UNCIG	Reizel	F						505
UNCIG	Etel	F						505
UNCIG	Mechel	M	married			Chana		505
UNCIG	Chana	F	married			Mechel		505
UNCIG	Rachel Gitel	F						505
UNCIG	Moshe	M	married			Malka		505
UNCIG	Malka	F	married			Moshe		505
UNCIG	Hanoch	M	married	Meir		Chana		505
UNCIG	Chana	F	married			Hanoch		505
UNCIG	Elke	F						505
UNCIG	Breine	F						505
UNCIG	Meir	M						505
UNCIG	Sura	F						505
UNCIG	Rivka	F						505
UNCIG	Leibish	M	married			Leah		505

UNCIG	Leah	F	married		Leibish			505
UNCIG	Etel	F						505
UNCIG	Yona	M						505
UNCIG	Sura	F		Meir				505
UNCIG	Yitzchak	M	married	Tsvi	Matl			505
UNCIG	Matl	F	married		Yitzchak			505
UNCIG	Sura	F						505
UNCIG	Meir	M						505
UNCIG	Etel	F						505
UNCIG	Sheindel	F						505
UNCIG	Eidel	F				her family		505
UNCIG	Yehosha	M	married		Elka			505
UNCIG	Elke	F	married		Yehosha			505
UNCIG	Etel	F						505
UNCIG	Sheindel	F						505
UNCIG	Chaya	F						505
UNCIG	Yecheskel	M	married		Beile			505
UNCIG	Beile	F	married		Yechezkel			505
UNCIG	Chana	F						505
UNCIG	Shlomo Chaim	M						505
UNCIG	Leah	F						505
UNCIG	Perl	F						505
UNCIG	Yitzchak	M	married		Cypa			505
UNCIG	Cypa	F	married		Yitzchak			505
UNCIG	Yisrael	M		Ezra		his family		505
UNTERBUCH	Rachel	F				her family		505
UNTERBUCH	Yosef	M	married		Feiga		Family with 5 family members	505
UNTERBUCH	Feiga	F	married		Yosef		Family with 5 family members	505
UNTERBUCH	Leibish	M	married		Cypa			505, 506
UNTERBUCH	Cypa	F	married		Leibish	children		505, 506
UNTERBUCH	Ester	F						505,

							506
UNTERBUCH	Bracha	F					505, 506
UNTERBUCH	Sura	F					505, 506
EDELSHTEIN	Tevel	M				his family	506
EDELSHTEIN	Nechama	F				her family	506
EDELSHTEIN	Yosel	M	married		Gitel		506
EDELSHTEIN	Gitel	F	married		Yosel		506
EDELSHTEIN	Yerachmiel	M					506
EDELSHTEIN	Baruch	M					506
EDELSHTEIN	Devorah	F					506
ELBOIM	Berish	M					506
ELBOIM	Hersh	M					506
ELBOIM	Hanoch	M		Shalom		his family	506
ELBOIM	Tsirel	F					506
ELBOIM	Leibish	M	married		Hinde		506
ELBOIM	Hinde	F	married		Leibish		506
ELBOIM	Hadasa	F					506
ELBOIM	Gitel	F					506
ELBOIM	Nechama	F					506
ELBOIM	Mordechai	M		Sender			506
ELBOIM	Hinde	F					506
ELBOIM	Freide	F					506
ELBOIM	Chaya	F					506
ELBOIM	Tevel	M		Mordechai		his family	506
ELBOIM	Hinde	F		Fishel			506
ELBOIM	Chava	F				her family	506
ELBOIM	Beniman	M			Hinde	his family	506
ELBOIM	Chaim	M			Hinde	his family	506
ELBOIM	Sender	M		Fishel		his family	506
ELBOIM	Chaim	M		Fishel		his family	506
ELBOIM	Niche	F		Fishel		her family	506
ELBOIM	Etel	F		Fishel		her family	506

ELBOIM	Racheli	F		Benyamin					506
ELBOIM	Pese	F	married			Meir			506
ELBOIM	Hanoch	M	married	Meir		Malka			506
ELBOIM	Malka	F	married			Hanoch			506
ELBOIM	Perl	F							506
ELBOIM	Benyamin	M		Meir			his family		506
ELBOIM	Yona	M	married			Gitel			506
ELBOIM	Gitel	F	married			Yona			506
ELBOIM	Liba	F							506
ELBOIM	Chaya	F							506
ELBOIM	Avram Yakov	M					his family	From Firsht family	506
ELBOIM	Pinchas	M					his family	From Firsht family	506
ELBOIM	Beile	F					her family	Maiden name FIRSHT	506
EIL	Sura	F					her family	Maiden name KNEBEL	506
EDELSHTEIN	Yehosha	M	married			Golda			506
EDELSHTEIN	Golda	F	married			Yehosha			506
APPELBOIM	Pinchas	M	married			Mindel			506
APPELBOIM	Mindel	F	married			Pinchas			506
APPELBOIM	Yisrael	M							506
APPELBOIM	Sura	F	married			Moshe Yakov			506
	Moshe Yakov	M	married			Sura			506
APPELBOIM	Yisrael	M							506
ARBESFELD	Milke	F	married			Todres			506
ARBESFELD	Perl	F							506
ARBESFELD	Duvid	M							506
ARBESFELD	Shepsel	M							506
ARBESFELD	Malka	F					her family	From Blizshev	506
ORDYNACHKY	Chaim	M	married			Zeltse			506
ORDYNACHKY	Zeltse	F	married			Chaim			506

ב Bet

BABAD	Shalom	M	married		Sura			506
BABAD	Sura	F	married		Shalom			506
BABAD	Yosef Aharon	M				his family		506
BABAD	Yitzchak	M	married		Rachel			506
BABAD	Rachel	F	married		Yitzchak			506
BABAD	Heshel	M						506
BABAD	Rachel Ratshe	F				her family		507
BABAD	Etel	F	married		Leibel			507
BABAD	Dov	M		Etel				507
BABAD	Chaim	M	married		Rachel		Family with 4 family members	507
BABAD	Rachel	F	married		Chaim		Family with 4 family members	507
BABAD	Reuven	M	married		Neomi		Family with 4 family members	507
BABAD	Neomi	F	married		Reuven		Family with 4 family members	507
BABAD	Yehosha	M	married		Nissel			507
BABAD	Nissel	F	married		Yehosha			507
BABAD	Yosel	M						507
BABAD	Berl	M						507
BABAD	Malka	F					Maiden name SHLEGEL	507
BABAD	Moshe	M		Malka				507
BABAD	Aharon							507
BABAD	Mordechai Yosef	M	married		Chaya		Family with 6 family members	507
BABAD	Chaya	F	married		Mordechai Yosef		Family with 6 family members	507
BABAD	Devorah	F						507
BABAD	Avram	M						507
BABAD	Heshel	M	married		Devorah			507
BABAD	Devorah	F	married		Heshel			507
	Meir Volf	M						507

	Michael	M				his family		507
	Sura	F		Yakov				507
	Mindel	F		Mosh'le			Daughter of Moshe'le the writer("HaSofer")	507
	Sime	F			Mindel			507
	Duvid	M		Mosh'le			Son of Moshe'le the writer("HaSofer")	507
	Avram	M	married			Miriam	there is a note "biniamolis"-not clear if it's a nickname or second surname	507
	Miriam	F	married			Avram		507
BURG	Shmuel Yosel	M	married			Rivka		507
BURG	Rivka	F	married			Shmuel Yosel		507
BURG	Tsipora	F						507
BURG	Yakov	M	married			Rachel		507
BURG	Rachel	F	married			Yakov		507
BURG	Reizel	F						507
BURG	Yeshayahu	M						507
BURG	Shlomo	M						507
BURG	Chaya	F						507
BURG	Yitzchak Meir	M			Chaya			507
BARENSHTEIN	Yona	M	married			Rachel		507
BARENSHTEIN	Rachel	F	married			Yona		507
BUKOVICH	Chaya	F						507
BUKOVICH	Gitel	F						507
BUKOVICH	Roize	F						507
BUKOVICH	Serl	M				his family		507
BIDLER	Avram	M	married			Sura	Family with 5 family members	507
BIDLER	Sura	F	married			Avram	Family with 5 family members	507
BLUZER	Leib	M	married			Ita		507

BLUZER	Ita	F	married		Leib			507
BLUZER	Yakov	M	married		Perl			507
BLUZER	Perl	F	married		Yakov			507
BLUZER	Riva	F						507
BLUZER	Moltshe	F						507
BLUZER	Yosef	M						507
BLUMSHTEIN	Mordechai Meir	M	married		Sime			507
BLUMSHTEIN	Sime	F	married		Mordechai Meir			507
BLUMSHTEIN	Henie	F						507
BLUMSHTEIN	Perl	F				her family		507
BLUMSHTEIN	Cheyka	F				her family		507
BLUMSHTEIN	Moshe	M	married		Etke			507
BLUMSHTEIN	Etke	F	married		Moshe			507
BLUMSHTEIN	Berl	M						507
BLUMSHTEIN	Chaya	F						507
BLICHT	Yitzchak	M	married		Chaya Beile		Family with 7 family members	507
BLICHT	Chaya Beile	F	married		Yitzchak		Family with 7 family members	507
BLEICHMAN	Hodes	F	married		Yetshe			507
BLEICHMAN	Avram	M	married		Toba			507
BLEICHMAN	Toba	F	married		Avram			507
BLEICHMAN	Rachel	F						507
BLEICHMAN	Shlomo	M					Family with 3 family members	507
BLEICHMAN	Leibel	M	married		Bracha		Family with 3 family members	507
BLEICHMAN	Bracha	F	married		Leibel			507
BLECHMAN	Tsvi	M				his family		507
BERGSHTEIN	Sara'le Gitels	F						507
BERGSHTEIN	Daniel	M				his family		507
BERGSHTEIN	Feiga	F	married		Chaim		Wife of Chaim the cantor ("Ha hazan")	507
BERGSHTEIN	Tsvi	M				his family		507

BERGSHTEIN	Isar	M				his family		508
BERLAND	Chaya Yehudit	F						508
BERLAND	Leibtshe	M	married		Ester			508
BERLAND	Ester	F	married		Leibtshe			508
BERLAND	Simcha	M						508
BERLAND	Sender	M						508
BERLAND	Moshe Yona	M						508
BERLAND	Cypa	F						508
BERLAND	Sura	F						508
BRODER	Baruch Eli	M	married		Tshernale			508
BRODER	Tsharne'le	F	married		Baruch Eli			508
BRODER	Tsvi	M						508
BRODER	Ester	F						508
BRODER	Perl	F						508
BRODER	Simcha	M	married		Chantshe		Family with 3 family members	508
BRODER	Chantshe	F	married		Simcha		Family with 3 family members	508
BRANSHTEIN	Chaim	M	married		Sura			508
BRANSHTEIN	Sura	F	married		Chaim			508
BRANSHTEIN	Gitel	F						508
BRANSHTEIN	Azriel	M					From Tsitishe	508
BRANSHTEIN	Reizel	F		Azriel				508
BRIKS	Hersh Leibel	M	married		Sura			508
BRIKS	Sura	F	married		Hersh Leibel			508
BRIKS	Devorah	F						508
BRIKS	Benyamin	M						508
BRIKHOLZ	Sura	F				her family		508
BRIKHOLZ	Rivka	F				her family		508
BRIKHOLZ	Beile	F				her family		508
BRIKHOLZ	Shmuel	M				his family		508
BRIKHOLZ	Hanoch	M				his family		508

BRIKHOLZ	Moshe	M				his family		508
BRIKHOLZ	Meir Mechel	M		Leibish				508

ג Gimmel

GOLDBRENER	Simcha	M	married		Sura		Family with 8 family members	508
GOLDBRENER	Sura	F	married		Simcha		Family with 8 family members	508
GOLDBRENER	Serke	F						508
GOLDBRENER	Rachel	F						508
GOLDBRENER	Ester	F						508
GOLDBRENER	Aharon	M						508
GOLDBERG	Moshe Yosel	M	married		Toba			508
GOLDBERG	Toba	F	married		Moshe Yosel			508
GOLDBERG	Efraim Zimel	M	married		Perl			508
GOLDBERG	Perl	F	married		Efraim Zimel			508
GOLDBERG	Tsipora	F						508
GOLDBERG	Rivka	F						508
GOLDBERG	Hersh	M						508
GOLDBERG	Cypa	F				her family		508
GOLDBERG	Yose	M	married		Chana'le			508
GOLDBERG	Chana'le	F	married		Yose			508
GOLDSHTEIN	Frimet	F						508
GOLDSHTEIN	Yeshayahu	M						508
GOLDSHTEIN	Yakov	M						508
GOLDSHTEIN	Nathan	M						508
GOLDSHTEIN	Chana	F						508
GOLDSHTEIN	Yahosha Duvid	M	married		Rachel			508
GOLDSHTEIN	Rachel	F	married		Yehosha Duvid			508
GOLDSHTEIN	Devorah	F						508
GOLDSHTEIN	Shalom	M						508

GOLDSHTEIN	Yosef	M							508
GOLDSHTEIN	Aharon	M							508
GOLDSHTEIN	Yitzchak	M	married			Yocheved			508
GOLDSHTEIN	Yocheved	F	married			Yitzchak			508
GOLDSHTEIN	Duvid	M							508
GOLDSHTEIN	Dov	M							508
GOLDSHTEIN	Baruch	M	married			Leah			508, 509
GOLDSHTEIN	Leah	F	married			Baruch			508, 509
GOLDSHTEIN	Sura	F							508, 509
GOLDSHTEIN	Devorah	F							508, 509
GOLDSHTEIN	Yosef	M	married			Rachel			509
GOLDSHTEIN	Rachel	F	married			Yosef			509
GOLDSHTEIN	Yisrael Yoel	M							509
GOLDSHTEIN	Devorah	F							509
GORTENKART	Ozer	M	married			Grone			509
GORTENKART	Grone	F	married			Ozer			509
GORTENKART	Mechtshe	F							509
GORTENKART	Sheindel	F							509
GORTENKART	Yosef	M							509
GORTENKART	Shmuel	M							509
GARBER	Fishel	M	married			Chaya			509
GARBER	Chaya	F	married			Fishel			509
GARBER	Leah	F							509
GOTHERZ	Gendel	F						From Tsitishe	509
GOTHERZ	Elimelech	M		Meir				his family	509
GURTLER	Tsvi	M	married	Zeinvil		Malka			509
GURTLER	Malka	F	married			Tsvi			509
GURTLER	Cypa	F							509
GURTLER	Gedaliahu	M		Moshe Itshe					509
GURTLER	Hanoch	M	married			Pesel			509

GURTLER	Pesel	F	married		Hanoch		509
GURTLER	Yakov	M					509
GURTLER	Chana	F					509
GURTLER	Yosef	M	married		Chaya		509
GURTLER	Chaya	F	married		Yosef		509
GURTLER	Shike	M	married				509
GURTLER		F	married				509
GURTLER	Hanoch	M	married	Moshe Beinis	Chana		509
GURTLER	Chana	F	married		Hanoch		509
GURTLER	Shmuel	M					509
GURTLER	Sura	F					509
GURTLER	Reizel	F					509
GURTLER		M	married		Dina		509
GURTLER	Dina	F	married		Bertshe		509
GURTLER	Shmuel	M					509
GURTLER	Chaya	F					509
GURTLER	Shmuel	M	married	Volf	Henie		509
GURTLER	Henie	F	married		Shmuel		509
GURTLER	Moshe	M	married		Reizel		509
GURTLER	Reizel	F	married		Moshe		509
GURTLER	Tsvi	M					509
GURTLER	Perl	F					509
GURTLER	Hinde	F					509
GURTLER	Hersh	M	married		Chaya		509
GURTLER	Chaya	F	married		Hersh		509
GURTLER	Moshe	M	married	Yakov	Sura		509
GURTLER	Sura	F	married		Moshe		509
GURTLER	Mindel	F					509
GURTLER	Perl	F					509
GURTLER	Shlomo	M					509
GURTLER	Shmuel	M	married	Lezer	Beile		509
GURTLER	Beile	F	married		Shmuel		509
GURTLER	Lezke	M	married		Sime		509

GURTLER	Sime	F	married		Lezke			509
GURTLER	Matl	M						509
GURTLER	Rachel	F						509
GURTLER	Mordchai	M	married		Elisheva			509
GURTLER	Elisheva	F	married		Mordechai			509
GURTLER	Finshte	M				his family		509
GURTLER	Chana	F		Yisraelish				509
GURTLER	Yente	F		Yisraelish				509
GURTLER	Yisrael	M		Aharon Volf				509
GURTLER	Tsvi	M	married		Beile		Family with 4 family members	509
GURTLER	Beile	F	married		Tsvi		Family with 4 family members	509
GURTLER	Moshe	M	married	Zeinvil	Golda			509
GURTLER	Golda	F	married		Moshe			509
GURTLER	Avram	M						509
GURTLER	Duvid	M						509
GURTLER	Falik	M	married		Primet			509
GURTLER	Frimet	F	married		Falik			509
GURTLER	Beile	F						509
GURTLER	Sura	F						509
GURTLER	Yisrael	M	married	Zeinvil	Yachtshe			509
GURTLER	Yachtshe	F	married		Yisrael			509
GURTLER	Nechemiia	M	married		Bracha			509, 510
GURTLER	Bracha	F	married		Nechemia			509, 510
GURTLER	Moshe	M						509, 510
GURTLER	Etel	F						509, 510
GURTLER	Chaya	F						510
GURTLER	Etel	F		Asher				510
GURTLER	Yakov	M		Lezer				510
GURTLER	Shmuel	M	married	Yakov	Sime			510
GURTLER	Sime	F	married		Shmuel			510

GURTLER	Eliezer	M		Shmuel	Sime				510
GURTLER	Eliezer	M		Yakov		his family			510
GURTLER	Shimon	M		Yakov		his family			510
GURTLER	Reuven	M		Yakov		his family			510
GURTLER	Perl	F							510
GURTLER	Shalom	M							510
GURTLER	Elimelech	M							510
GURTLER	Yakov	M		Chaim Tevel		his family			510
GURTLER	Avigdor	M							510
GURTLER	Azriel	M	married		Sura				510
GURTLER	Sura	F	married		Azriel				510
GURTLER	Feiga	F				her family			510
GURTLER	Eliezer	M		Chaim Tevel		his family			510
GITER	Yitzchak	M	married		Ita		From Tsitishe		510
GITER	Ita	F	married		Yitzchak				510
GITER	Rivka	F							510
GITER	Arie	M							510
GITER	Moshe	M							510
GITER	Avram	M							510
GITER	Velvel	M	married		Tsetel				510
GITER	Tsetel	F	married		Velvel				510
GITER	Chana	F							510
GITER	Rivka	F							510
GITER	Yitzchak	M							510
GITER	Eliezer	M							510
GITER	Leah	F		Elazar					510
GITER	Sura	F		Elazar					510
GEISTAT	Tsvi	M	married		Chaya				510
GEISTAT	Chaya	F	married		Tsvi				510
GEISTAT	Michael	M							510
GEISTAT	Yakov	M							510
GEISTAT	Meir	M							510

GEISTAT	Yakov	M	married	Meir	Rachel			510
GEISTAT	Rachel	F	married		Yakov			510
GEISTAT	Meir	M						510
GEISTAT	Mechel	M						510
GEISTAT	Hersh Mechel	M				his family	From Zabretshne	510
GEIST	Reuven	M						510
GLOTER	Yehosha	M	married		Feiga			510
GLOTER	Feiga	F	married		Yehosha			510
GLOTER	Leah	F						510
GLOTER	Gitel	F						510
GLOTER	Yisrael	M				his family		510
GLOTER	Moshe	M				his family		510
GLOTER	Yona	M	married		Ester			510
GLOTER	Ester	F	married		Yona			510
GLOTER	Leah	F						510
GLIK	Yehosha	M	married		Bina		Family with 6 family members	510
GLIK	Bina	F	married		Yehosha		Family with 6 family members	510
GLISTMAN	Baruch	M	married		Devorah			510
GLISTMAN	Devorah	F	married		Baruch			510
GLISTMAN	Ester	F						510
GLISTMAN	Roza	F						510
GLISTMAN	Chana	F						510
GLISTMAN	Duvid	M						510
GLIKMAN	Efraim Yoel	M	married		Yentel			510
GLIKMAN	Yentel	F	married		Efraim Yoel			510
GLIKMAN	Velvel	M						510
GLIKMAN	Berish	M		Yosef Yehosha		his family		510
GLIKMAN	Hanoch	M	married		Sura			510, 511
GLIKMAN	Sura	F	married		Hanoch			510, 511

GLIKMAN	Nachum	M						510, 511
GLIKMAN	Mendel	M						510, 511
GLIKMAN	Devorah	F						510, 511
GLIKMAN	Tsipora	F						510, 511
GLIKMAN	Chaya	F						510, 511
GLIKMAN	Eliezer	M	married			Sura		511
GLIKMAN	Sura	F	married			Elazar		511
GLIKMAN	Nachum	M						511
GLIKMAN	Tsipora	F						511
GEZNER	Hersh	M	married			Zlate	Family with 5 family members	511
GEZNER	Zlate	F	married			Hersh	Family with 5 family members	511
GELERNTER	Shmuel Zeinvil	M	married			Chana		511
GELERNTER	Chana	F	married			Shmuel Zeinvil		511
GELERNTER	Feiga	F						511
GELERNTER	Gedaliahu	M					his family	511
GROSS	Moshe	M	married			Chaya Bine		511
GROSS	Chaya Bine	F	married			Moshe		511
GROSS	Elchanan	M						511
GROSS	Chana	F						511
GROSS	Malka	F						511
GROSMAN	Shimon	M		Chaim Shlomo				511
GROSMAN	Duvid	M		Chaim Shlomo			his family	511
GROSMAN	Eliezer	M		Chaim Shlomo			his family	511
GERY	Kresel	F		Leibish				511
GERY	Moshe Yitzchak	M	married			Devorah		511

GERY	Devorah	F	married		Moshe Yitzchak		511
GERY	Hersh Avram	M					511
GERY	Chaim	M					511
GERY	Meir	M					511
GERY	Perl	F					511
GERY	Feiga	F					511
GERY	Rechtshe	F					511
GERY	Elchanan	M				whole family	511
GRINBOIM	Shimon	M		Yakov			511
GRINBOIM	Avram	M					511
GRINBOIM	Aharon	M					511
GRINBOIM	Leah	F					511
GRINBOIM	Chaya	F					511
GRINBOIM	Elihau	M		Leibish			511
GRINBOIM	Yitzchak	M	married	Leibish	Hinde		511
GRINBOIM	Hinde	F	married		Yitzchak		511
GRINBOIM	Yehuda	M					511
GRINBOIM	Arie	M					511
GRINBOIM	Chaya	F					511
GRINBOIM	Hadasa	F					511
GRINBOIM	Reizel	F					511
GRINBOIM	Moshe	M				Profession:carter	511
GRINBOIM	Berish	M	married		Rivka		511
GRINBOIM	Rivka	F	married		Berish		511
GRINBOIM	Yehudit	F					511
GRINBOIM	Leah	F		Berish		her family	511
GRINBOIM	Teme	F		Leibish			511
GRINBOIM	Chaya	F					511
GRINBOIM	Chana	F					511
GRINBOIM	Moshe	M	married	Yakov	Chava		511
GRINBOIM	Chava	F	married		Moshe		511
GRINBOIM	Velvel	M					511

GRINBOIM	Chaya Eidel	F						511
GRINBOIM	Ester	F		Yitzchak Aizik			From Nimerovke	511
GRINBOIM	Marese	F						511
GRINBOIM	Chaya	F						511
GRINBOIM	Sura	F						511
GRINBOIM	Mordechai	M						511
GRINBOIM	Yitzchak Moshe Aizik	M	married		Hadel			511
GRINBOIM	Hadel	F	married		Yitzchak Moshe Aizik			511

ד **Dalet**

DORNFELD	Avram	M	married		Shifra			512
DORNFELD	Shifra	F	married		Avram		Maiden name GLISTMAN	512
DORNFELD	Perl	F						512
DORNFELD	Ester	F						512
DINER	Rachel	F						512
DINER	Shlomo	M		Rachel				512
DINER	Michael	M				his family		512
DICHTERMAN	Shlomo	M	married		Nechama			512
DICHTERMAN	Nechama	F	married		Shlomo			512
DICHTERMAN	Shmuel	M						512
DICHTERMAN	Yisrael	M	married		Toba			512
DICHTERMAN	Toba	F	married		Yisrael			512
DICHTERMAN	Yosel	M		Yisrael	Toba			512
DICHTERMAN	Roize	F						512
DICHTERMAN	Mordechai	M						512
DICHTERMAN	Ester	F						512
DICHTERMAN	Chaim	M						512
DICHTERMAN	Beile	F						512
DICHTERMAN	Miriam	F						512

DICHTERMAN	Rivka	F			Miriam				512
DICHTERMAN	Hanoch	M	married			Sura		Family with 4 family members	512
DICHTERMAN	Sura	F	married			Hanoch		Family with 4 family members	512
DICHTERMAN	Gitel	F							512
DICHTERMAN	Abish Itshe	M	married			Ita			512
DICHTERMAN	Ita	F	married			Abish Itshe			512
DRUNG	Daniel	M	married			Reizel			512
DRUNG	Reizel	F	married			Daniel		Maiden name BABAD	512
DRUNG	Avram	M							512
DRUNG	Moshe	M							512

ה Hey

HOZ	Moshe	M	married	Zev		Shashke			512
HOZ	Shashke	F	married			Moshe			512
HOZ	Velvel	M							512
HOZ	Yeshayahu	M							512
HOZ	Avram	M		Zev			his family		512
HOZ	Yehosha	M		Zev			his family		512
HALPERN	Tsirel	F						Family with 5 family members	512
HALPERN	Devorah	F							512
HALPERN	Daniel	M							512
HOLZ	Yosef	M	married			Feiga			512
HOLZ	Feiga	F	married			Yosef		From Chtkiev(supossed to be Chitkov)	512
HOLZBERG	Bonem	M	married			Reizke			512
HOLZBERG	Reizke	F	married			Bonem			512
HOLZBERG	Rivka	F							512
HOLZBERG	Tsvi	M							512
HOLZBERG	Arie	M							512
HOLZBERG	Shlomo	M							512

HOLZBERG	Menachem	M							512
HOLZBERG	Shlomo	M	married			Hinde			512
HOLZBERG	Hinde	F	married			Shlomo		Maiden name	512
HOLZBERG	Bonem	M							512
HOLZBERG	Avram	M							512
HANDELSMAN	Asher	M							512
HAF	Nachum	M	married			Ester			512
HAF	Ester	F	married			Nachum		Maiden name GURTLER	512
HAF	Yosef	M							512
HAF	Mindel	F							512
HAF	Sura	F							512
HAKMAN	Cherna	F							512
HARNDREXLER	Azriel	M	married			Sura			512
HARNDREXLER	Sura	F	married			Azriel			512
HARNDREXLER	Chaya	F					her family			512
HARNDREXLER	Elihau	M	married			Roize			512
HARNDREXLER	Roize	F	married			Elihau			512
HEISMAN	Pesach Moshe	M							512
HEISMAN	Leizke	M							512
HEISMAN	Avish	M							512
HELFMAN	Pesach	M	married			Chana			512, 513
HELFMAN	Chana	F	married			Pesach			512, 513
HELFMAN	Ita	F							512, 513
HELFMAN	Moshe	M							512, 513
HELFMAN	Tevel	M							512, 513
HELFMAN	Yosef	M							512, 513
HELFMAN	Benamin	M	married			Chaya		Family with 4 family members	513

HELFMAN	Chaya	F	married			Benyamin		Family with 4 family members	513
HELFMAN	Sura	F	married			Mendel	children		513
	Mendel	M	married			Sura	children		513
HELFMAN	Yitzchak Zeev	M	married			Liba Devorah			513
HELFMAN	Liba Devorah	F	married			Yitzchak Zev			513
HELFMAN	Moshe	M							513
HELFMAN	Pese	F							513
HELFMAN	Mashe	F							513
HELFMAN	Ita	F							513
HELFMAN	Yakov	M							513
HELFMAN	Bracha	F	married			Moshe			513
	Moshe	M	married			Bracha			513
HELFMAN	Rivka	F							513
HELFMAN	Leah	F							513
HERBSMAN	Avram	M	married			Feiga			513
HERBSMAN	Feiga	F	married			Avram		Maiden name LANGER	513
HERBSMAN	Moshe	M							513
HERBSMAN	Leibel	M							513
HERBSMAN	Chana	F							513
HERING	Dvashe	F						Maiden name BERGSHTEIN	513
HERZBERG	Elisheva	F							513
HERZBERG	Gitel	F							513
HERZBERG		F			Gitel				513
	Dov	M	married			Sime			513
	Sime	F	married			Dov		Maiden name TENTSER	513

ו Vav

VEINTRUB	Zev	M	married			Leah			513
VEINTRUB	Leah	F	married			Zev			513
VEINTRUB	Leizer	M	married			Beile			513
VEINTRUB	Beile	F	married			Leizer			513

VEINTRUB	Rachel	F					513
VEINTRUB	Aharon	M					513
VEINTRUB	Gershon	M					513
VEINRACH	Leibish	M	married		Henie		513
VEINRACH	Henie	F	married		Leibish		513
VAISLEDER	Michael	M	married		Rachel		513
VAISLEDER	Rachel	F	married		Michael		513
VAISLEDER	Shlomo	M					513
VAISLEDER	Avram	M					513
VAISLEDER	Yisrael	M					513
VAISFISH	Yitzchak Hersh	M	married		Chantshe		513
VAISFISH	Chantshe	F	married		Yitzchak Hersh		513
VAISFISH	Sini	M					513
VAISFISH	Beile	F					513
VAISFISH	Roize	F					513
VAISFISH	Yehosha	M	married		Rive		513
VAISFISH	Rive	F	married		Yehosha		513
VAISFISH	Toba	F					513
VAISFISH	Tape	F					513
VAISFISH	Yisrael	M					513
VELTSHER	Mendel	M	married		Malka		513
VELTSHER	Malka	F	married		Mendel		513
VELTSHER	Arie	M					513
VELTSHER	Moshe	M					513
VELTSHER	Yitzchak	M	married		Reizel		513
VELTSHER	Reizel	F	married		Yitzchak		513
VELTSHER	Etel	F					513
VELTSHER	Arie	M					513
VELTSHER	Elazar	M	married		Hinde		513
VELTSHER	Hinde	F	married		Elazar		513
VELTSHER	Arie	M					513
VEXLER	Duvid	M				From Chitkov	513

VEXLER	Yehosha	M	married		Malka			513
VEXLER	Malka	F	married		Yehosha			513
VEXLER	Chana	F						513
VEXLER	Berl	M						513
VEXLER	Gitel	F						513
VEXLER	Shmuel	M				his family		513
VEXLER	Beril	M	married		Tsirel	children		513
VEXLER	Tsirel	F	married		Beril	children		513

ז Zayin

JAMSKI	Beinish	M	married		Ester		Family with 4 family members	514
JAMSKI	Ester	F	married		Beinish		Family with 4 family members	514
ZAIONTS	Chaim Yodel	M	married		Miriam		Family with 4 family members	514
ZAIONTS	Miriam	F	married		Chaim Yodel		Family with 4 family members	514
ZOMLER	Hersh Leib	M				his family	From the Burg family	514
ZAK	Meir	M		Ben-Tsion		his family		514
ZAK	Duvid	M		Ben-Tsion		his family		514
ZIGELMAN	Moshe	M	married		Hinde			514
ZIGELMAN	Hinde	F	married		Moshe			514
ZIGELMAN	Chana Gishe	F						514
ZILBERGELD	Nachum	M	married		Etel			514
ZILBERGELD	Etel	F	married		Nachum		Maiden name MAZABIS	514
ZILBERSHTEIN	Itshe	M	married		Tsirel		Family with 4 family members	514
ZILBERSHTEIN	Tsirel	F	married		Itshi		Family with 4 family members	514
ZILBERSHTEIN	Gershon Hanoch	M	married		Perl		Family with 4 family members	514
ZILBERSHTEIN	Perl	F	married		Gershon Hanoch		Family with 4 family members	514

ZEIDEL	Gitel	F					Maiden name VEINTRUB	514
ZEIFMAN	Alter	M	married		Chana Sura			514
ZEIFMAN	Chana Sura	F	married		Alter			514
ZIMERMAN	Chana	F						514
ZIMERMAN	Avram	M	married		Gitel			514
ZIMERMAN	Gitel	F	married		Avram			514
ZIMERMAN	Chase	F						514
ZIMERMAN	Temtshe	F				children	Family with 3 family members	514
ZIMERMAN	Azriel	M				his family		514
ZINGER	Shaul	M	married		Shashe			514
ZINGER		F	married		Shaul		Maiden name FUKS	514
ZITSER	Itsheli	M	married		Zlate			514
ZITSER	Zlate	F	married		Itsheli			514
ZITSER	Sura	F						514
ZITSER	Etel	F						514
ZITSER	Yakov	M						514
ZITSER	Leib	M				his family		514
ZITSER	Meshulam	M				his family		514
ZITSER	Chaim	M				his family		514
ZELTSER	Yisrael Yakov	M		Shalom		his family		514

ט Tet

TORM	Chana	F		Avram Abish		her family		514
TORM	Hershel	M						514
TORM	Rechtshe	F						514
TORM	Yachtshe	F						514
TENTSER	Beile	F						514
TENTSER	Valvish	M	married		Sheindel			514
TENTSER	Sheindel	F	married		Valvish			514
TENTSER	Shmuel	M						514
TENTSER	Mordechai	M						514

TENTSER	Sura	F				514
TENTSER	Miriam	F				514
TENTSER	Yakov	M	married		Feiga	514
TENTSER	Feiga	F	married		Yakov	514
TENTSER	Shmuel	M	married		Sura Rive	514
TENTSER	Sura Rive	F	married		Shmuel	514
TENTSER	Berl	M				514
TENTSER	Pinchas	M				514
TENTSER	Elimelech	M	married		Feiga	514
TENTSER	Feiga	F	married		Elimelech	514
TENTSER	Berl	M				514
TENTSER	Yitzchak	M				514
TENTSER	Betsalel	M				514

כ Kaf

COHEN	Yosef	M	married		Hinde	514
COHEN	Hinde	F	married		Yosef	514
COHEN	Feiga	F				514
COHEN	Yakov	M	married		Breine	515
COHEN	Breine	F	married		Yakov	515
CATZ	Shpesel Meir	M	married		Sura	515
CATZ	Sura	F	married		Shepsel Meir	515
CATZ	Zise	F				515
CATZ	Chaya	F				515
CATZ	Yakov	M				515
CATZ	Rivka	F				515
CATZ	Eliezer	M				515

ל Lamed

LAM	Leizer	M	married		Etel	515
LAM	Etel	F	married		Leizer	515
LAM	Berish	M				515
LAM	Rivka	F				515

LAM	Yakov	M						515
LAM	Yosef	M	married	Leizer	Roize		Family with 3 family members	515
LAM	Roize	F	married		Yosef		Family with 3 family members	515
LAM	Yosef	M	married	Berish	Chava			515
LAM	Chava	F	married		Yosef			515
LAM	Zisel	F						515
LAM	Berish	M						515
LAM	Moshe	M						515
LAM	Yakov	M	married		Chana			515
LAM	Chana	F	married		Yakov			515
LAM	Berish	M						515
LAM	Base	F						515
LAM	Feiga	F						515
LANAIL	Shimon	M		Mordechai				515
LANGER	Sura	F						515
LANGER	Devorah	F				her family		515
LANGER	Baruch Volf	M	married		Sheindel			515
LANGER	Sheindel	F	married		Baruch Volf			515
LANGER	Chana	F						515
LANGER	Devorah	F						515
LANGER	Leibel	M	married		Leah			515
LANGER	Leah	F	married		Leibel			515
LANGER	Hanoch	M						515
LANGER	Devorah	F						515
LANGER	Avram	M	married		Perl			515
LANGER	Perl	F	married		Avram			515
LANGER	Hanoch	M						515
LANGFELD	Eliezer	M	married		Sime			515
LANGFELD	Sime	F	married		Eliezer			515
LANGFELD	Shmuel	M				his family		515
LANGFELD	Malka	F				her family		515

LANGFELD	Sura Feiga	F				her family	515
LANGFELD	Tsvi	M				his family	515
LOCHFELD	Yisrael Asher	M	married	Aharon	Base		515
LOCHFELD	Base	F	married		Yisrael Asher		515
LOCHFELD	Bat-Sheva	F		Aharon			515
LIAN	Meir	M	married		Pese		515
LIAN	Pese	F	married		Meir		515
LIAN	Shmuel	M					515
LIAN	Mirel	F					515
LIAN	Ester	F					515
LIAN	Sura	F					515
LIAN	Yakov	M	married		Liba	Family with 6 family members	515
LIAN	Liba	F	married		Yakov	Family with 6 family members	515
LIAN	Shlomo	M					515
LIAN	Moshe	M					515
LIAN	Shalom	M					515
LIBEL	Mordechai	M					515
LIBEL	Eliezer	M				his family	515
LIBEL	Shimon	M	married	Mordechai	Beile		515
LIBEL	Beile	F	married		Shimon		515
LIBEL	Yocheved	F					515
LIBEL	Chana	F					515
LIBEL	Reizel	F					515
LIBEL	Shaul	M				his family	515
LIBEL	Elihau	M	married		Leah'ke		515
LIBEL	Leah'ke	F	married		Elihau		515
LIBEL	Chava	F				Grandaughter of Elihau and Leah'ke	515
LIBEL	Shimon	M	married		Nechama		516
LIBEL	Nechama	F	married		Shimon		516

LIBEL	Sura	F					516
LIBEL	Mordechai	M		Shimon		his family	516
LIBER	Chaim	M	married		Teltshe		516
LIBER	Teltshe	F	married		Chaim		516
LIBER	Netanel	M					516
LIBER	Benyamin	M					516
LIBER	Naftaly	M					516
LIBER	Chana	F					516
LICHTFELD	Yosel	M	married		Zeptel		516
LICHTFELD	Zeptel	F	married		Yosel		516
LICHTFELD	Perl	F					516
LICHTFELD	Gitel	F					516
LICHTFELD	Sura	F					516
LIFSH	Natan	M	married		Feiga		516
LIFSH	Feiga	F	married		Nathan		516
LIFSH	Yisrael	M					516
LIFSH	Chaya	F					516
LIFSH	Eidel	F					516
LEIZEROVICH	Shimon	M	married		Breine		516
LEIZEROVICH	Breine	F	married		Shimon		516
LEIZEROVICH	Chava	F					516
LEIZEROVICH	Gitel	F					516
LEIZEROVICH	Feiga	F					516
LEITER	Yakov Leib	M				his family	516
LEDER	Yakov	M				his family	516
LEDERMAN	Toba	F					516
LEDERMAN	Hinde	F					516
LEDERMAN	Gitel	F					516
LEDERMAN	Brashe	F					516
LEDERMAN	Bracha	F					516
LEDERMAN	Nachum	M	married		Chaytshe		516
LEDERMAN	Chaitshe	F	married		Nachum		516
LEDERMAN	Yeshayahu	M					516

LEDERMAN	Yosef	M					her family		516
LEDERMAN	Yitzchak	M							516
LEDERMAN	Ester	F					her family	Relatives of the Lefler family	516
LEVINFUS	Shmuel	M	married			Pese			516
LEVINFUS	Pese	F	married			Shmuel			516
LEVINFUS	Mordechai	M	married			Beiltshe			516
LEVINFUS	Beiltshe	F	married			Mordechai			516
LEVINFUS	Yitzchak	M							516
LEVINFUS	Moshe	M							516
LEVINFUS	Avigdor	M							516
LEVINFUS	Frimet	F							516
LEVINFUS	Duvid	M	married			Malka			516
LEVINFUS	Malka	F	married			Duvid			516
LEVINFUS	Etel	F							516
LEVINFUS	Reizel	F							516
LEVINFUS	Chana	F							516
LEVINFUS	Ester	F							516
LEVINFUS	Hersh Pinchas	M	married			Sura		Family with 4 family members	516
LEVINFUS	Sura	F	married			Hersh Pinchas		Family with 4 family members	516
LEFLER	Yitzchak	M	married	Sender		Matl			516
LEFLER	Matl	F	married			Yitzchak			516
LEFLER	Hersh	M	married			Rivka			516
LEFLER	Rivka	F	married			Hersh			516
LEFLER	Sura	F							516
LEFLER	Nachum	M	married	Sender		Elke Rachel			516
LEFLER	Elke Rachel	F	married			Nachum			516
LEFLER	Arie	M							516
LEFLER	Yona	M							516
LEFLER	Yehosha	M		Nachum			his family		516
LEFLER	Moshe	M	married			Roize			516
LEFLER	Roize	F	married			Moshe		Maiden name SHTRAKER	516

LEFLER	Hinde	F						516
LEFLER	Shmuel	M	married		Pese			516
LEFLER	Pese	F	married		Shmuel		Maiden name SHTRAKER	516
LEFLER	Feiga	F						516
LEFLER	Yehosha	M		Chaim Shlomo		his family		516
LERNER	Rachel	F						516, 517
LERNER	Chaya	F						516, 517
LERNER	Ita	F						516, 517
LERNER	Moshe	M	married		Ester			517
LERNER	Ester	F	married		Moshe			517
LERNER	Yitzchak	M						517
LERNER	Avram	M						517
LERNER	Beile	F						517
LERNER	Leibish	M	married		Sura			517
LERNER	Sura	F	married		Leibish			517
LERNER	Chana	F						517
LERNER		F						517
LERNER	Yoel	M				his family	From Hishin	517
LERNER	Elihau	M	married		Miriam			517
LERNER	Miriam	F	married		Elihau			517
LERNER	Yoel	M						517
LERNER	Duvid	M						517
LERNER	Avram	M	married		Chana			517
LERNER	Chana	F	married		Avram		Maiden name ELBOIM	517
LERNER	Meir Leizer	M	married		Teme		Family with 6 family members	517
LERNER	Teme	F	married		Meir Leizer		Family with 6 family members	517
LERNER	Aharon	M						517

מ Mem

MOZES	Yose	M	married		Pese			517
MOZES	Pese	F	married		Yose			517
MOZES	Zisel	F						517
MOZES	Sura	F						517
MOZES	Nechemiia	M						517
MOZES	Benyamin	M						517
MOZES	Shmuel Leib	M	married		Machla			517
MOZES	Machle	F	married		Shmuel Leib			517
MOZES	Tsvi	M						517
	Yakov	M	married		Hudes			517
	Hudes	F	married		Yakov			517
	Rive	F						517
	Simcha	M						517
	Mirel	F				her family		517
MANDEL	Nachum	M	married		Sura		Family with 5 family members	517
MANDEL	Sura	F	married		Nachum		Family with 5 family members	517
MANDEL	Azriel	M						517
MANDEL	Leibel	M	married		Sura			517
MANDEL	Sura	F	married		Leibel			517
MANDEL	Mordechai	M	married		Toba			517
MANDEL	Toba	F	married		Mordechai		Maiden name UNCIG	517
MANDEL	Chava	F						517
MANDEL	Tsvi	M						517
MANDEL	Yosef	M						517
MORGENSHTERN	Yakov Meir	M						517
MORGENSHTERN	Naftaly	M				his family		517
MORGENSHTERN	Chaim Hersh	M				his family		517
MARER	Chaya	F						517
MARER	Shlomo	M						517
MARER	Rivka	F						517

MARER	Yosel	M						517
MARER	Yodel	M						517
MARER	Avram	M				his family		517
MARER	Yente	F				her family		517
MARER	Leah	F				her family		517
MARER	Heshel	M	married		Mirel			517
MARER	Mirel	F	married		Heshel			517
MARER	Rachel	F						517
MARER	Moshe	M						517
MOND	Yechiel	M	married		Ita			517
MOND	Ita	F	married		Yechiel		Maiden name MARGALIOT	517
MOND	Pinchas Asher	M		Yechiel	Ita			517
MAIZLES	Roize	F						517
MAIZLES	Moshe	M						517
MAIZLES	Yechezkel	M						517
MILTZ	Aharon Shmuel	M						517,518
MILTZ	Chana	F						517,518
MILTZ	Yakov	M						517,518
MILTZ	Leibish	M						517,518
MILTZ	Duvid Tevel	M	married		Rivka			518
MILTZ	Rivka	F	married		Duvid Tevel			518
MITSNER	Itshe	M	married		Freide		Family with 4 family members	518
MITSNER	Freide	F	married		Itshe		Family with 4 family members	518
MITSNER	Mechel	M	married		Perl			518
MEIER	Perl	F	married		Mechel			518
MARGALIOT	Rabbi Menachem Monish	M	married		Ester Tsirel			518
MARGALIOT	Ester Tsirel	F	married		Menahem Monish			518

MARGALIOT	Moshe Levi	M		Menachem Monis	Ester Tsirel				518

נ Nun

NAGEL	Avram	M		Naftaly			his family		518
NAGEL	Sura Teme	F							518
NAGEL	Toba	F							518
NAGEL	Etel	F							518
NIKELSBERG	Rabbi Naftaly Hertz	M	married			Fetel			518
NIKELSBERG	Fetel	F	married			Naftaly Hertz			518
NIKELSBERG	Nachum	M							518
NIKELSBERG	Sheindel	F							518
NIKELSBERG	Hadasa	F							518
NIRENSHTEIN	Moshe	M	married			Feiga			518
NIRENSHTEIN	Feiga	F	married			Moshe		Maiden name GARTENKRAUT	518
NIRENSHTEIN	Avram	M							518

ס Samech

SUSHCHAK	Avram Meir	M	married			Keile			518
SUSHCHAK	Keile	F	married			Avram Meir			518
SUSHCHAK	Chava	F							518
SUSHCHAK	Hinde	F							518
SUSHCHAK	Yisrael Shlomo	M							518
SUSHCHAK	Chana	F							518
SUSHCHAK	Shalom	M							518

ע Ayin

ENTNER	Efraim	M	married			Chaytshe			518
ENTNER	Chaytshe	F	married			Efraim			518
ENTNER	Peretz	M							518
ENTNER	Cypa	F							518

ENTNER	Sura	F						518
ENTNER	Golda	F						518
ENTNER	Levi	M	married		Chana Shifra		Family with 4 family members	518
ENTNER	Chana Shifra	F	married		Levy		Family with 4 family members	518
ENTNER	Shmuel Yosel	M				his family		518
ENTNER	Perl	F						518
ENTNER	Tsvi	M		Perl				518
ENTNER	Yoel	M	married		Rachel			518
ENTNER	Rachel	F	married		Yoel			518
ENTNER	Feiga	F						518
ENTNER	Shaul	M				his family		518
ERLICH	Getsel	M	married		Matl			518
ERLICH	Matl	F	married		Getsel			518
ERLICH	Tsvi	M						518
ERLICH	Yisasschar	M						518
ERLICH	Sime	F						518
ERLICH	Ita	F						518

פ Peh

FALB	Miriam	F				her family	Maiden name KNEBIL	518
PAPIR	Yakov	M	married		Toba		Family with 5 family members	518
PAPIR	Toba	F	married		Yakov		Family with 5 family members	518
FARBER	Mendel	M	married		Blume			518,519
FARBER	Blume	F	married		Mendel			518,519
FARBER	Avram	M						518,519
FARBER	Yisrael	M						518,519
FARBER	Ester	F						518,519
FUKS	Yitzchak	M	married		Devorah			519

FUKS	Devorah	F	married		Yitzchak			519
FUKS	Leah	F						519
FUKS	Feiga	F						519
FUKS	Moshe	M						519
FUKS	Mendel	M						519
FUKS	Berish	M	married	Yitzchak	Sura			519
FUKS	Sura	F	married		Berish			519
FUKS	Mordechai	M						519
FUKS	Feiga	F						519
FUKS	Meir	M	married		Ester			519
FUKS	Ester	F	married		Meir			519
FUKS	Berish	M	married	Yakov	Leah			519
FUKS	Leah	F	married		Berish			519
FUKS	Moshe	M						519
FUKS	Fetel	F						519
FUKS	Freide	F						519
FUKS	Yakov	M						519
FUKS	Chaim	M						519
FUKS	Miriam	F						519
FUKS	Pese	F						519
FUKS	Hinde	F						519
FUKS	Elimelech	M				his family		519
FUKS	Meir	M	married		Nese			519
FUKS	Nese	F	married		Meir			519
FUKS	Kresel	F						519
FOIGEL	Moshe	M	married		Ita			519
FOIGEL	Ita	F	married		Moshe			519
FOIGEL	Yisrael	M						519
FOIGEL	Leizer	M	married		Chana			519
FOIGEL	Chana	F	married		Leizer			519
FOIGEL	Reizel	F						519
FOIGEL	Shalom	M						519
FOIGEL	Perl	F						519

FOIGEL	Tsvi	M	married			Bluma		519
FOIGEL	Bluma	F	married			Tsvi		519
FOIGEL	Shalom	M						519
FOIGEL	Sura	F						519
FOIGEL	Ita	F						519
FOIGEL	Dov	M						519
FOIGEL	Yehosha	M	married			Golda		519
FOIGEL	Golda	F	married			Yehosha		519
FOIGEL	Yosef	M						519
FOIGEL	Sura	F	married			Yehosha		519
	Yehosha	M	married			Sura		519
FOIGEL	Yosef	M						519
FIRSHT	Yosef	F	married	Efraim		Ita		519
FIRSHT	Ita	M	married			Yosef		519
FIRSHT	Yisrael Tsvi	M						519
FIRSHT	Aba	F	married	Efraim		Rivka		519
FIRSHT	Rivka	M	married			Aba		519
FIRSHT	Sender	M						519
FIRSHT	Gdal	M		Efraim				519
FEINGOLD	Devorah	F						519
FEINGOLD	Yosel	M						519
FEINGOLD	Yisrael	M						519
FEIER	Meitshe	M	married			Toba		519
FEIER	Toba	F	married			Meitshe	Maiden name LANGER	519
FEIER	Henie	F						519
FEIER	Noach	M						519
FISHEL	Shalom	M	married			Perl		519
FISHEL	Perl	F	married			Shalom		519
FISHEL	Yechezkel	M						519
FLUG	Leibish	M	married			Maltshe		519
FLUG	Maltshe	F	married			Leibish		519
FLUG	Leah	F						519

FLUG	Yehuda	M					519
FLAMENBOIM	Avram Baruch	M	married		Hadel		519
FLAMENBOIM	Hadel	F	married		Avram Baruch		519
FLAMENBOIM	Hadasa	F					519
FLAMENBOIM	Duvid	M					519
FLAMENBOIM	Pinchas	M					519
FLAMENBOIM	Azriel	M					519
PECHER	Hersh	M					519
FEFER	Mordechai Ber	M	married		Pesi		520
FEFER	Pesi	F	married		Mordechai Ber		520
FEFER	Yitzchak	M					520
FEFER	Roize	F					520
FEFER	Ester	F					520
FEFER	Leah	F					520
FERDER	Yisrael	M	married		Perl		520
FERDER	Perl	F	married		Yisrael	From Radashtsh	520
FERDER	Rachel	F					520
FERDER	Chana	F					520
FERDER	Rivka	F					520
FERDER	Chava	F					520
FERDER	Berish	M	married		Liba	Family with 4 family members	520
FERDER	Liba	F	married		Berish	Family with 4 family members	520
FRUMER	Hersh	M	married		Bluma		520
FRUMER	Bluma	F	married		Hersh	Maiden name TENTSER	520
FRUMER	Berl	M					520
FRUMER	Shalom	M					520
FRID						From Chitkov village	520
FRIDLENDER	Pese	F				Maiden name EILBOIM	520
FRIDLENDER	Keile	F					520

FRIDLENDER	Chana	F						520
FRIDLENDER	Yakov	M	married		Feiga		Family with 5 family members	520
FRIDLENDER	Feiga	F	married		Yakov		Family with 5 family members	520
FRIDLENDER	Rivka	F						520
FRIMERMAN	Chantshe	F						520
FREILICH	Michael	M	married		Rivka			520
FREILICH	Rivka	F	married		Michael		Maiden name GERY	520
FREILICH	Chava	F						520
FREILICH	Shlomo	M						520
FREIMAN	Moshe Aharon	M	married		Liba			520
FREIMAN	Liba	F	married		Moshe Aharon			520
FREIMAN	Rivka	F						520
FREIMAN	Feiga	F						520
FREIND	Avram Yakov	M	married		Ester			520
FREIND	Ester	F	married		Avram Yakov			520
FREIND	Tsvi	M	married		Tila			520
FREIND	Tila	F	married		Tsvi			520
FREIND	Tishe	F						520
FREIND	Zisel	F						520
FREIND	Etel	F						520
FREIND	Moshe	M						520
FREIND	Benyamin	M	married		Reitse			520
FREIND	Reitse	F	married		Benyamin			520
FREIND	Malka	F						520
FREIND	Rivka	F						520

צ Tzadik

TSVEKIN	Yakov	M				his family		520
TSUKER	Hersh	M	married		Malka			520

TSUKER	Malka	F	married			Hersh		Maiden name ELBOIM	520
TSITRIN	Zelman	M							520
TSITRIN	Freide	F							520
TSITRIN	Heshel	M					his family		520
TSITRIN	Yakov	M					his family		520
TSITRIN	Sura	F					her family		520

קּ Kof

KAVENSHTOCK	Nechamiia	M							520
KAVENSHTOCK	Bracha	F							520
KAVENSHTOCK	Chaya	F							520
KAVENSHTOCK	Batse	F							520
KAVENSHTOCK	Elihau	M					his family		520
KAVENSHTOCK	Finie	M					his family		520
KAVENSHTOCK	Edel	F					her family		521
KAVENSHTOCK	Mordechai	M	married			Chantshe			521
KAVENSHTOCK	Chantshe	F	married			Mordechai			521
KAVENSHTOCK	Rivka	F							521
KAVENSHTOCK	Shifra	F							521
KAM	Ben-Tsion	M	married			Cypa			521
KAM	Cypa	F	married			Ben-Tsion			521
KAM	Feiga	F							521
KAM	Rive	F					her family		521
KAM	Yosef	M					his family		521
KAM	Moshke	M	married			Perl			521
KAM	Perl	F	married			Moshe'ke			521
KAM	Yakov	M							521
KANDEL	Eliezer	M					his family		521
KANDEL	Gershon	M					his family		521
KANDEL	Itshe	M	married			Chantshe		Family with 4 family members	521
KANDEL	Chantshe	F	married			Itshe		Family with 4 family members	521
KANDEL	Zise	F							521

KOPEL	Etel	F						521
KOPEL	Efraim	M	married	Yosel		Miriam		521
KOPEL	Miriam	F	married			Efraim		521
KOPEL	Zev	M						521
KOPEL	Duvid	M						521
KOPEL	Tsvia	F						521
KOPEL	Yosel	M						521
KOPEL	Mordechai	M	married	Yosel		Sura Yocheved		521
KOPEL	Sura Yocheved	F	married			Mordechai		521
KOPEL	Shlomo	M						521
KOPEL	Tsipora	F						521
KOPEL	Yosel	M						521
KOPEL	Berl	M						521
KOPEL	Etel	F						521
KATSMAN	Yosef	M					his family	521
KATSMAN	Aharon	M						521
KATSMAN	Roize	F					her family	521
KUPIETS	Shlomo	M	married	Menashe		Beile Cypa		521
KUPIETS	Beila Cypa	F	married			Shlomo		521
KUPIETS	Yitzchak Meir	M						521
KUPIETS	Yehudit	F						521
KUPIETS	Rivka	F		Yetshe				521
KUPIETS	Feiga	F						521
KUPIETS	Rishe	F						521
KUPIETS	Yitzchak	M						521
KUPIETS	Rive	F					her grand-children	521
KUPIETS	Rachel	F		Moshe				521
KUPIETS	Sura Rachel	F		Moshe				521
KUPIETS	Shlomo Todres	M		Moshe				521
KUPIETS	Mirtshe	F						521

KUPIETS	Avram	M					521
KUPIETS	Bine	F					521
KUPIETS	Chana	F					521
KUPIETS	Shlomo Ozer	M	married		Leah		521
KUPIETS	Leah	F	married		Shmuel Ozer		521
KUPIETS	Michael	M					521
KUPIETS	Elke	F					521
KUPIETS	Mendel	M					521
KUPIETS	Menachem	M					521
KUPIETS	Shlomo	M					521
KUPIETS	Leibke	M	married		Sura		521
KUPIETS	Sura	F	married		Leibke		521
KUPIETS	Miriam	F					521
KUPIETS	Reizel	F					521
KUPIETS	Shlomo	M					521
KUPIETS	Ita	F					521
KUPIETS	Etel	F					521
KUPIETS	Shmuel	M	married	Arish	Bina Rachel		521
KUPIETS	Bina Rachel	F	married		Shmuel		521
KUPIETS	Yosef	M					521
KUPIETS	Shlomo	M					521
KUPIETS	Yekutiel	M		Yisrael			522
KUPIETS	Hanoch	M		Yisrael			522
KUPIETS	Yosel	M		Yisrael			522
KUPER	Moshe	M					522
KUPER	Nute	M					522
KUPER	Shimon	M		Avram			522
KUPER	Sender	M					522
KUPERSHTEIN	Noach	M	married		Dina		522
KUPERSHTEIN	Dina	F	married		Noach	From Chitkov	522
KUPERSHTEIN	Chaya	F					522

KLEINER	Aharon Gershon	M	married		Sura		522
KLEINER	Sura	F	married		Aharon Gershon		522
KLEINER	Leibel	M					522
KLEINER	Avram Yakov	M					522
KLEINER	Feiga	F					522
KLEINER	Sheindel	F					522
KLEINER	Michael	M	married		Etel		522
KLEINER	Etel	F	married		Michael		522
KLEINER	Yehosha	M	married		Sura		522
KLEINER	Sura	F	married		Yehosha	Maiden name UNCIG	522
KLEINER	Moshe	M					522
KLEINER	Tsvi	M					522
KLEINER	Chaya Liba	F				her family Relatives of the Lefler family	522
KNEBEL	Berl	M	married		Chana		522
KNEBEL	Chana	F	married		Berl		522
KNEBEL	Rachel	F					522
KNEBEL	Ester	F					522
KNEBEL	Elimelech	M	married		Etke		522
KNEBEL	Etke	F	married		Elimelech		522
KNEBEL	Hertsel	M					522
KNEBEL	Mordechai	M	married		Chana		522
KNEBEL	Chana	F	married		Mordechai		522
KNEBEL	Chaya	F					522
KNEBEL	Rivka	F					522
KNEBEL	Ester	F					522
KNEBEL	Pinchas	M					522
KNEBEL	Perets	M					522
KNEBEL	Shlomo	M					522
KNEBEL	Aba	M	married		Golda		522
KNEBEL	Golda	F	married		Aba		522
KNEBEL	Shlomo	M					522

KNEBEL	Itsheli	M					522
KERER	Meir	M	married		Chana		522
KERER	Chana	F	married		Meir		522
KERER	Yocheved	F					522
KERER	Leizer	M					522
KERER	Shimon	M					522
KERER	Sheindel	F					522
KERER	Shimon	M	married		Leah		522
KERER	Leah	F	married		Shimon		522
KERER	Aharon	M					522
KERER	Leibish	M					522
KERER	Gedaliahu	M					522
KERER	Yehosha	M		Zelman Ber		his family	522
KERER	Mechel	M		Zelman Ber		his family	522
KERER	Chaim	M		Zelman Ber		his family	522
KRAMER	Reuven	M	married		Mindel		522
KRAMER	Mindel	F	married		Reuven		522
KRAMER	Elke	F					522
KRAMER	Sura	F					522
KRAMER	Yitzchak	M					522
KRAMER	Duvid	M					522
KRAMER	Feiga	F					522
KRAMER	Yakov Ber	M					522
KRAMER	Malka	F					522
KRAMER	Reuvele	M					522
KREIDEN	Feiga	F					522
KREIDEN	Roize	F				her family	522
KREIDEN	Freide	F				her family	522
KREIDEN	Yakov Hersh	M	married		Beile		522
KREIDEN	Beile	F	married		Yakov Hersh		522

KRELMAN	Bonem	M	married		Pese			522, 523
KRELMAN	Pese	F	married		Bonem			522, 523
KRELMAN	Moshe	M						522, 523
KRELMAN	Pinchas	M	married		Rachel			523
KRELMAN	Rachel	F	married		Pinchas			523
KRELMAN	Freide	F						523
KRELMAN	Moshe	M	married		Cypa			523
KRELMAN	Cypa	F	married		Moshe			523
KRELMAN	Rivka	F						523
KRELMAN	Yitzchak	M						523
KRELMAN	Hersh	M						523
KRELMAN	Yosef	M						523
KRELMAN	Perl	F						523
KRELMAN	Freide	F						523
KRELMAN	Hanoch	M						523
KRELMAN	Meir	M	married		Sura			523
KRELMAN	Sura	F	married		Meir			523
KRELMAN	Beiltshe	F						523
KRELMAN	Tanchum	M						523
KRELMAN	Shmuel	M						523
KRELMAN	Chaim	M						523

ר Resh

ROTHEIZER	Michael	M	married		Rachel			523
ROTHEIZER	Rachel	F	married		Michael			523
ROTHEIZER	Feiga	F						523
ROTHEIZER	Primet	F						523
ROTHEIZER	Yakov Hersh	M	married		Itke			523
ROTHEIZER	Itke	F	married		Yakov			523
ROTHEIZER	Sura	F						523
ROTHEIZER	Velvel	M	married		Feiga			523
ROTHEIZER	Feiga	F	married		Velvel			523

ROTHEIZER	Pinchas	M						523
ROTHEIZER	Shprintse	F						523
RAPER	Reizel	F					Maiden name ZIMERMAN	523
RAPER	Gitel	F						523
RAPER	Avram	M						523
RAPER	Feiga	F						523
RAPER	Leah	F						523
RAPER	Yehosha	M		Duvid		his family		523
RAPER	Aharon	M	married		Sura			523
RAPER	Sura	F	married		Aharon			523
ROZENFELD	Bintshe	M	married		Maltshe			523
ROZENFELD	Maltshe	F	married		Bintshe			523
ROZENFELD	Rachel	F						523
ROZENFELD	Mordechai	M						523
ROZENFELD	Heshel	M						523
ROZENFELD	Mendel	M					Tsheshler	523
ROZENFELD	Grone	F				her family		523
ROTMAN	Chaim	M	married		Chaya			523
ROTMAN	Chaya	F	married		Chaim			523
ROITER	Duvid	M	married		Chana		Family with 4 family members	523
ROITER	Chana	F	married		Duvid		Family with 4 family members	523
RUND	Avram Berish	M						523
RUND	Rivka	F						523
RUND	Rachel	F						523
RUND	Yosef	M		Shmuel				523
RUND	Malka	F		Shmuel				523
RUND	Sime	F		Shmuel				523
RUND	Zindel	M		Tsvi				523
RUND	Avigdor	M		Tsvi				523
REINER	Yakov Leib	M	married		Rivka			523
REINER	Rivka	F	married		Yakov Leib			523

REINER	Nachum	M						523
REIF	Chaim Zelman	M	married		Chana			523
REIF	Chana	F	married		Chaim Zelman			523
REIF	Avram	M						523
REIF	Bracha	F						523
RENDLER	Sheindel Ester	F						523
RENDLER	Shmuel	M	married		Rivka		Family with 4 family members	523
RENDLER	Rivka	F	married		Shmuel		Family with 4 family members	523
RENDLER	Yona	M						523
RENDLER	Moshe Yehosha	M				his family		523
RENDLER	Shalom Aharon	M	married		Chava	children		523
RENDLER	Chava	F	married		Shalom Aharon	children		523
RENDLER	Duvid	M	married		Sura	children		523
RENDLER	Sura	F	married		Duvid	children		523
RENDLER	Chana Reizel	F					From Chitkov	524
RENDLER	Leibish	M						524
RENDLER	Golda	F		Moshe Yakov				524
RENDLER	Duvid	M		Moshe Yakov				524
RENDLER	Yosel	M		Moshe Yakov		his family		524

Shin

SHATS	Leizer	M				his family		524
SHATS	Abish	M				his family		524
SHAK	Berl	M	married		Base		Family with 6 family members	524
SHAK	Bashe	F	married		Berl		Family with 6 family members	524
SHUCH	Tsvi	M	married		Reichel			524

SHUCH	Reichel	F	married		Tsvi			524
SHUCH	Moshe	M						524
SHUCH	Henie	F						524
SHUCH	Rachel	F						524
SHUCH	Yosef	M						524
SHUCH	Aizik	M						524
SHPEIZMAN	Yehosha	M	married		Rachel Leah		Family with 5 family members	524
SHPEIZMAN	Rachel Leah	F	married		Yehosha		Family with 5 family members	524
SHTOKHAMER	Nachman	M	married		Beile Base			524
SHTOKHAMER	Beile Base	F	married		Nachman			524
SHTOKHAMER	Shimon	M						524
SHTOKHAMER	Ester	F						524
SHTOKHAMER	Yente	F				her family		524
SHTOKHAMER	Pinchas	M				his family		524
SHTARKER	Rachel	F						524
SHTARKER	Yitzchak	M	married		Ester Hadasa			524
SHTARKER	Ester Hadasa	F	married		Yitzchak			524
SHTARKER	Zev	M						524
SHTARKER	Freide	F						524
SHTARKER	Zelman	M	married		Rivka			524
SHTARKER	Rivka	F	married		Zelman			524
SHTARKER	Leibish	M						524
SHTARKER	Feiga	F						524
SHTIBEL	Beile	F						524
SHTEINBERG	Mindel	F						524
SHTEINBERG	Tsvi	M						524
SHTEINBERG	Moshe	M						524
SHTEINBERG	Gitel	F		Leibish				524
SHTEINBERG	Sonie	F						524
SHTEINBERG	Avram	M						524
SHTEINBERG	Blume	F						524

SHTEINBERG	Gitel	F		Dov Yehuda			children	Family with 5 family members	524
SHTRIKLER	Chaim Reuven	M	married			Matl			524
SHTRIKLER	Matl	F	married			Chaim Reuven			524
SHTREICHER	Toba	F					her family		524
SHTREICHER	Gitel	F					her family		524
SHTREICHER	Hersh	M					his family		524
SHTREICHER	Bracha	F					her family		524
SHTEMER	Tevel	M		Itsheli Yosels					524
SHTEMER	Yitzchak	M	married			Etel			524
SHTEMER	Etel	F	married			Yitzchak			524
SHTEMER	Elazar	M		Leib					524
SHTEMER	Ozer	M	married			Hinde	children		524
SHTEMER	Hinde	F	married			Ozer	children		524
SHTEMER	Pese	F							524
SHTEMER	Sura	F							524
SHTEMER	Rachel	F							524
SHTEMER	Eliezer	M	married			Freide			524
SHTEMER	Freide	F	married			Eliezer			524
SHTEMER	Yitzchak	M							524
SHTEMER	Mahse	F							524
SHEIDVASER	Yosef Aharon	M	married			Nechama		Profession: Shochat	524, 525
SHEIDVASER	Nechama	F	married			Yosef Aharon			524, 525
SHEIDVASER	Mordechai	M							524, 525
SHEIDVASER	Chava	F							524, 525
SHEIDVASER	Bine	F							524, 525
SHEIDVASER	Shmuel	M							524, 525
SHEIDVASER	Yakov	M							524, 525

SHEIDVASER	Rive	F		Moshe			Daughter of a "shochat"	525
SHLEGEL	Fishel	M	married		Toba			525
SHLEGEL	Toba	F	married		Fishel			525
SHLEGEL	Moshe	M						525
SHLEGEL	Yehosha	M						525
SHLEGEL	Chaya	F						525
SHLEGEL	Etel	F					Maiden name TENTSER	525
SHLEGEL	Chaya	F						525
SHLEGEL	Dobe	F						525
SHLEGEL	Malka	F	married		Artshe			525
SHLEGEL	Chaya	F						525
SHNOR	Elke	F	married		Avram			525
SHNOR	Moshe	M	married		Yocheved			525
SHNOR	Yocheved	F	married		Moshe			525
SHNOR	Ita	F						525
SHNOR	Dobe	F						525
SHNOR	Gershon	M						525
SHNOR	Yehosha	M	married		Roize			525
SHNOR	Roize	F	married		Yehosha			525
SHNOR	Gershon	M						525
SHNOR	Tsipora	F						525
SHNOR	Sime	F		Mordechai		children		525
SHECHTER	Rachel	F					From Majdan Sopocki	525
SHECHTER	Perl	F						525
SHECHTER	Toba	F						525
SHECHTER	Gitel	F						525
SHECHTER	Hanoch	M				his family		525
SHECHTER	Refael	M	married		Chaya			525
SHECHTER	Chaya	F	married		Refael			525
SHECHTER	Rachel	F						525
SHERMAN	Kelman	M	married		Hinde			525

SHERMAN	Hinde	F	married			Kelman			525
SHERMAN	Bracha	F							525
SHPORER	Gershon	M							525
SHPIZAIZEN	Moshe	M	married			Freide			525
SHPIZAIZEN	Freide	F	married			Moshe			525
SHPIZAIZEN	Perl	F							525
SHPIZAIZEN	Shmuel	M	married			Mashe	children	Family with 6 family members	525
SHPIZAIZEN	Mashe	F	married			Shmuel	children	Family with 6 family members	525
SHPEICHER	Aharon Leizer	M							525
SHPEICHER	Yakov	M							525
SHPEICHER	Mordechal	M							525
SHPEICHER	Cypa	F							525
SHPEICHER	Chana Sime	F							525
SHPEICHER	Feiga Rachel	F							525
SHPEICHER	Yosef Leib	M	married			Pese			525
SHPEICHER	Pese	F	married			Yosef Leib			525
SHPEICHER	Rivka	F							525
SHPEICHER	Chaya	F							525
SHPEICHER	Pesach	M							525
SHPINDEL	Yosef Mendel	M	married			Beile			525
SHPINDEL	Beile	F	married			Yosef Mendel			525
SHPINDEL	Cypa	F							525
SHPINDEL	Yosef	M							525
SHPINDEL	Sone	M						his family	525
SHPERLING	Itshe Ber	M	married			Beile			525
SHPERLING	Beile	F	married			Itshe Ber			525
SHPERLING	Chava	F							525
SHPERLING	Feiga	F							525
SHPERLING	Rivka	F							525

SHPERLING	Yakov	M							525
SHPERLING	Toba	F							525
SHPERLING	Azriel	M	married			Yocheved	children		525
SHPERLING	Yocheved	F	married			Azriel	children		525

NAME INDEX

www.ingramcontent.com/pod-product-compliance
Lightning Source LLC
Chambersburg PA
CBHW050411110426
42812CB00006BA/1861